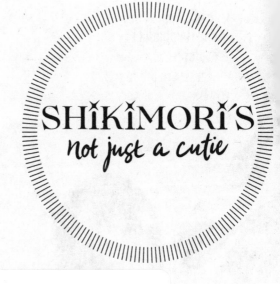

SHiKiMORi'S
not just a cutie

D1377052

KEIGO MAKI

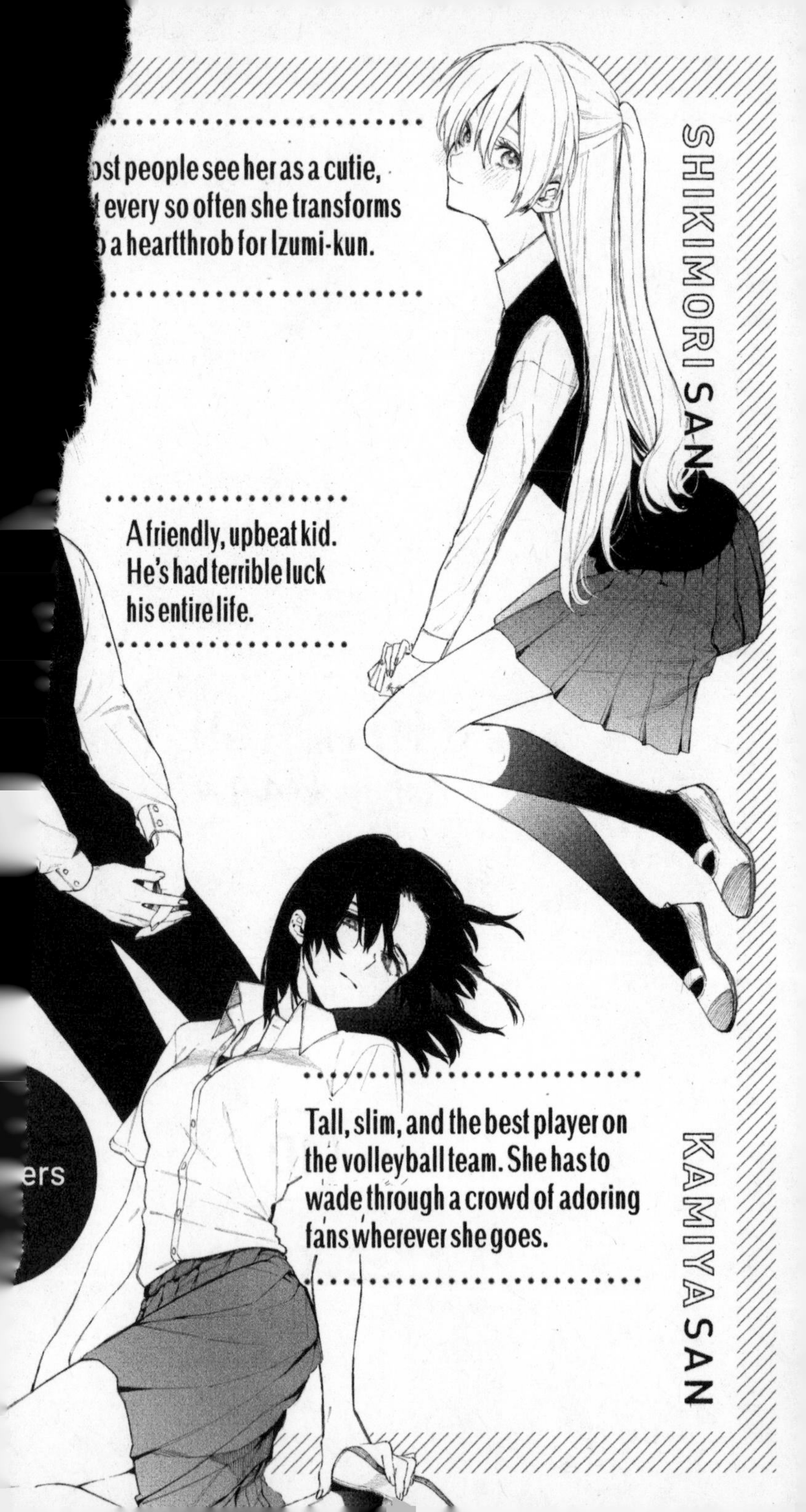
SHIKIMORI SAN
ost people see her as a cutie,
t every so often she transforms
o a heartthrob for Izumi-kun.
A friendly, upbeat kid. He's had terrible luck his entire life.
KAMIYA SAN
Tall, slim, and the best player on the volleyball team. She has to wade through a crowd of adoring fans wherever she goes.
ers

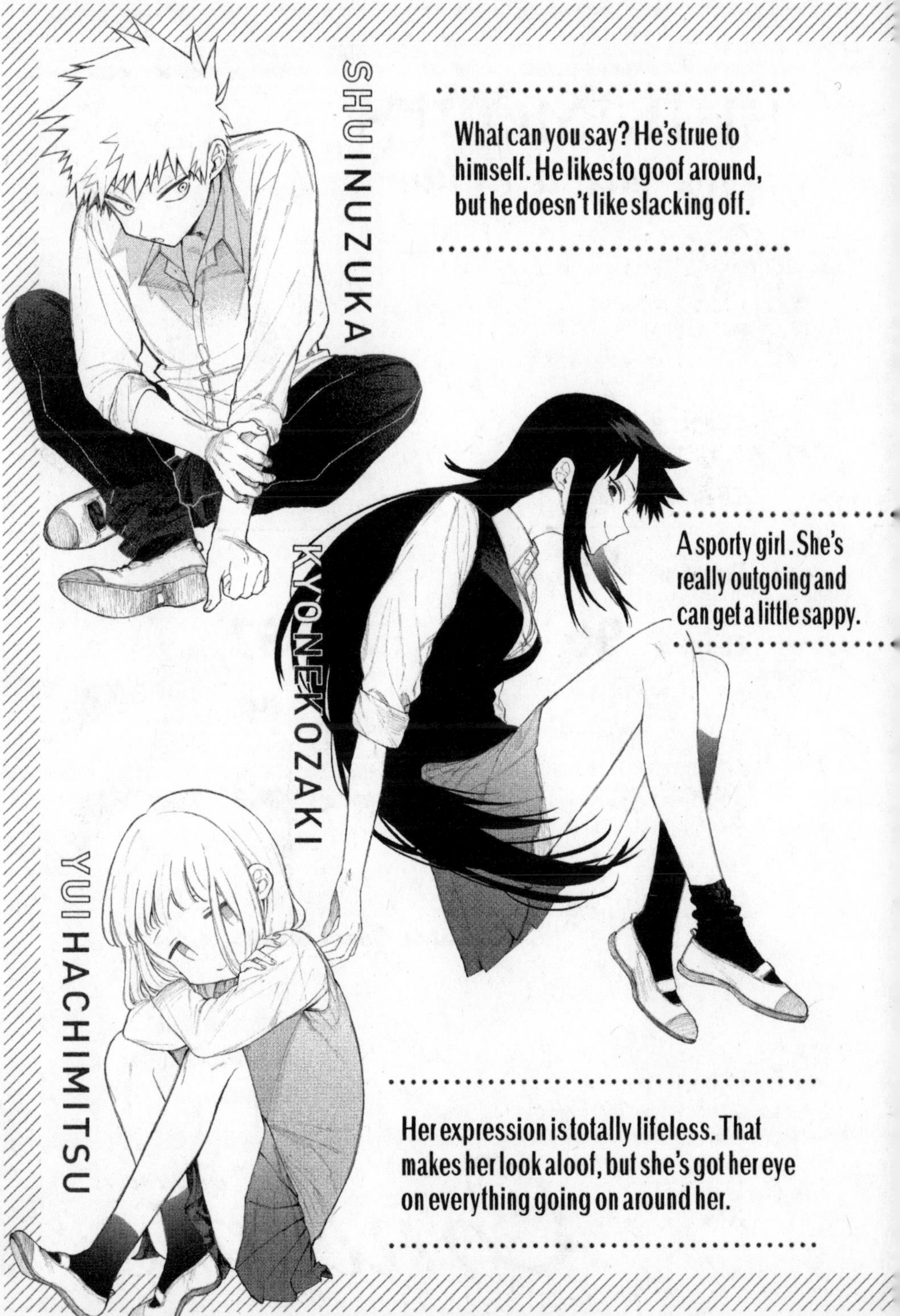
SHU INUZUKA
What can you say? He's true to himself. He likes to goof around, but he doesn't like slacking off.
KYO NEKOZAKI
A sporty girl . She's really outgoing and can get a little sappy.
YUI HACHIMITSU
Her expression is totally lifeless. That makes her look aloof, but she's got her eye on everything going on around her.

SHIKIMORI'S
not just a cutie

volume.10
Contents

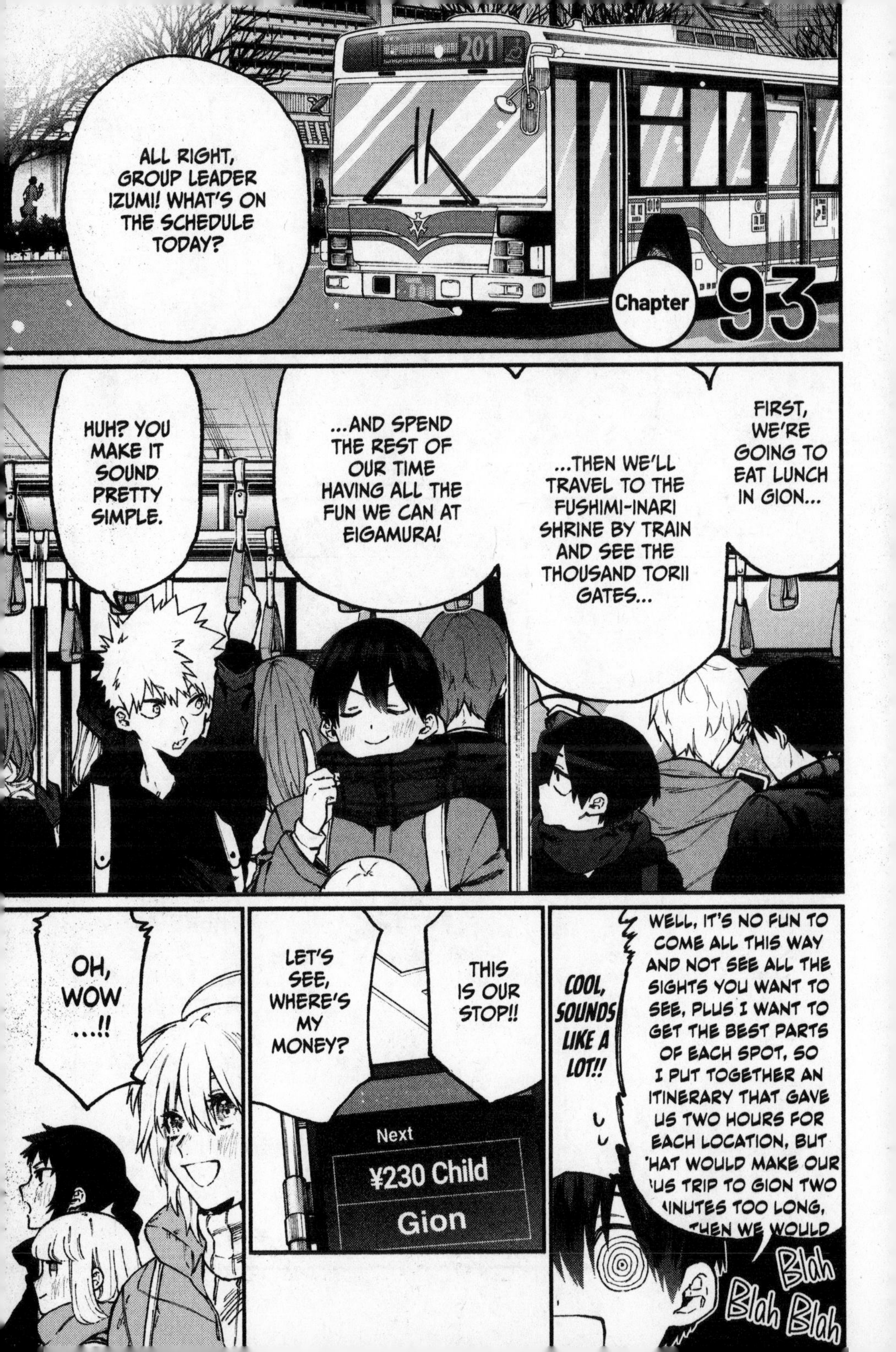
ALL RIGHT, GROUP LEADER IZUMI! WHAT'S ON THE SCHEDULE TODAY?
Chapter 93
FIRST, WE'RE GOING TO EAT LUNCH IN GION...
...THEN WE'LL TRAVEL TO THE FUSHIMI-INARI SHRINE BY TRAIN AND SEE THE THOUSAND TORII GATES...
...AND SPEND THE REST OF OUR TIME HAVING ALL THE FUN WE CAN AT EIGAMURA!
HUH? YOU MAKE IT SOUND PRETTY SIMPLE.
WELL, IT'S NO FUN TO COME ALL THIS WAY AND NOT SEE ALL THE SIGHTS YOU WANT TO SEE, PLUS I WANT TO GET THE BEST PARTS OF EACH SPOT, SO I PUT TOGETHER AN ITINERARY THAT GAVE US TWO HOURS FOR EACH LOCATION, BUT 'HAT WOULD MAKE OUR 'US TRIP TO GION TWO ΜINUTES TOO LONG, THEN WE WOULD
COOL, SOUNDS LIKE A LOT!!
Blah Blah Blah
THIS IS OUR STOP!!
LET'S SEE, WHERE'S MY MONEY?
Next
¥230 Child
Gion
OH, WOW ...!!

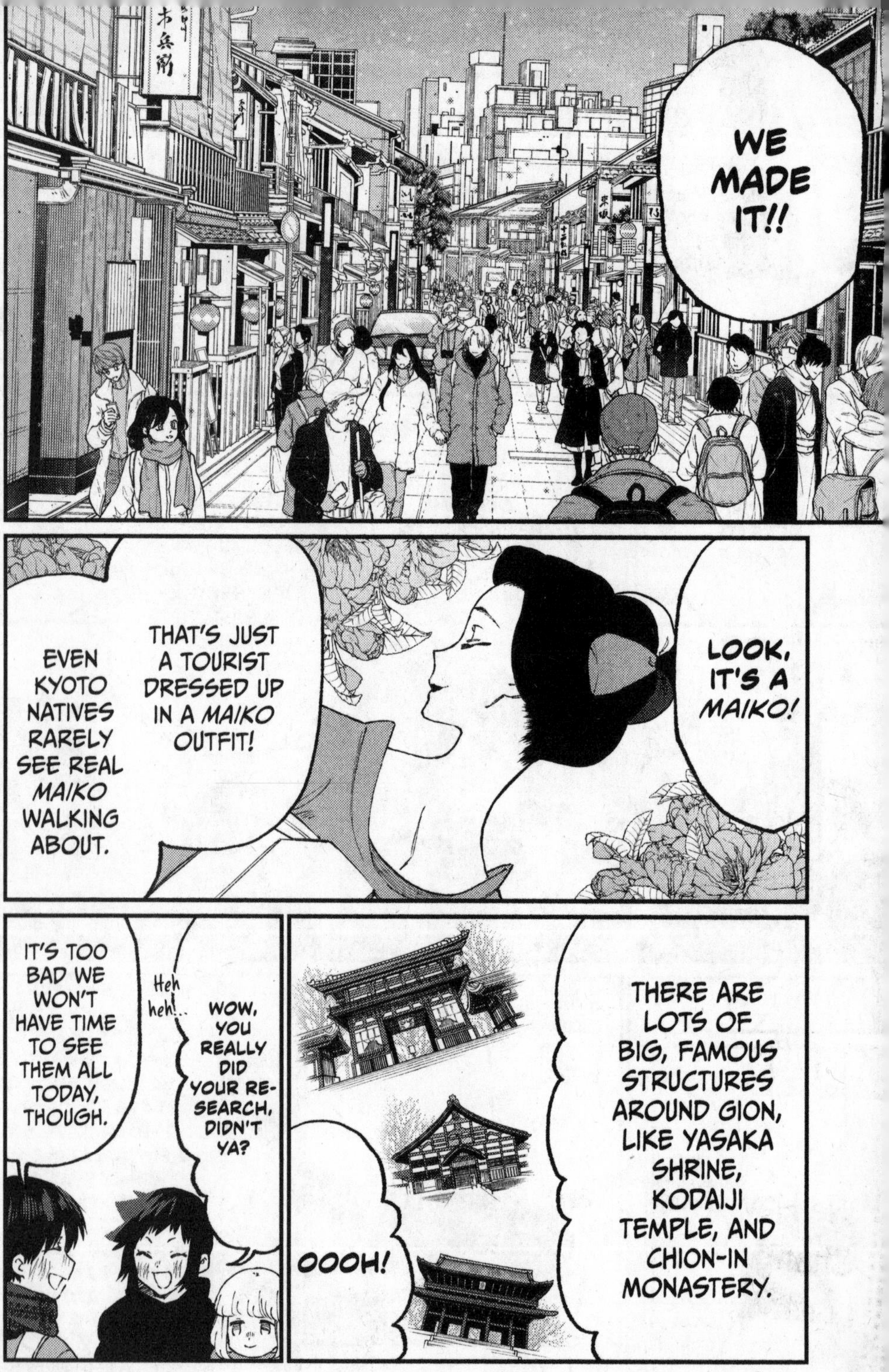

WE MADE IT!!
LOOK, IT'S A *MAIKO*!
THAT'S JUST A TOURIST DRESSED UP IN A *MAIKO* OUTFIT!
EVEN KYOTO NATIVES RARELY SEE REAL *MAIKO* WALKING ABOUT.
THERE ARE LOTS OF BIG, FAMOUS STRUCTURES AROUND GION, LIKE YASAKA SHRINE, KODAIJI TEMPLE, AND CHION-IN MONASTERY.
OOOH!
WOW, YOU REALLY DID YOUR RE-SEARCH, DIDN'T YA?
Heh heh!...
IT'S TOO BAD WE WON'T HAVE TIME TO SEE THEM ALL TODAY, THOUGH.

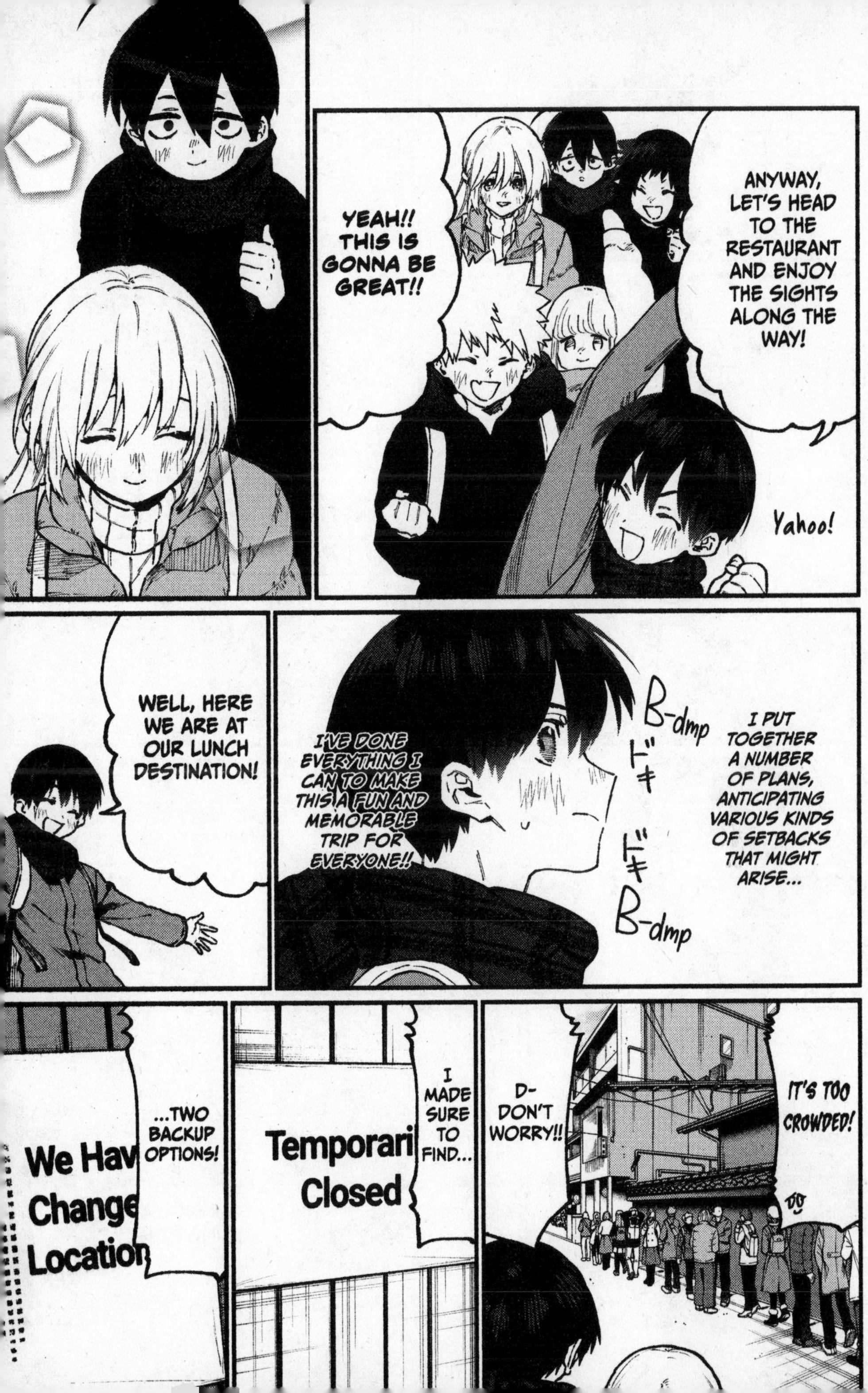
ANYWAY, LET'S HEAD TO THE RESTAURANT AND ENJOY THE SIGHTS ALONG THE WAY!
Yahoo!
YEAH!! THIS IS GONNA BE GREAT!!
I PUT TOGETHER A NUMBER OF PLANS, ANTICIPATING VARIOUS KINDS OF SETBACKS THAT MIGHT ARISE...
B-dmp
ドキ
ドキ
B-dmp
I'VE DONE EVERYTHING I CAN TO MAKE THIS A FUN AND MEMORABLE TRIP FOR EVERYONE!!
WELL, HERE WE ARE AT OUR LUNCH DESTINATION!
IT'S TOO CROWDED!
D-DON'T WORRY!!
I MADE SURE TO FIND...
Temporari
Closed
...TWO BACKUP OPTIONS!
We Hav
Change
Location

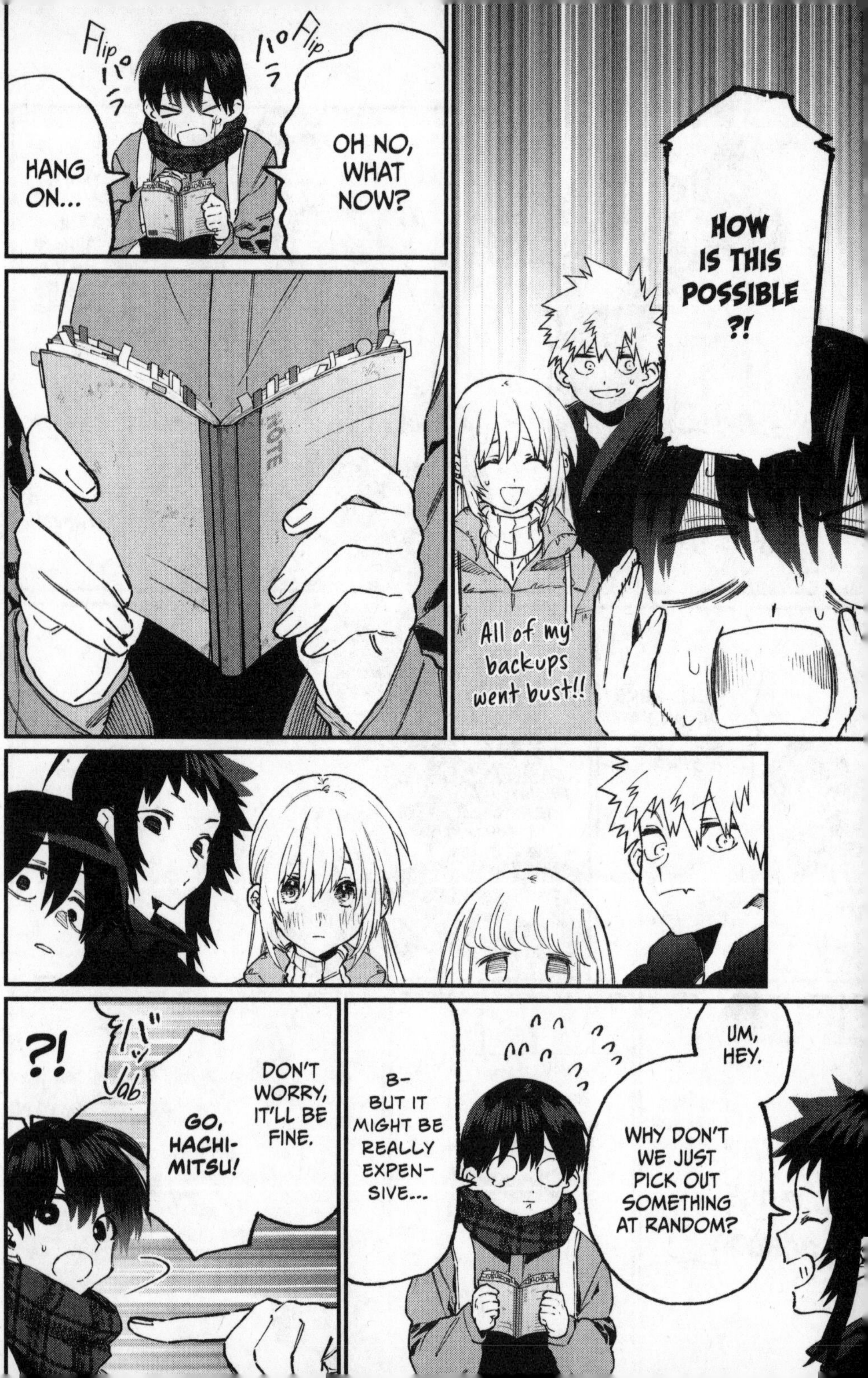
HOW IS THIS POSSIBLE?!
All of my backups went bust!!
Flip ハラ
Flip パラ
OH NO, WHAT NOW?
HANG ON...
NOTE
UM, HEY.
WHY DON'T WE JUST PICK OUT SOMETHING AT RANDOM?
B- BUT IT MIGHT BE REALLY EXPENSIVE...
DON'T WORRY, IT'LL BE FINE.
GO, HACHIMITSU!
Jab バッ
?!

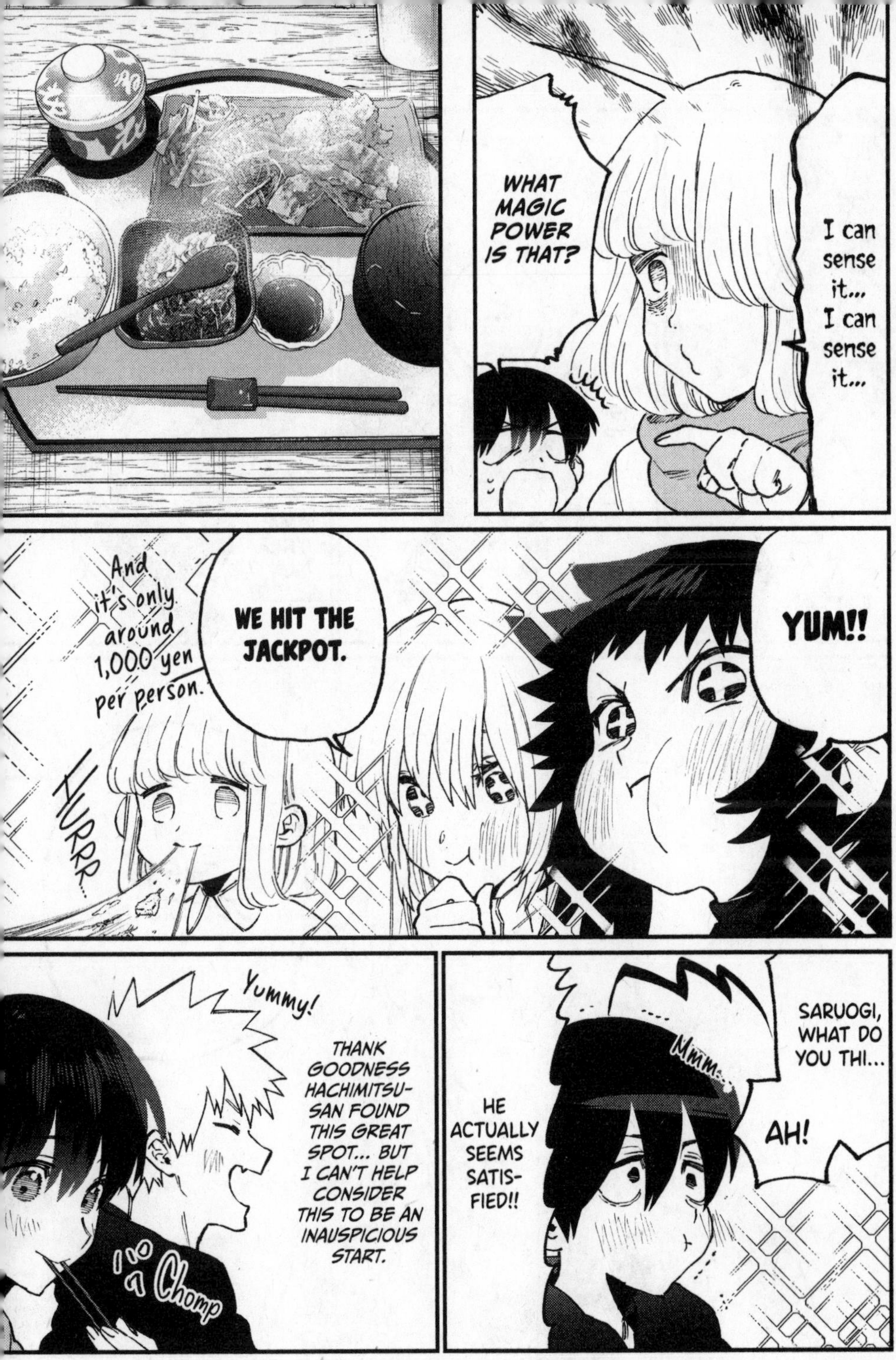
I can sense it... I can sense it...
WHAT MAGIC POWER IS THAT?
YUM!!
WE HIT THE JACKPOT.
And it's only around 1,000 yen per person.
HURRR
SARUOGI, WHAT DO YOU THI...
AH!
Mmm...
HE ACTUALLY SEEMS SATIS-FIED!!
Yummy!
THANK GOODNESS HACHIMITSU-SAN FOUND THIS GREAT SPOT... BUT I CAN'T HELP CONSIDER THIS TO BE AN INAUSPICIOUS START.
Chomp

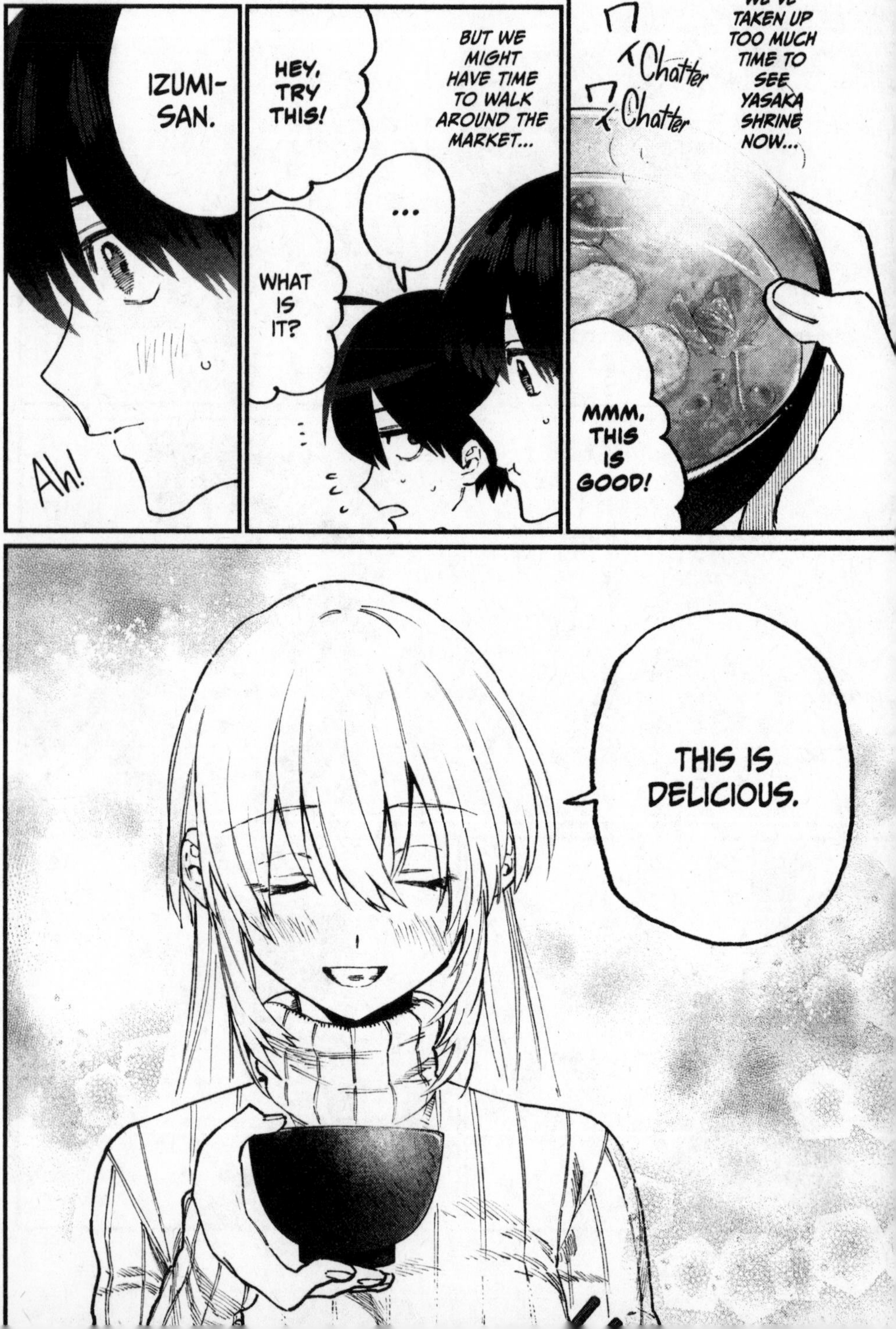
WE'VE TAKEN UP TOO MUCH TIME TO SEE YASAKA SHRINE NOW...
Chatter
Chatter
MMM, THIS IS GOOD!
BUT WE MIGHT HAVE TIME TO WALK AROUND THE MARKET...
HEY, TRY THIS!
...
WHAT IS IT?
IZUMI-SAN.
Ah!
THIS IS DELICIOUS.

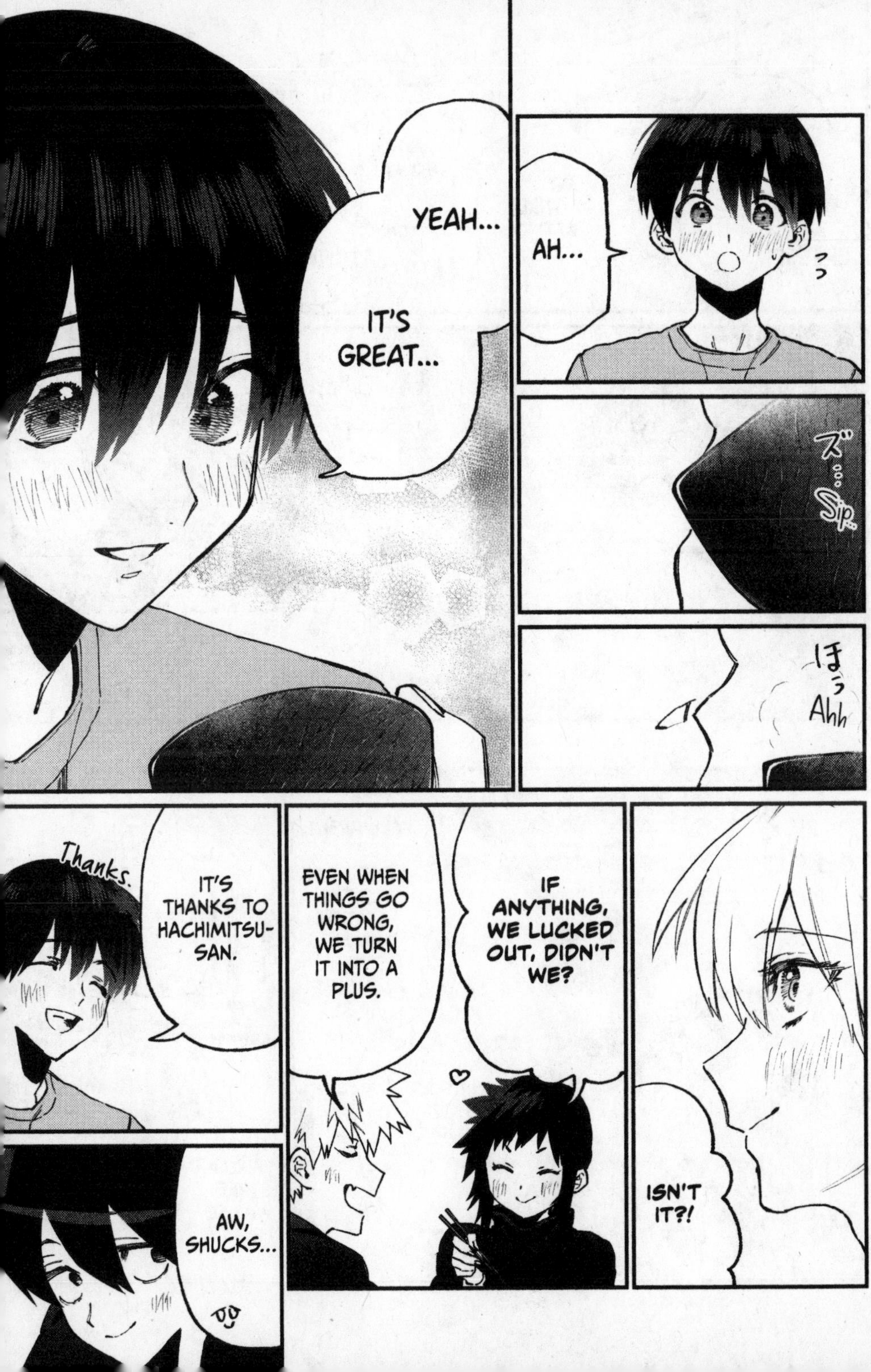
AH...
ズ... Sip
ほっ Ahh
YEAH...
IT'S GREAT...
ISN'T IT?!
IF ANYTHING, WE LUCKED OUT, DIDN'T WE?
EVEN WHEN THINGS GO WRONG, WE TURN IT INTO A PLUS.
IT'S THANKS TO HACHIMITSU-SAN.
Thanks.
AW, SHUCKS...

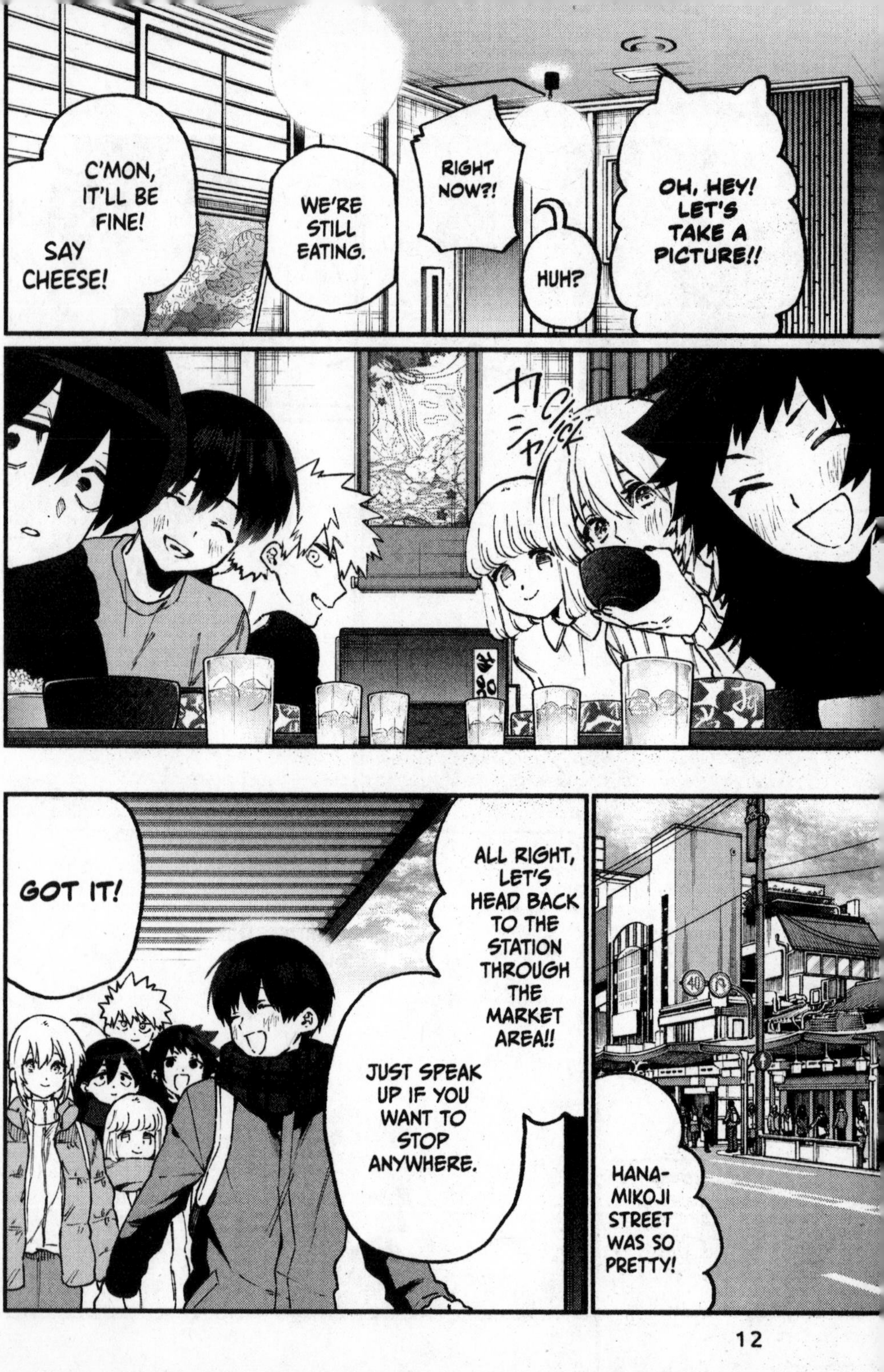
OH, HEY! LET'S TAKE A PICTURE!!
HUH?
RIGHT NOW?!
WE'RE STILL EATING.
C'MON, IT'LL BE FINE!
SAY CHEESE!
カシャ
CLICK
HANA-MIKOJI STREET WAS SO PRETTY!
ALL RIGHT, LET'S HEAD BACK TO THE STATION THROUGH THE MARKET AREA!!
JUST SPEAK UP IF YOU WANT TO STOP ANYWHERE.
GOT IT!

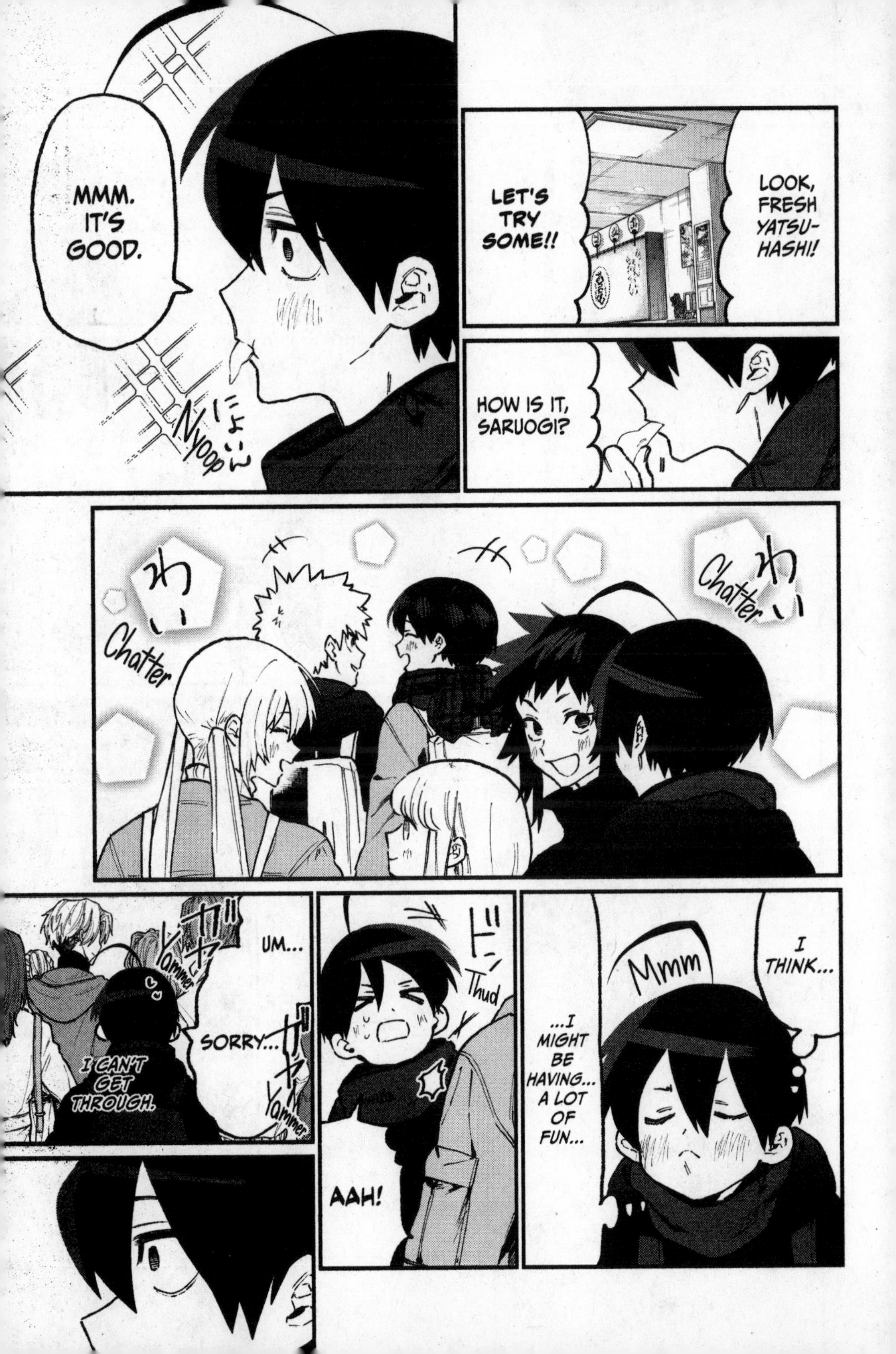
LOOK, FRESH YATSU-HASHI!
LET'S TRY SOME!!
HOW IS IT, SARUOGI?
MMM. IT'S GOOD.
にょいん
Nyoop
わい
Chatter
わい
Chatter
I THINK...
...I MIGHT BE HAVING... A LOT OF FUN...
Mmm
ドン
Thud
AAH!
ガヤ
Yammer
UM...
SORRY...
ガヤ
Yammer
I CAN'T GET THROUGH.

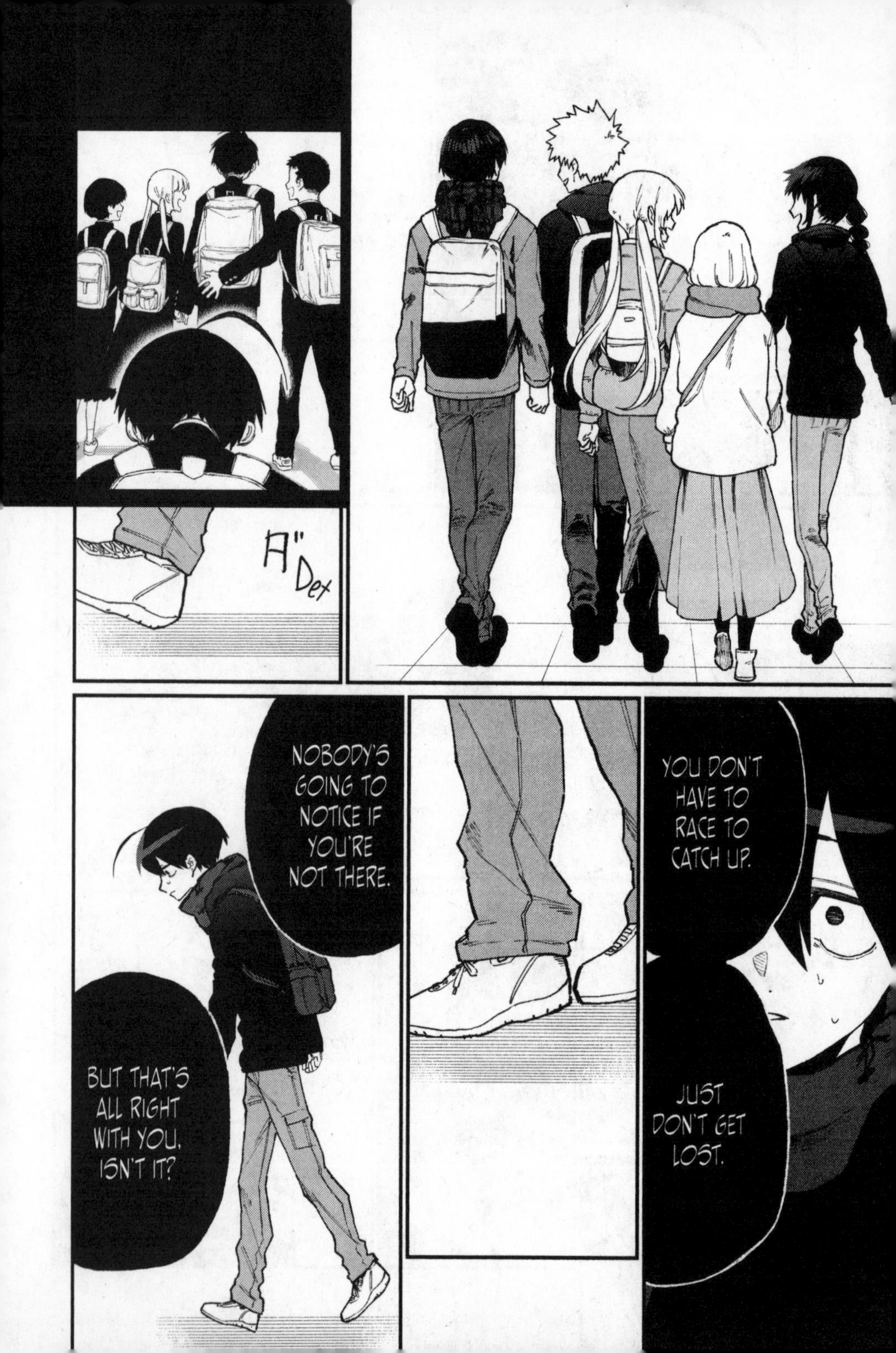
YOU DON'T HAVE TO RACE TO CATCH UP.
JUST DON'T GET LOST.
NOBODY'S GOING TO NOTICE IF YOU'RE NOT THERE.
BUT THAT'S ALL RIGHT WITH YOU, ISN'T IT?

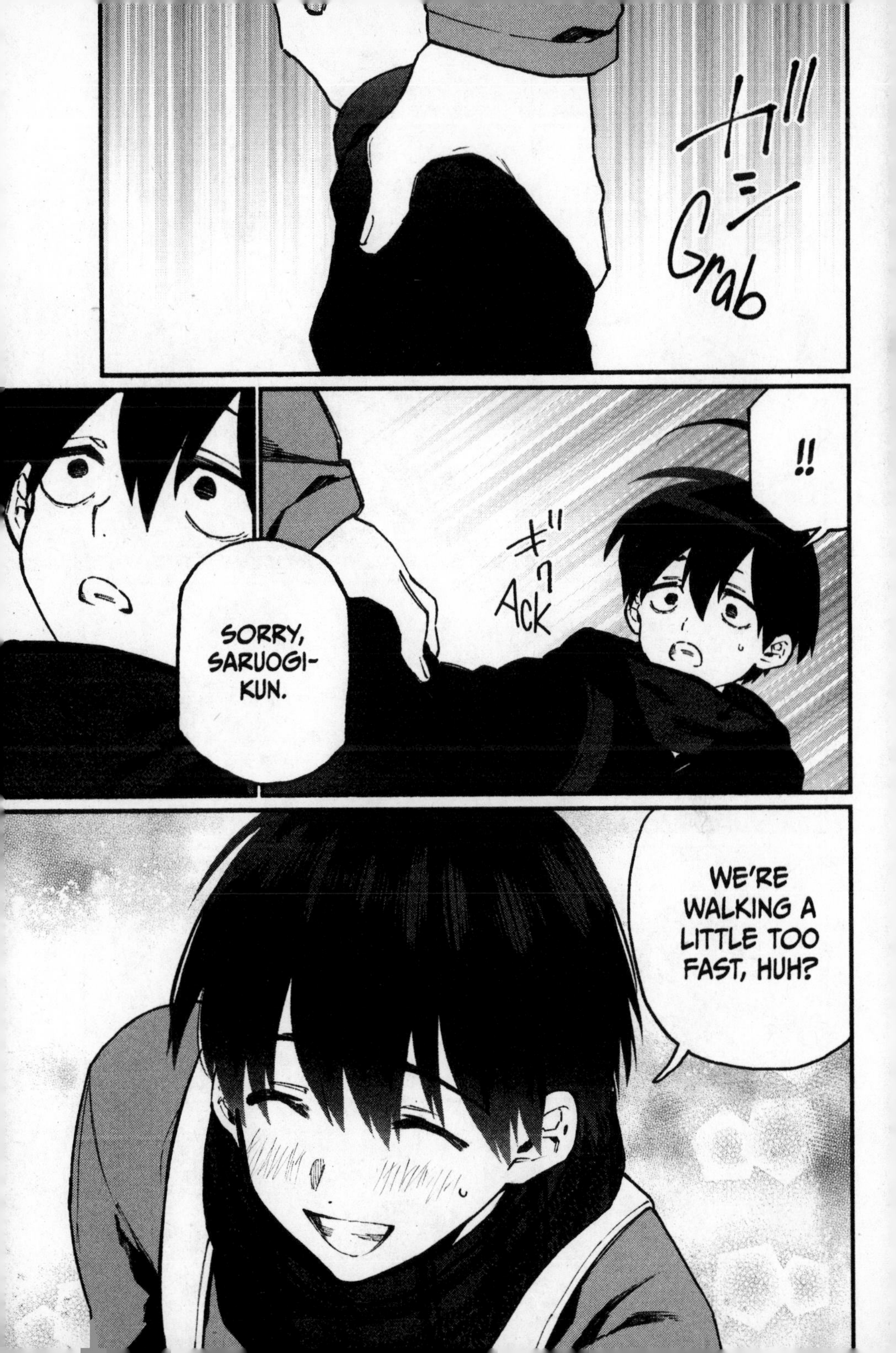

ガシ
Grab
!!
ギク
Ack
SORRY, SARUOGI-KUN.
WE'RE WALKING A LITTLE TOO FAST, HUH?

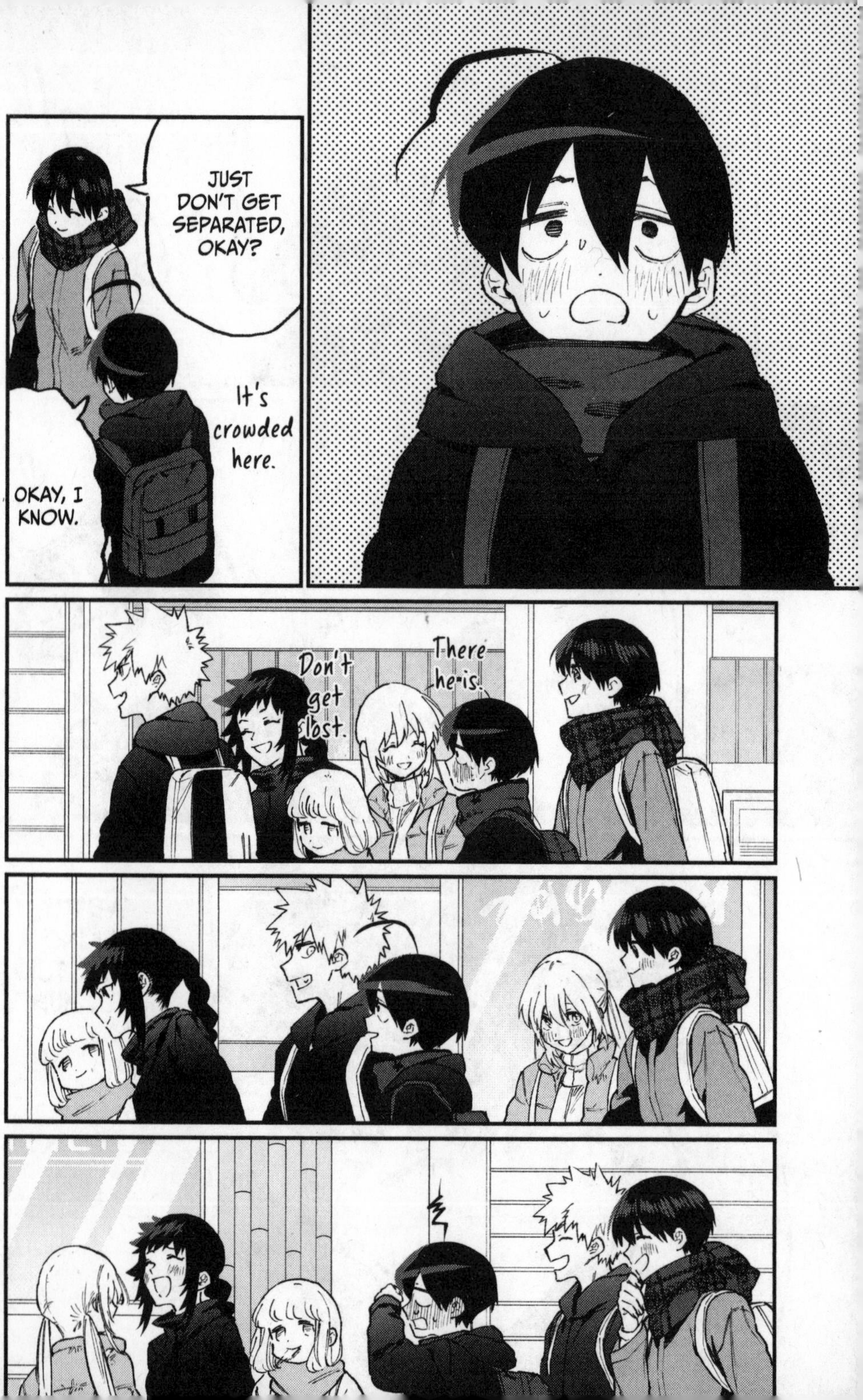
JUST DON'T GET SEPARATED, OKAY?
It's crowded here.
OKAY, I KNOW.
There he is.
Don't get lost.

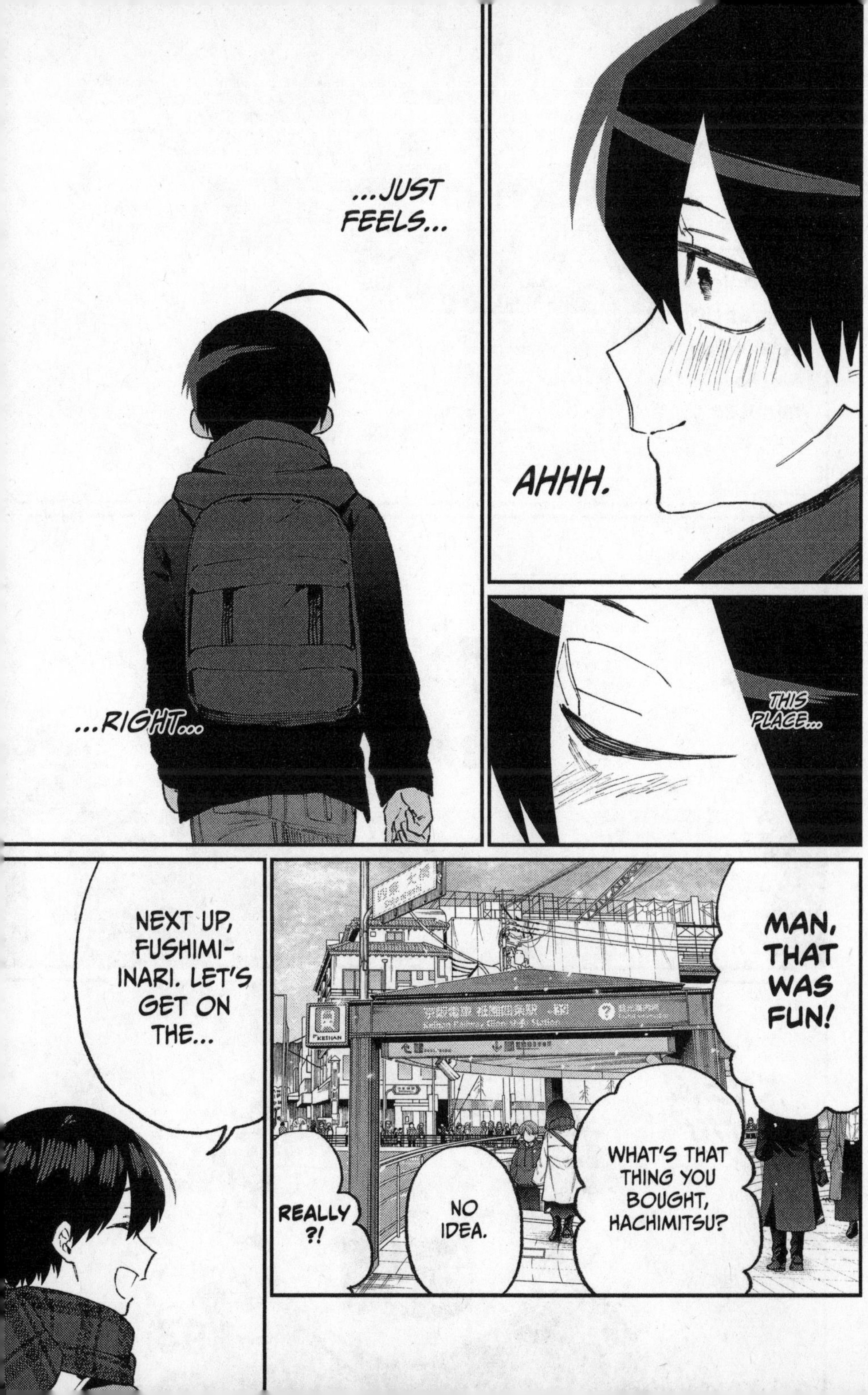
AHHH.
THIS PLACE...
...JUST FEELS...
...RIGHT...
MAN, THAT WAS FUN!
WHAT'S THAT THING YOU BOUGHT, HACHIMITSU?
NO IDEA.
REALLY?!
NEXT UP, FUSHIMI-INARI. LET'S GET ON THE...

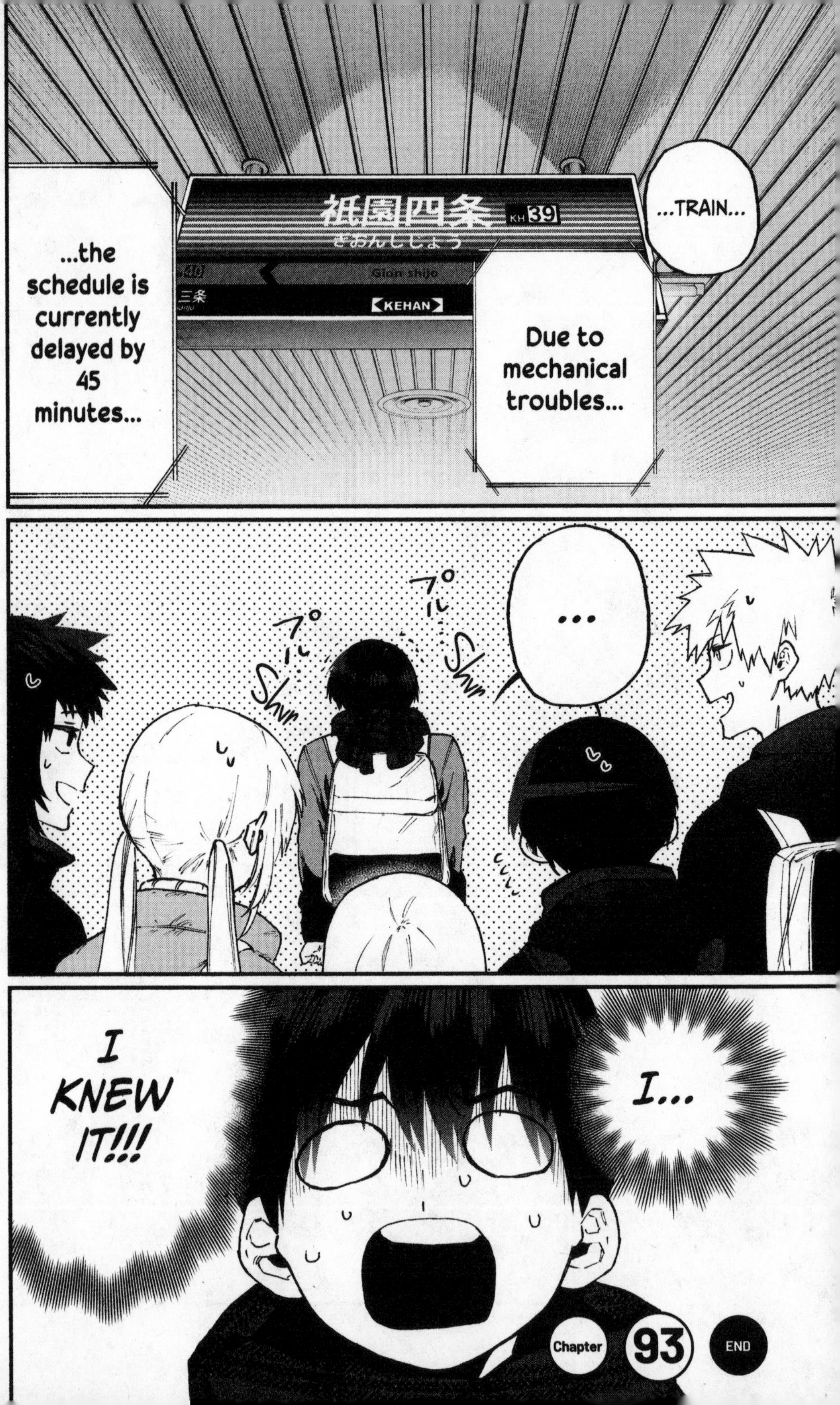
...TRAIN...
祇園四条
KH 39
ぎおんしじょう
Gion shijo
三条
KEHAN
Due to mechanical troubles...
...the schedule is currently delayed by 45 minutes...
...
プル
Shvr
プル
Shvr
I...
I KNEW IT!!!
Chapter 93 END

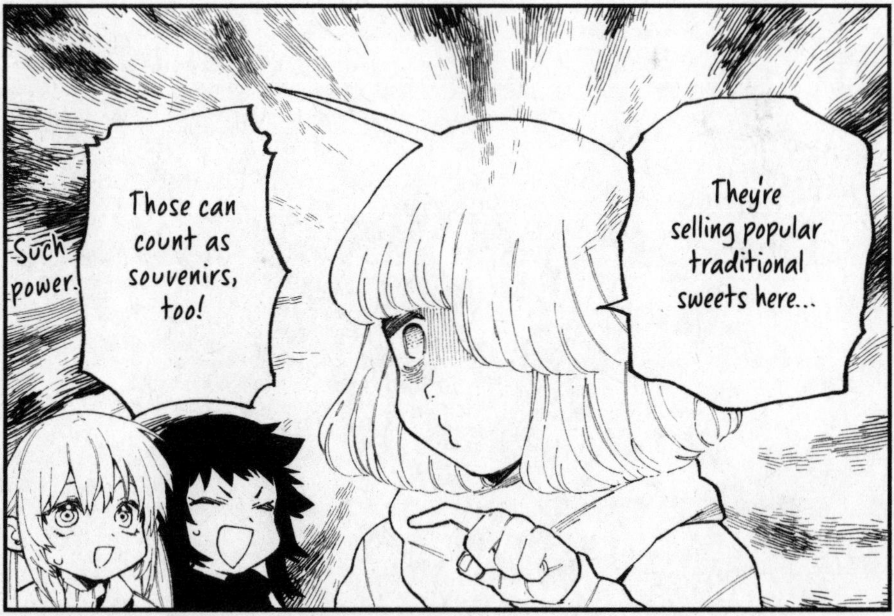
They're selling popular traditional sweets here...
Those can count as souvenirs, too!
Such power.

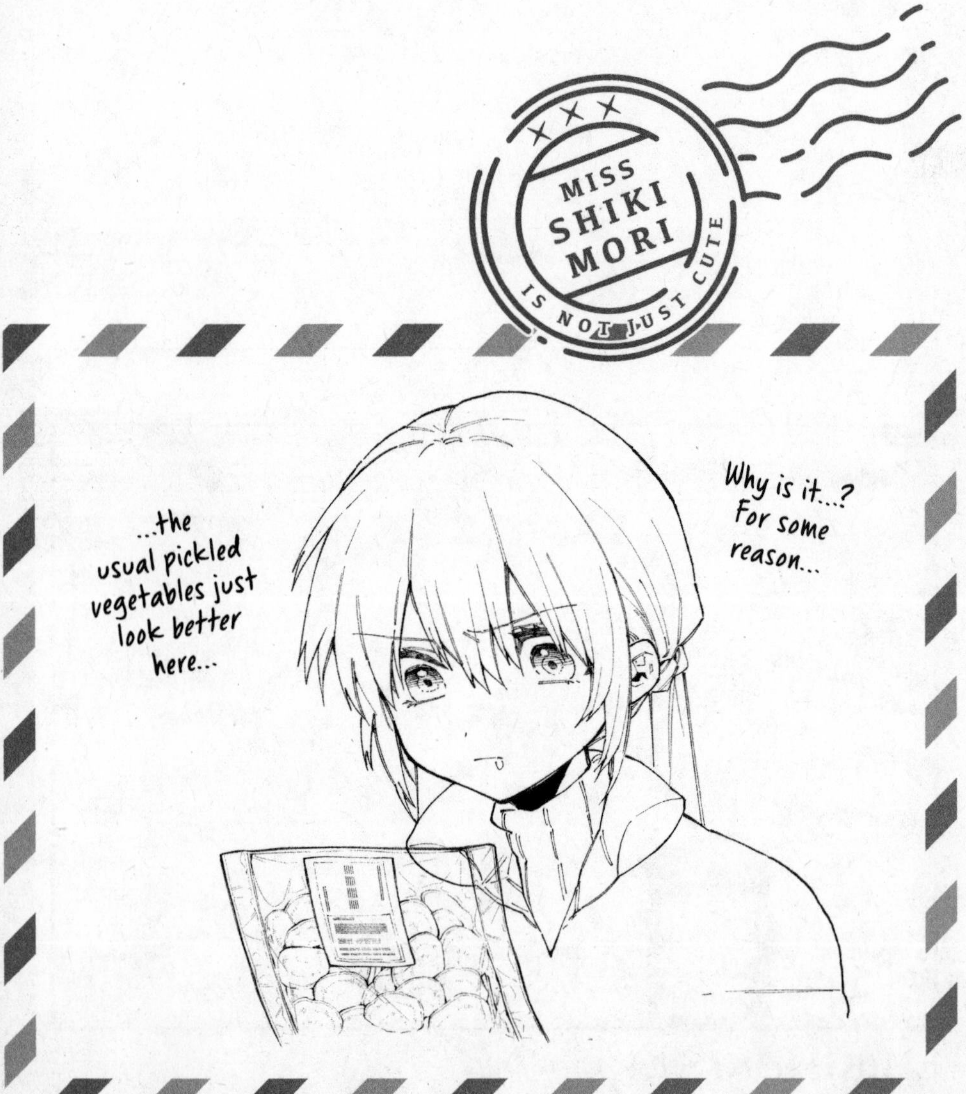
MISS SHIKI MORI
IS NOT JUST CUTE
Why is it...? For some reason...
...the usual pickled vegetables just look better here...

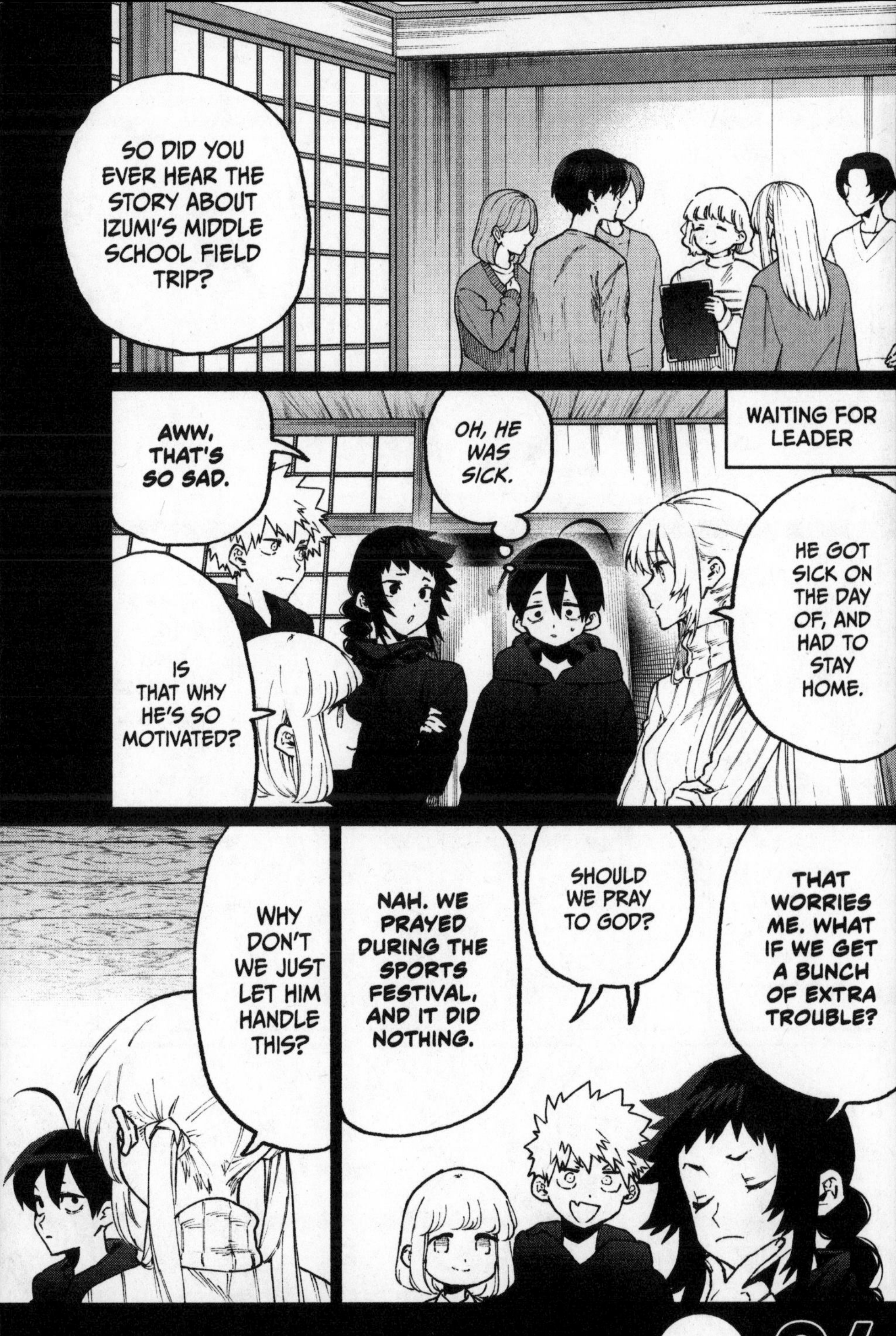
SO DID YOU EVER HEAR THE STORY ABOUT IZUMI'S MIDDLE SCHOOL FIELD TRIP?
WAITING FOR LEADER
HE GOT SICK ON THE DAY OF, AND HAD TO STAY HOME.
OH, HE WAS SICK.
AWW, THAT'S SO SAD.
IS THAT WHY HE'S SO MOTIVATED?
THAT WORRIES ME. WHAT IF WE GET A BUNCH OF EXTRA TROUBLE?
SHOULD WE PRAY TO GOD?
NAH. WE PRAYED DURING THE SPORTS FESTIVAL, AND IT DID NOTHING.
WHY DON'T WE JUST LET HIM HANDLE THIS?

Chapter 94

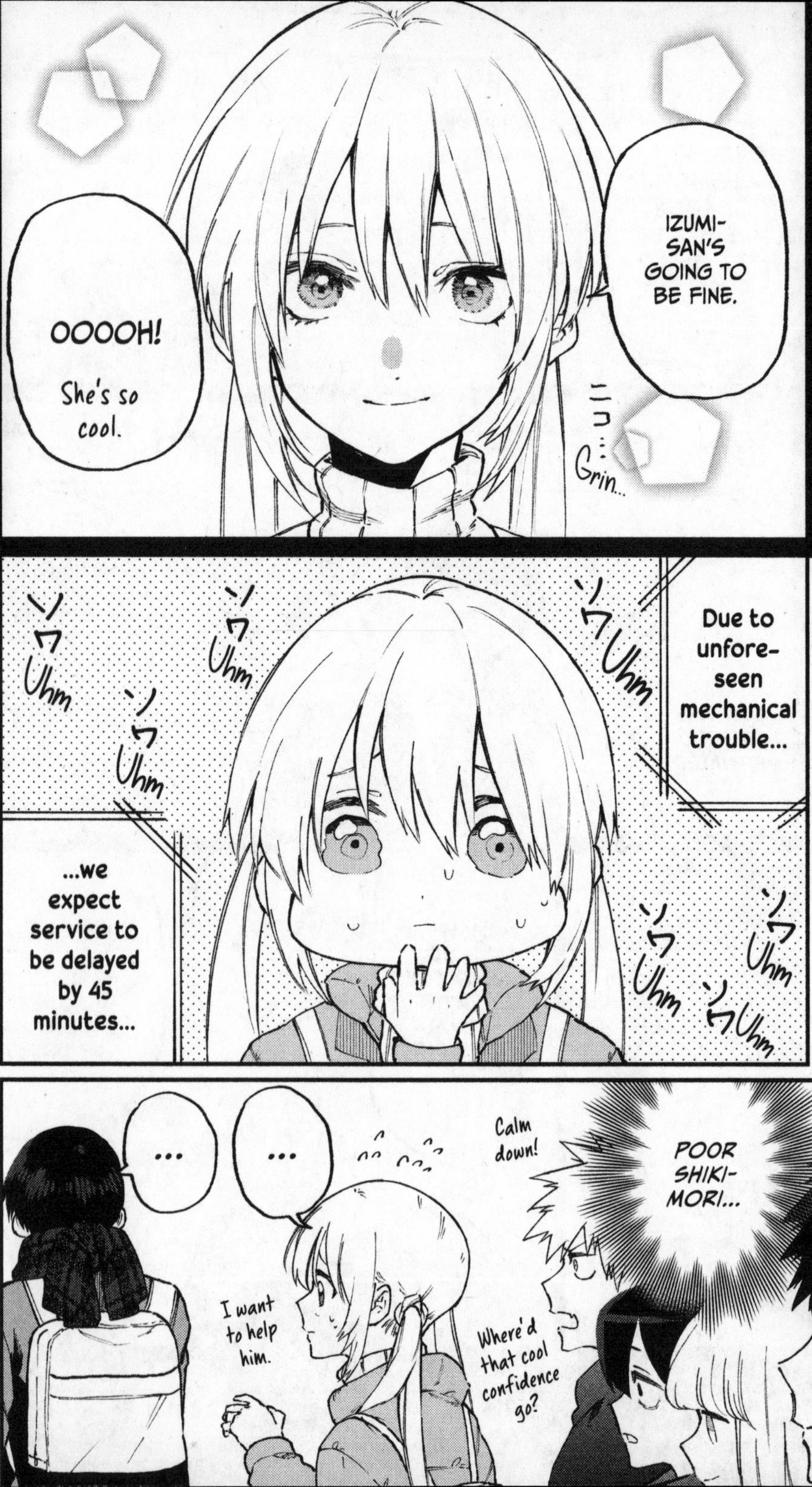
IZUMI-SAN'S GOING TO BE FINE.
ニコ…
Grin...
OOOOH!
She's so cool.
Due to unfore-seen mechanical trouble...
ソワ Uhm
ソワ Uhm
ソワ Uhm
ソワ Uhm
...we expect service to be delayed by 45 minutes...
ソワ Uhm
ソワ Uhm
ソワ Uhm
POOR SHIKI-MORI...
Calm down!
Where'd that cool confidence go?
I want to help him.
...
...

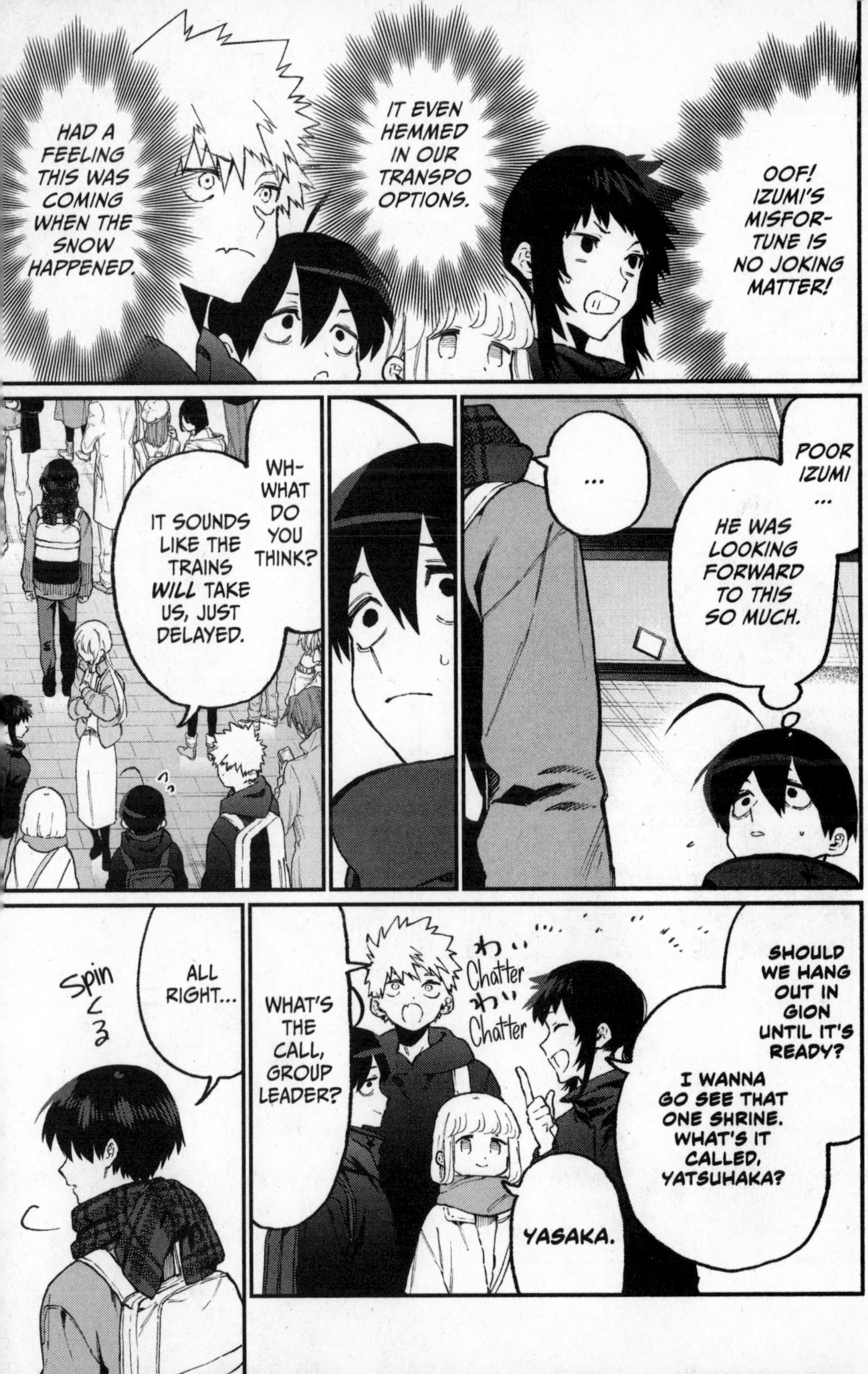
OOF! IZUMI'S MISFOR-TUNE IS NO JOKING MATTER!
IT EVEN HEMMED IN OUR TRANSPO OPTIONS.
HAD A FEELING THIS WAS COMING WHEN THE SNOW HAPPENED.
POOR IZUMI ...
HE WAS LOOKING FORWARD TO THIS SO MUCH.
...
WH-WHAT DO YOU THINK?
IT SOUNDS LIKE THE TRAINS WILL TAKE US, JUST DELAYED.
SHOULD WE HANG OUT IN GION UNTIL IT'S READY?
I WANNA GO SEE THAT ONE SHRINE. WHAT'S IT CALLED, YATSUHAKA?
Chatter
Chatter
WHAT'S THE CALL, GROUP LEADER?
YASAKA.
ALL RIGHT...
Spin

LET'S SWITCH IT UP AND TAKE THE BUS!

WHY DON'T WE HEAD OVER TO THE STOP?

ドロッ
Shine

HE'S TOTALLY FINE...

HUH...?

UMMM

IT'LL TAKE 20 MINUTES LONGER, AND THERE ARE LOTS OF TRANSFERS...

...SO WE'LL HAVE TO BE CARE-FUL NOT TO GET ON THE WRONG ONE.

ALL PLANNED OUT

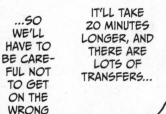

?

WHAT'S WRONG? LET'S GO!

UH... SURE!

Where's my map?

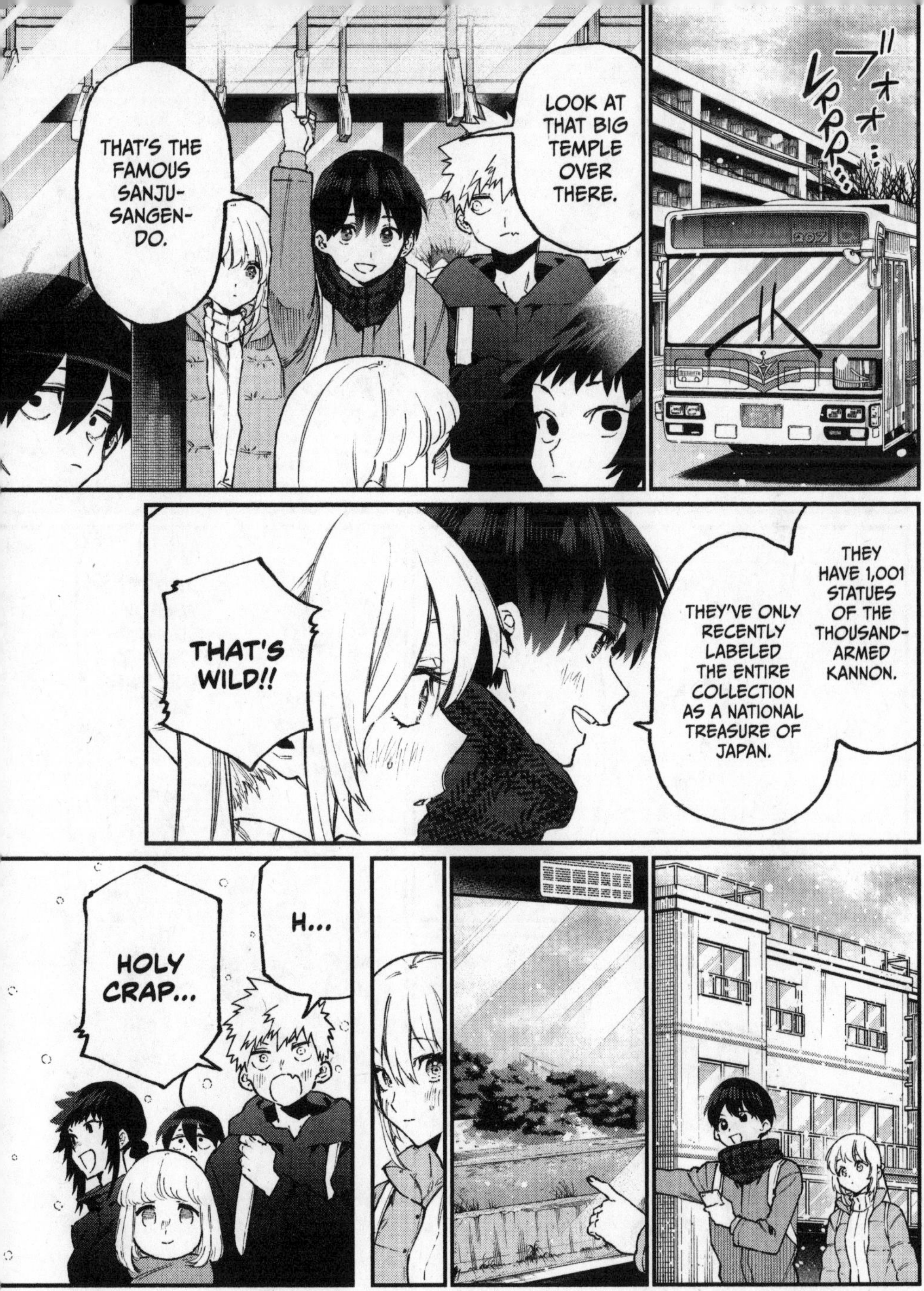

ブォォ…
VRRR...
LOOK AT THAT BIG TEMPLE OVER THERE.
THAT'S THE FAMOUS SANJU-SANGEN-DO.
THEY HAVE 1,001 STATUES OF THE THOUSAND-ARMED KANNON.
THEY'VE ONLY RECENTLY LABELED THE ENTIRE COLLECTION AS A NATIONAL TREASURE OF JAPAN.
THAT'S WILD!!
H...
HOLY CRAP...

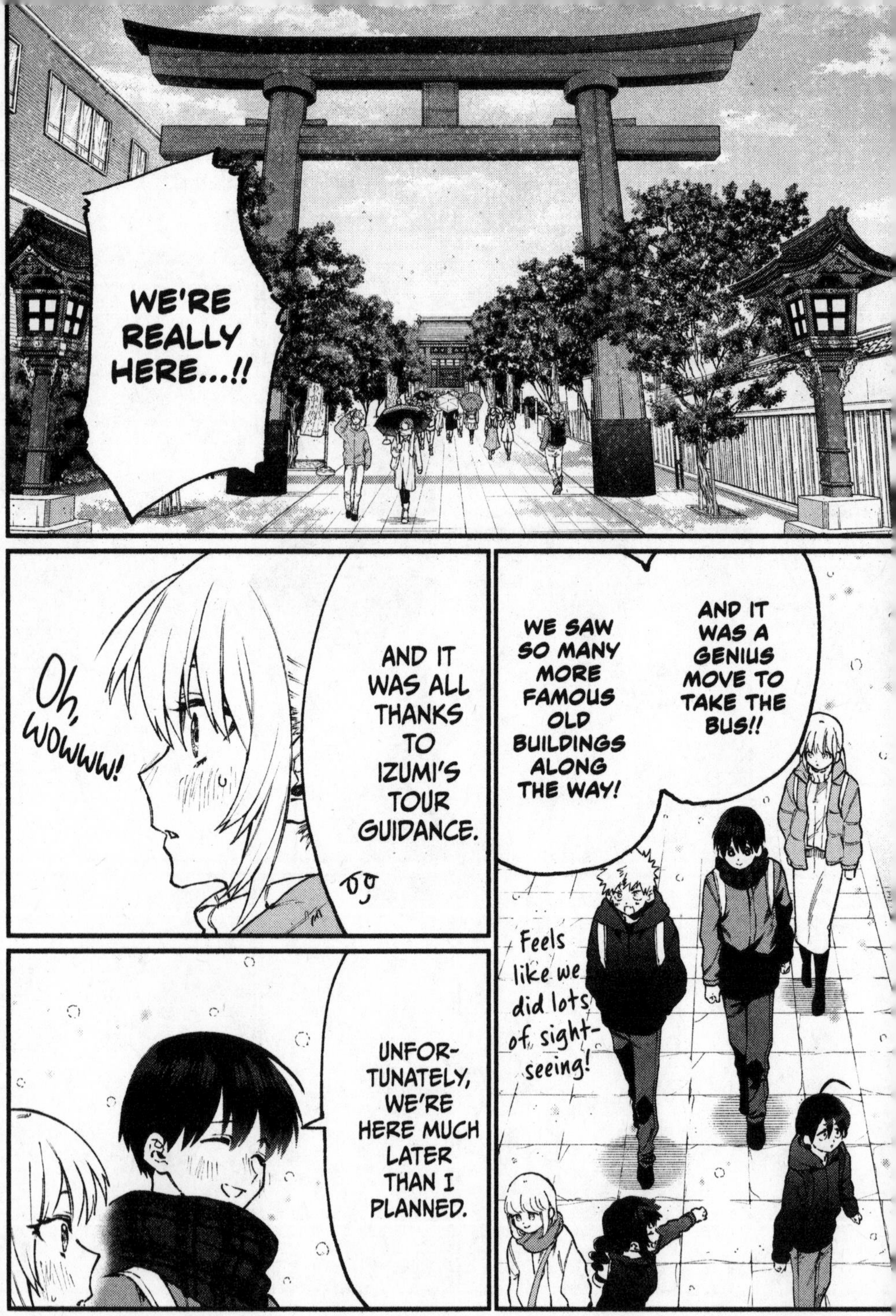
WE'RE REALLY HERE...!!
AND IT WAS A GENIUS MOVE TO TAKE THE BUS!!
WE SAW SO MANY MORE FAMOUS OLD BUILDINGS ALONG THE WAY!
Feels like we did lots of sight-seeing!
AND IT WAS ALL THANKS TO IZUMI'S TOUR GUIDANCE.
Oh, wowww!
UNFOR-TUNATELY, WE'RE HERE MUCH LATER THAN I PLANNED.

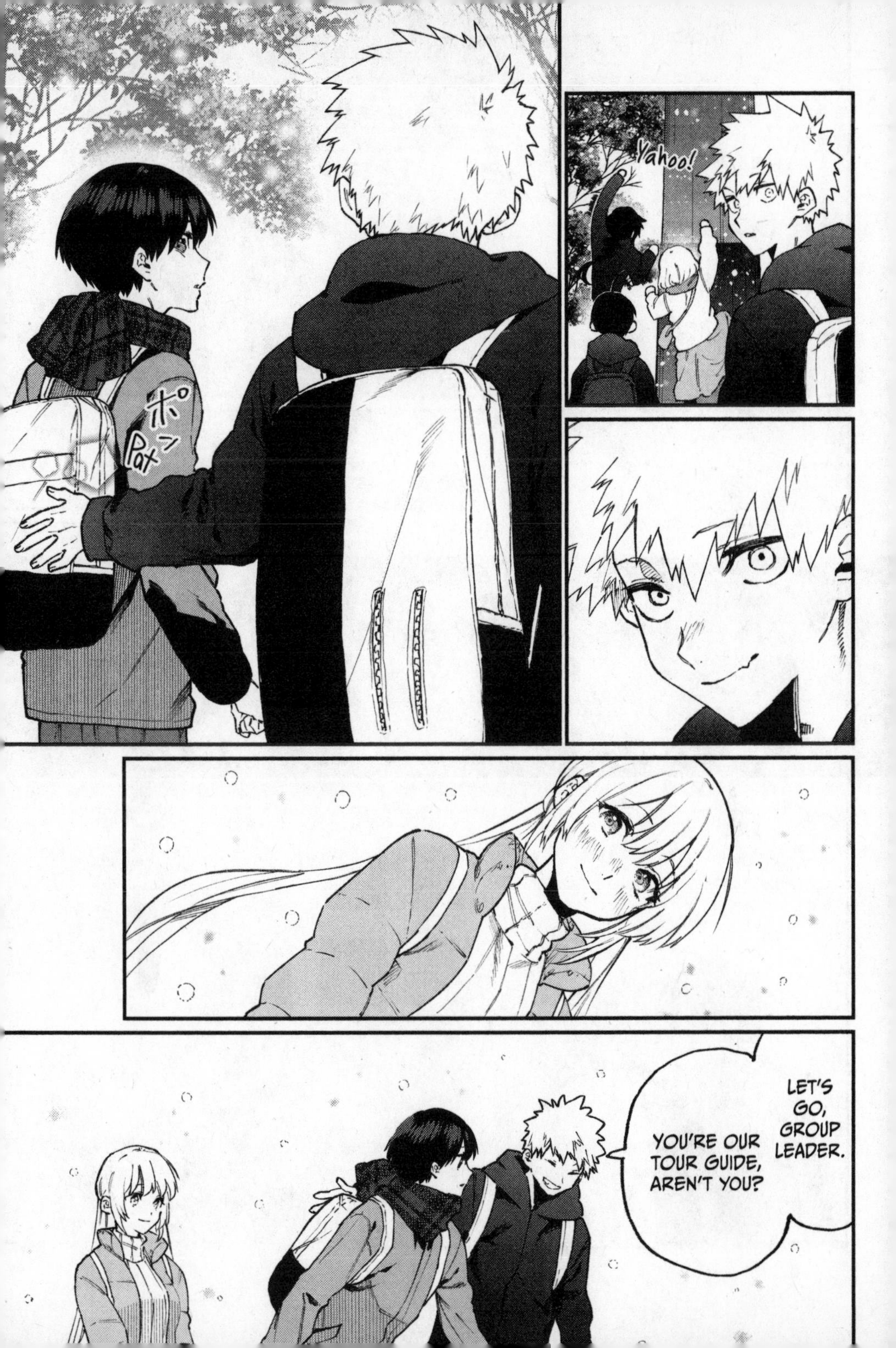

Yahoo!
ポン
Pat
LET'S GO, GROUP LEADER.
YOU'RE OUR TOUR GUIDE, AREN'T YOU?

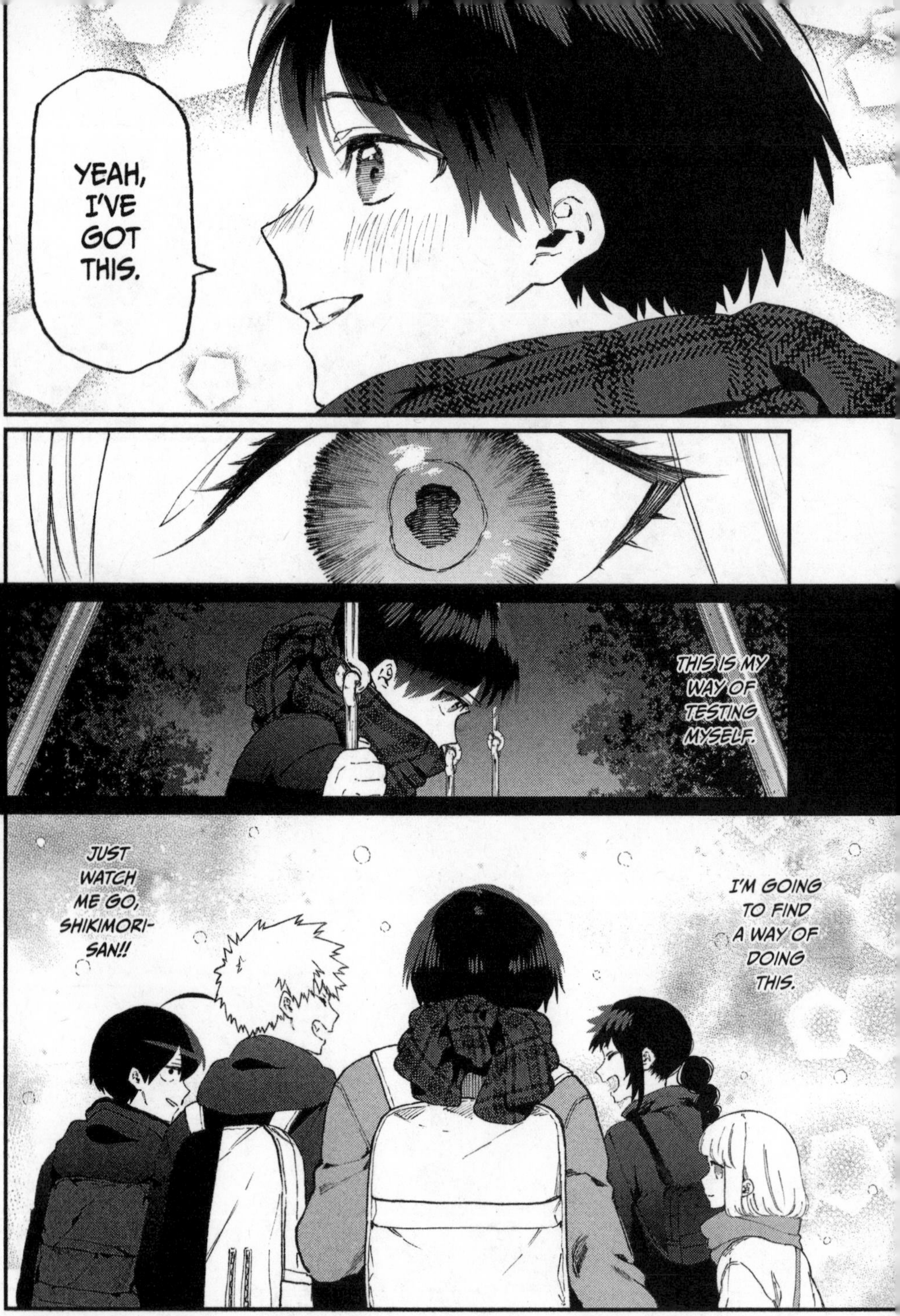
YEAH, I'VE GOT THIS.
THIS IS MY WAY OF TESTING MYSELF.
I'M GOING TO FIND A WAY OF DOING THIS.
JUST WATCH ME GO, SHIKIMORI-SAN!!

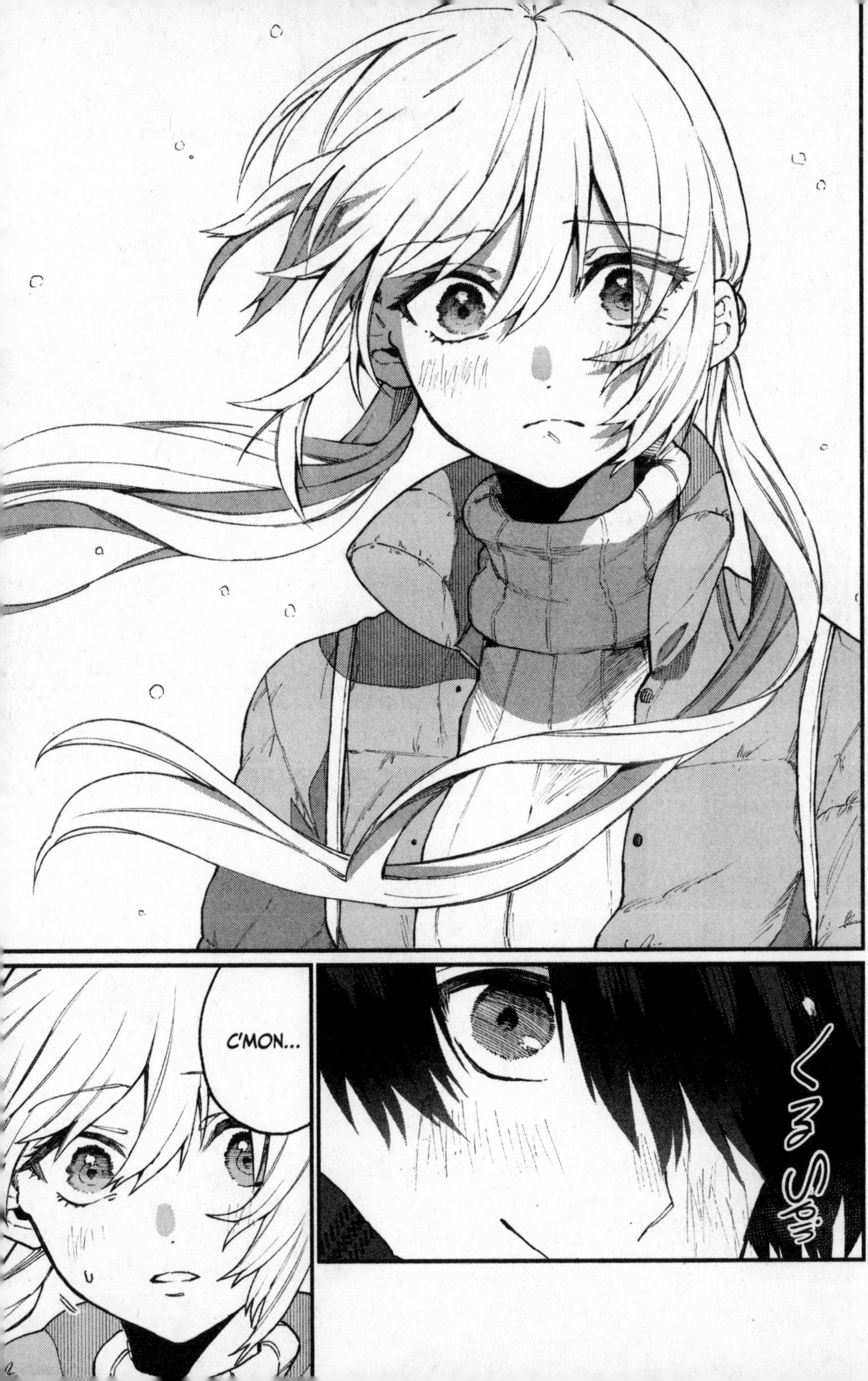
Spin
C'MON...

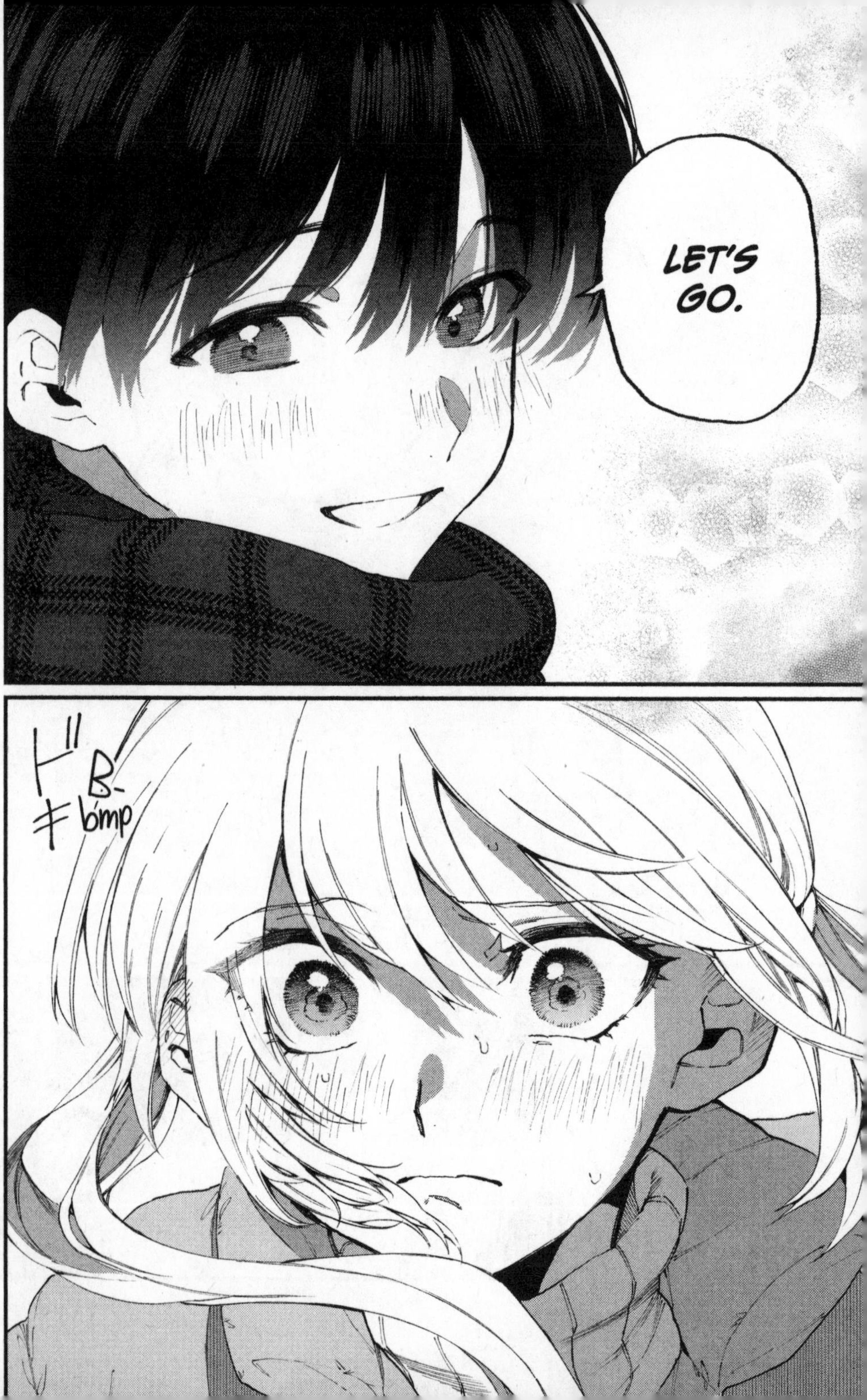
LET'S GO.
ドキ
B-bmp

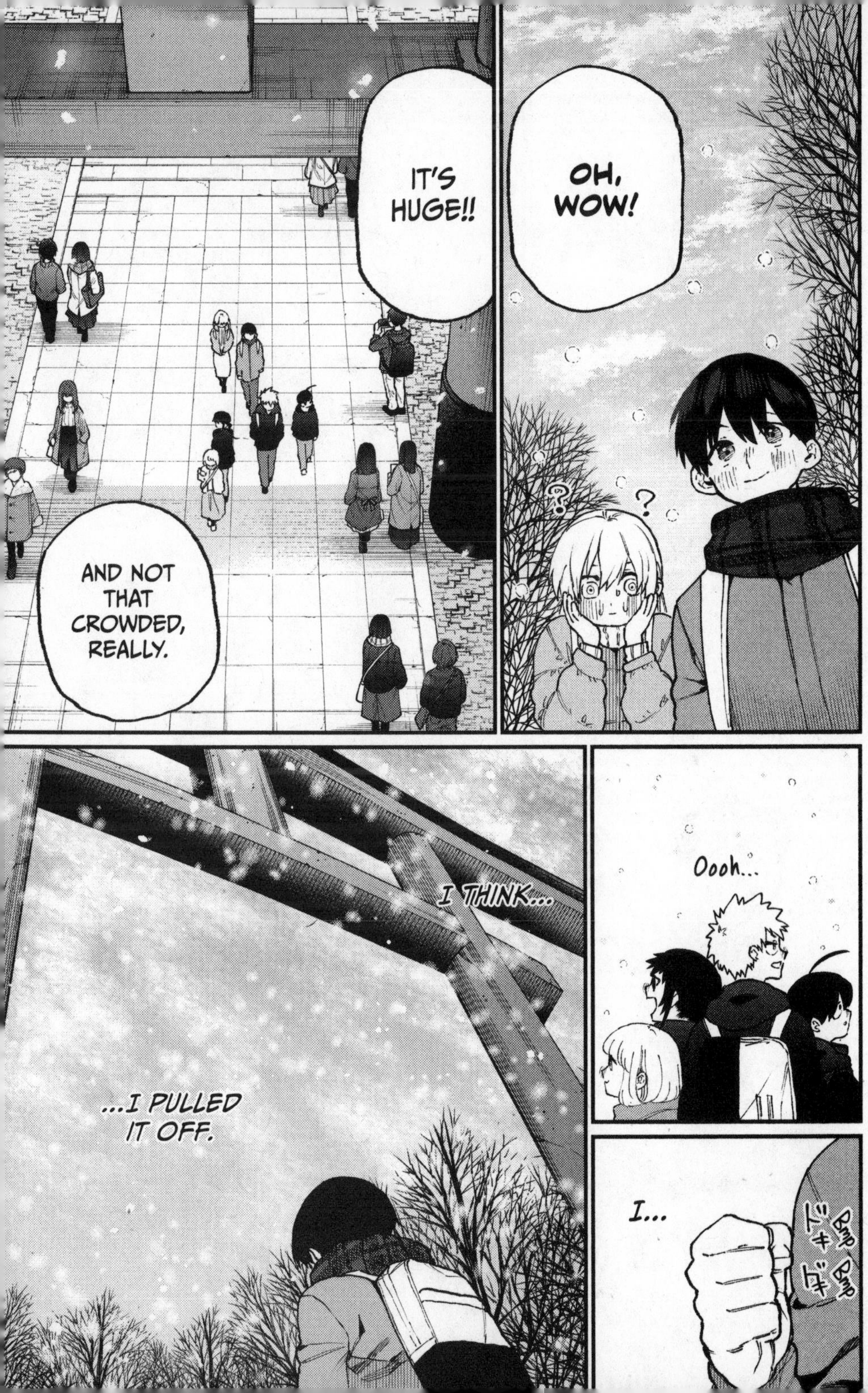
OH, WOW!
IT'S HUGE!!
AND NOT THAT CROWDED, REALLY.
Oooh...
I...
ドキドキ
Bmp Bmp
I THINK...
...I PULLED IT OFF.

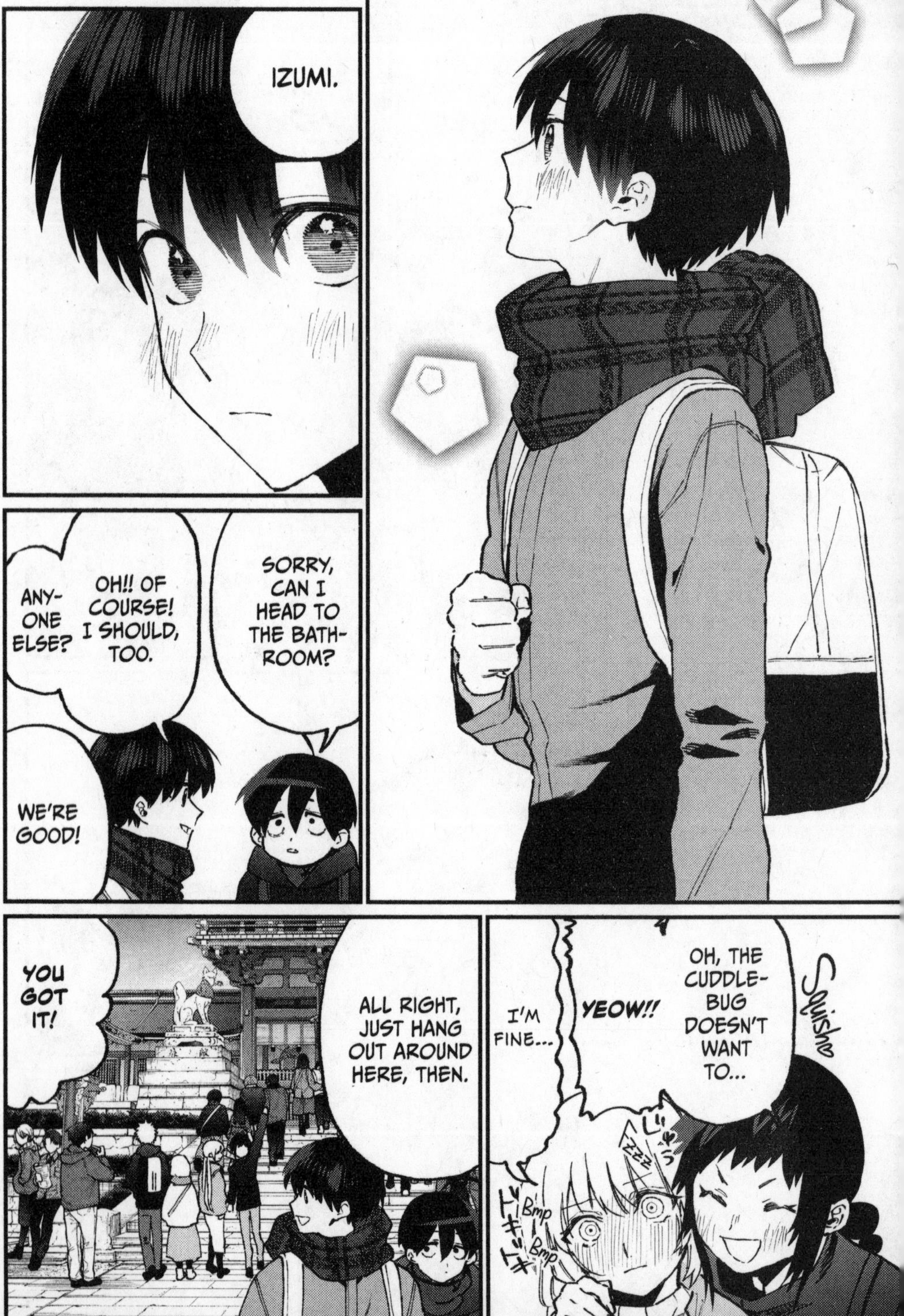
IZUMI.
SORRY, CAN I HEAD TO THE BATHROOM?
OH!! OF COURSE! I SHOULD, TOO.
ANYONE ELSE?
WE'RE GOOD!
Squish
OH, THE CUDDLEBUG DOESN'T WANT TO...
YEOW!!
I'M FINE...
Bmp Bmp
ALL RIGHT, JUST HANG OUT AROUND HERE, THEN.
YOU GOT IT!

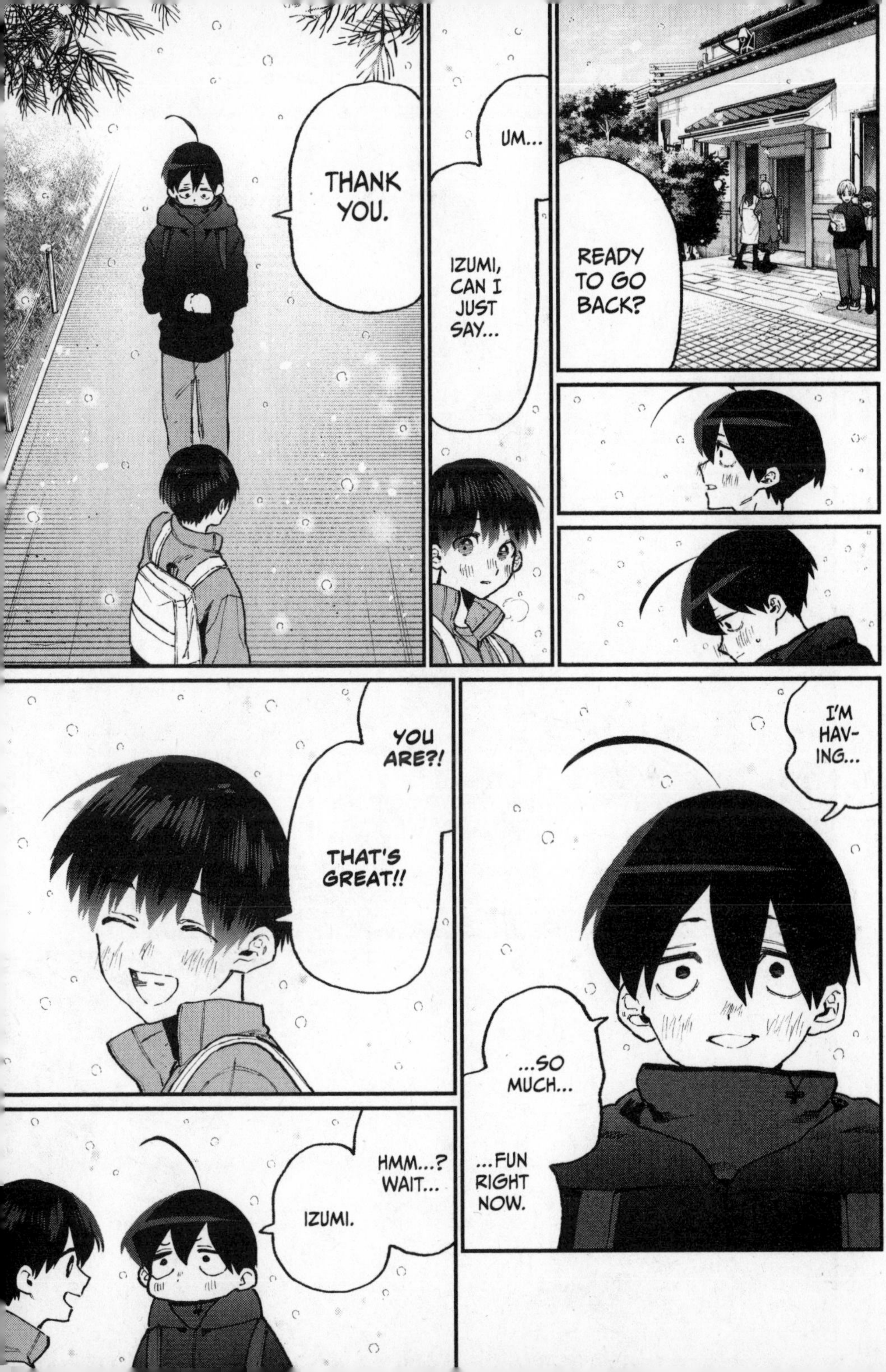
READY TO GO BACK?
UM...
IZUMI, CAN I JUST SAY...
THANK YOU.
I'M HAV-ING...
...SO MUCH...
...FUN RIGHT NOW.
YOU ARE?!
THAT'S GREAT!!
HMM...? WAIT...
IZUMI.

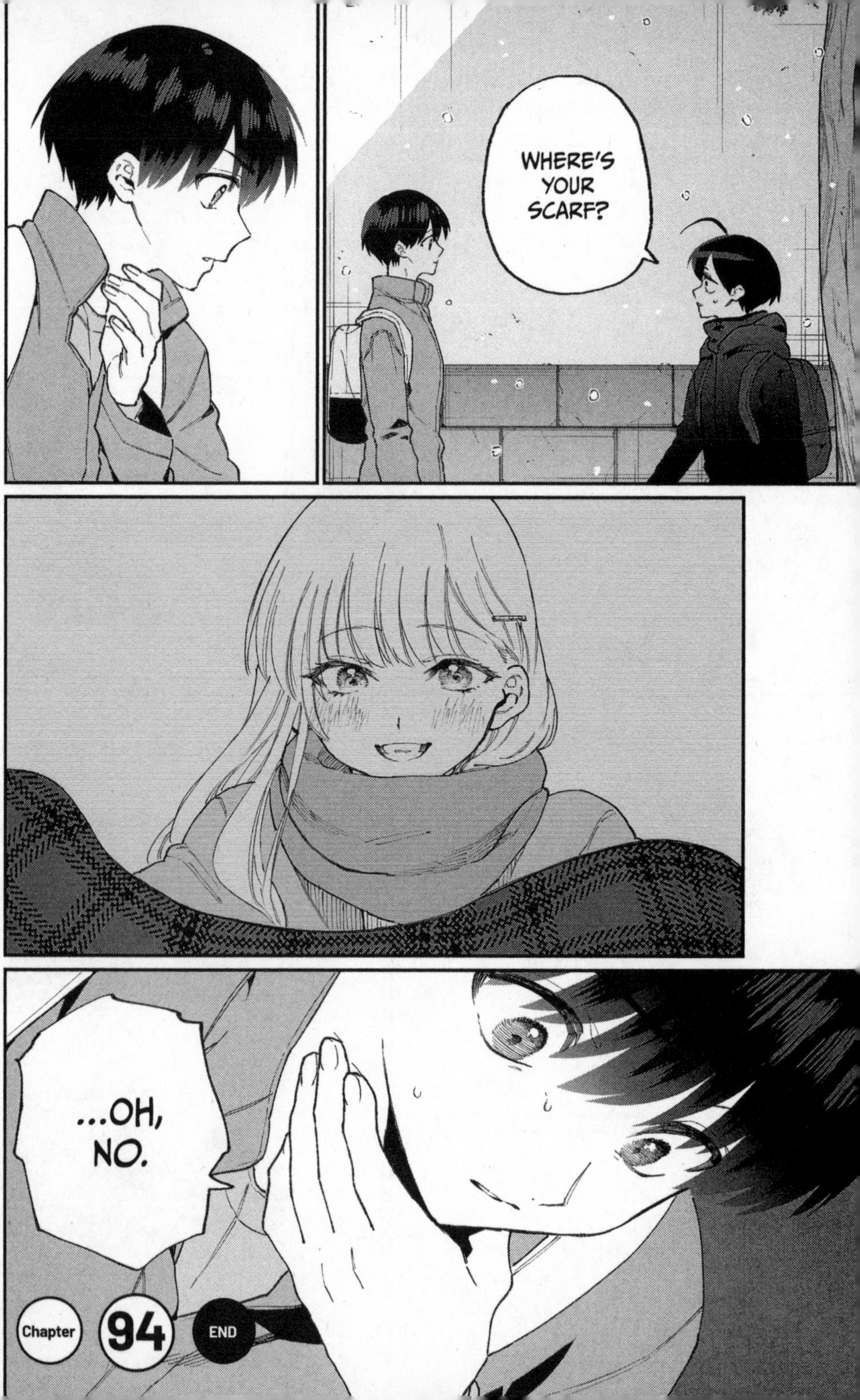
WHERE'S YOUR SCARF?
...OH, NO.
Chapter 94 END

SHIKIMORI'S not just a cutie

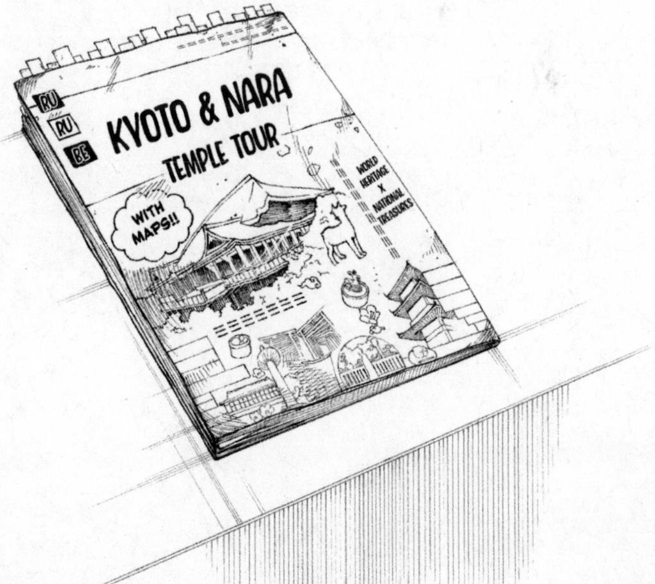
RU
RU
BE
KYOTO & NARA
TEMPLE TOUR
WITH MAPS!!
WORLD HERITAGE X NATIONAL TREASURES

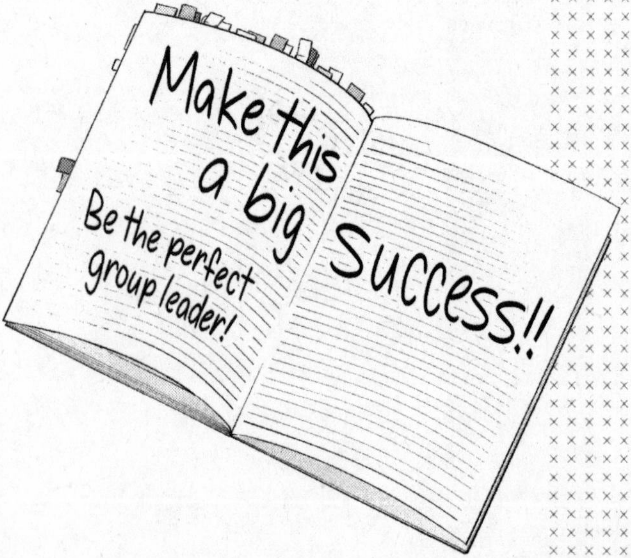
Make this a big Success!!
Be the perfect group leader!

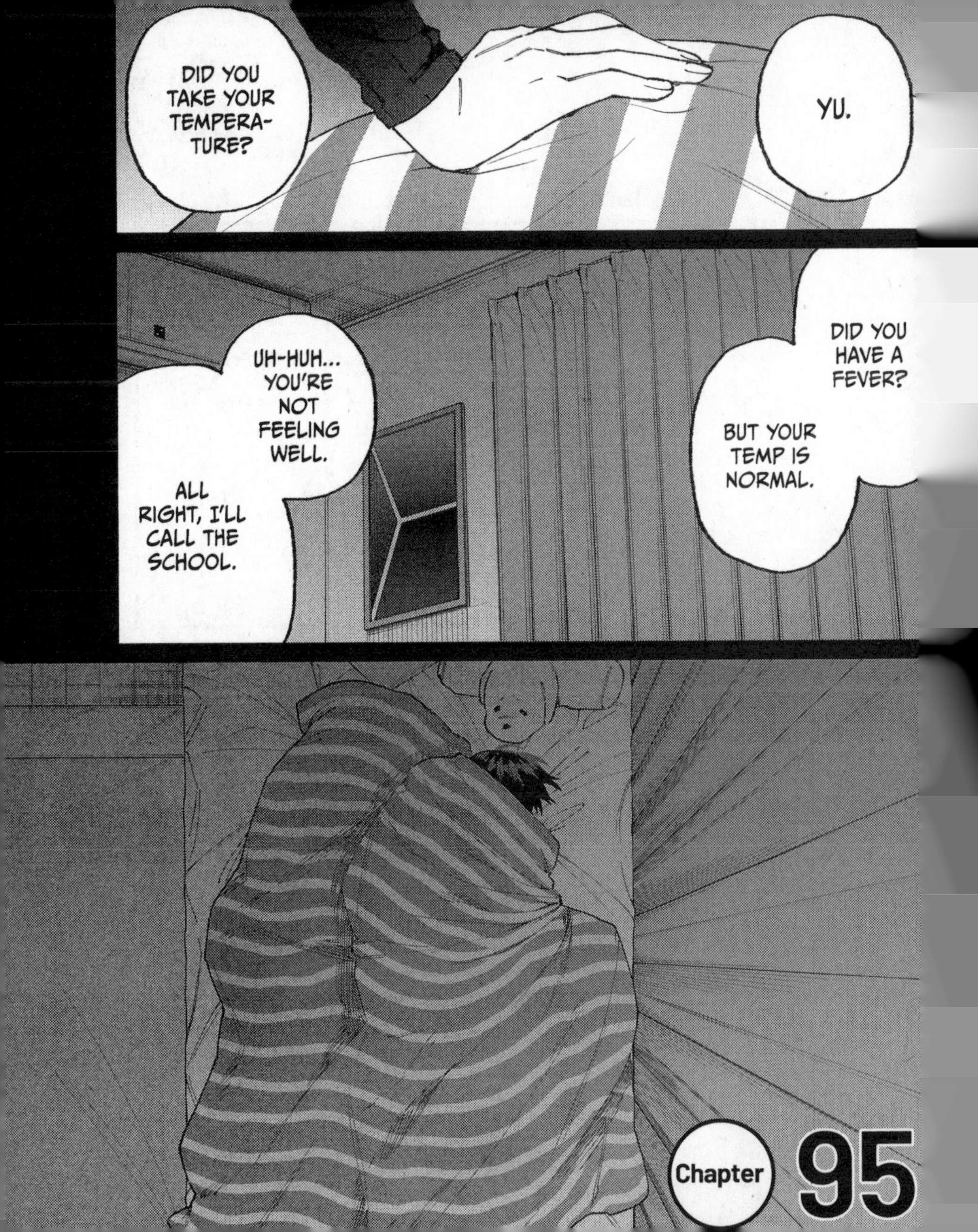
YU.
DID YOU TAKE YOUR TEMPERA-TURE?
DID YOU HAVE A FEVER?
BUT YOUR TEMP IS NORMAL.
UH-HUH... YOU'RE NOT FEELING WELL.
ALL RIGHT, I'LL CALL THE SCHOOL.
Chapter 95

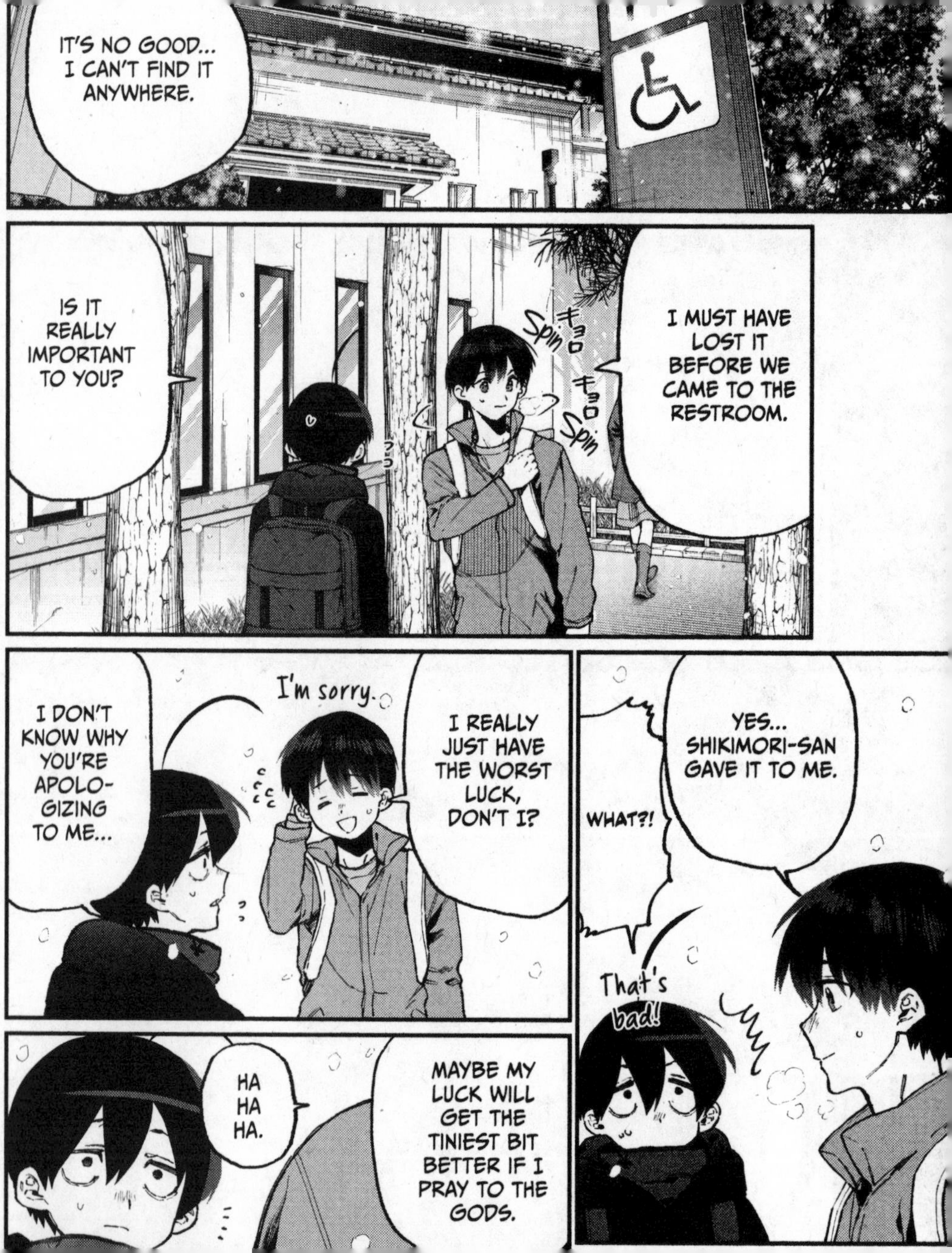
IT'S NO GOOD... I CAN'T FIND IT ANYWHERE.
I MUST HAVE LOST IT BEFORE WE CAME TO THE RESTROOM.
キョロ Spin
キョロ Spin
IS IT REALLY IMPORTANT TO YOU?
YES... SHIKIMORI-SAN GAVE IT TO ME.
WHAT?!
That's bad!
I REALLY JUST HAVE THE WORST LUCK, DON'T I?
I'm sorry.
I DON'T KNOW WHY YOU'RE APOLO-GIZING TO ME...
MAYBE MY LUCK WILL GET THE TINIEST BIT BETTER IF I PRAY TO THE GODS.
HA HA HA.

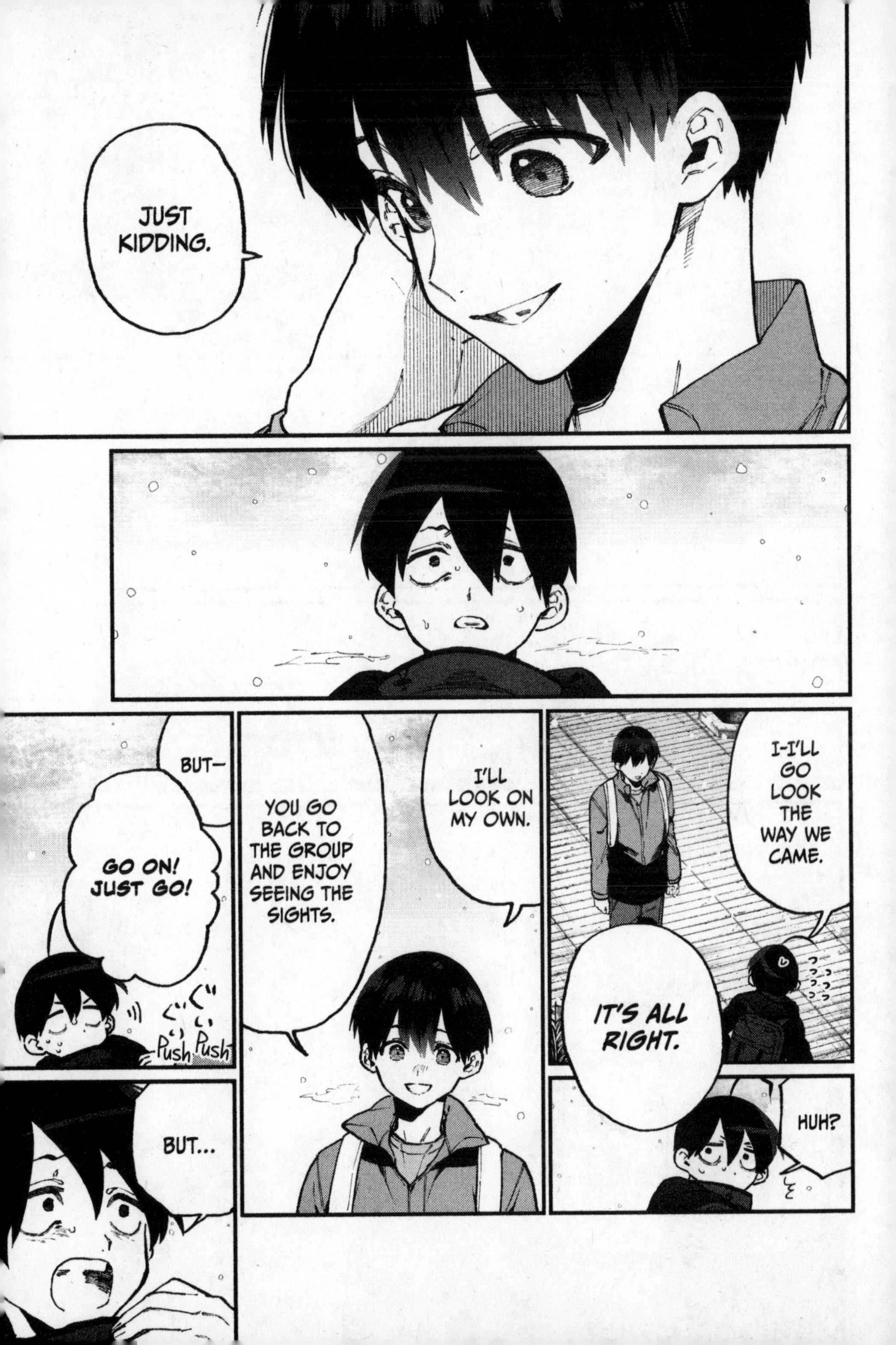
JUST KIDDING.
I-I'LL GO LOOK THE WAY WE CAME.
IT'S ALL RIGHT.
HUH?
I'LL LOOK ON MY OWN.
YOU GO BACK TO THE GROUP AND ENJOY SEEING THE SIGHTS.
BUT—
GO ON! JUST GO!
Push Push
BUT...

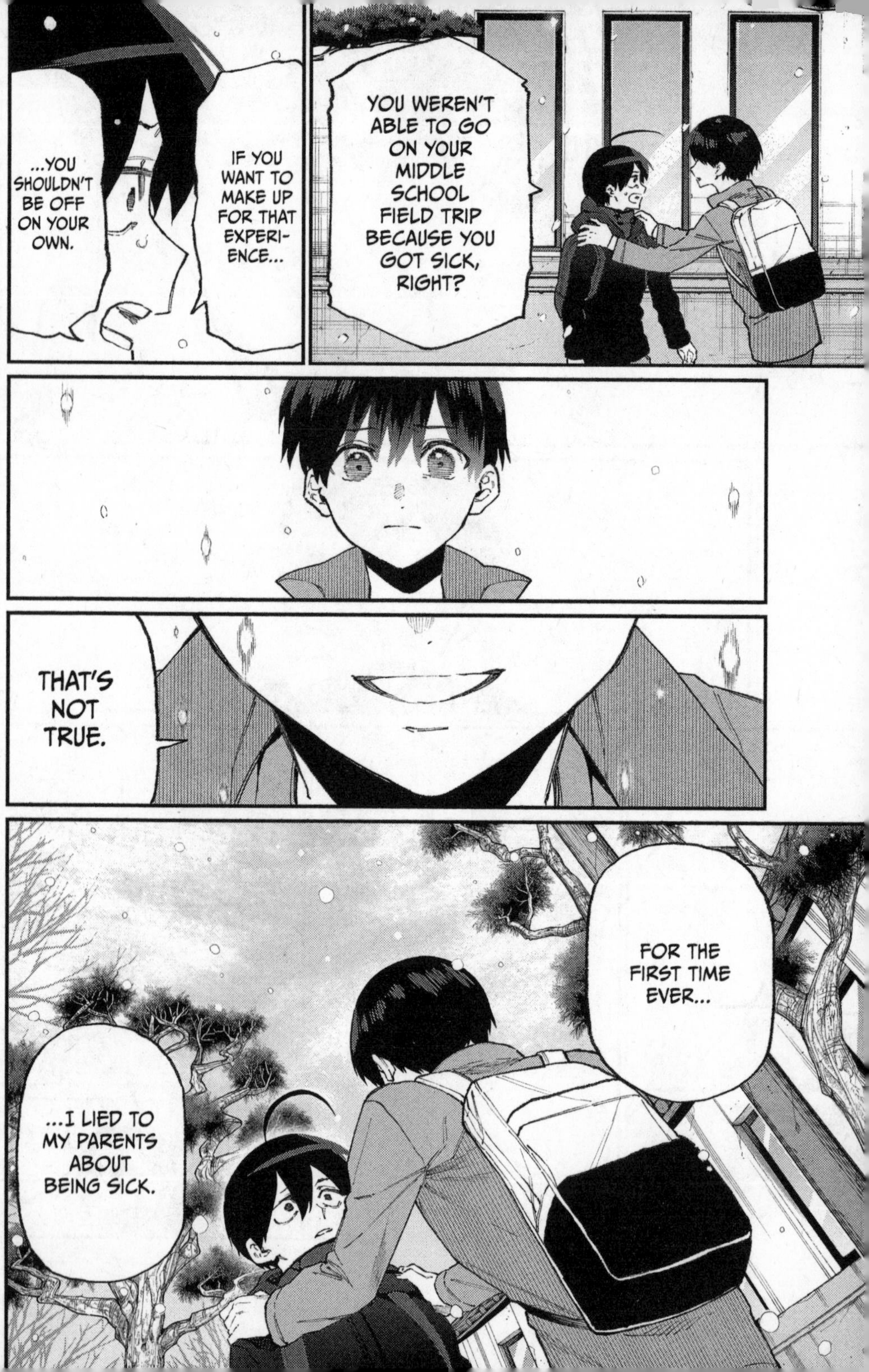
YOU WEREN'T ABLE TO GO ON YOUR MIDDLE SCHOOL FIELD TRIP BECAUSE YOU GOT SICK, RIGHT?
IF YOU WANT TO MAKE UP FOR THAT EXPERI-ENCE...
...YOU SHOULDN'T BE OFF ON YOUR OWN.
THAT'S NOT TRUE.
FOR THE FIRST TIME EVER...
...I LIED TO MY PARENTS ABOUT BEING SICK.

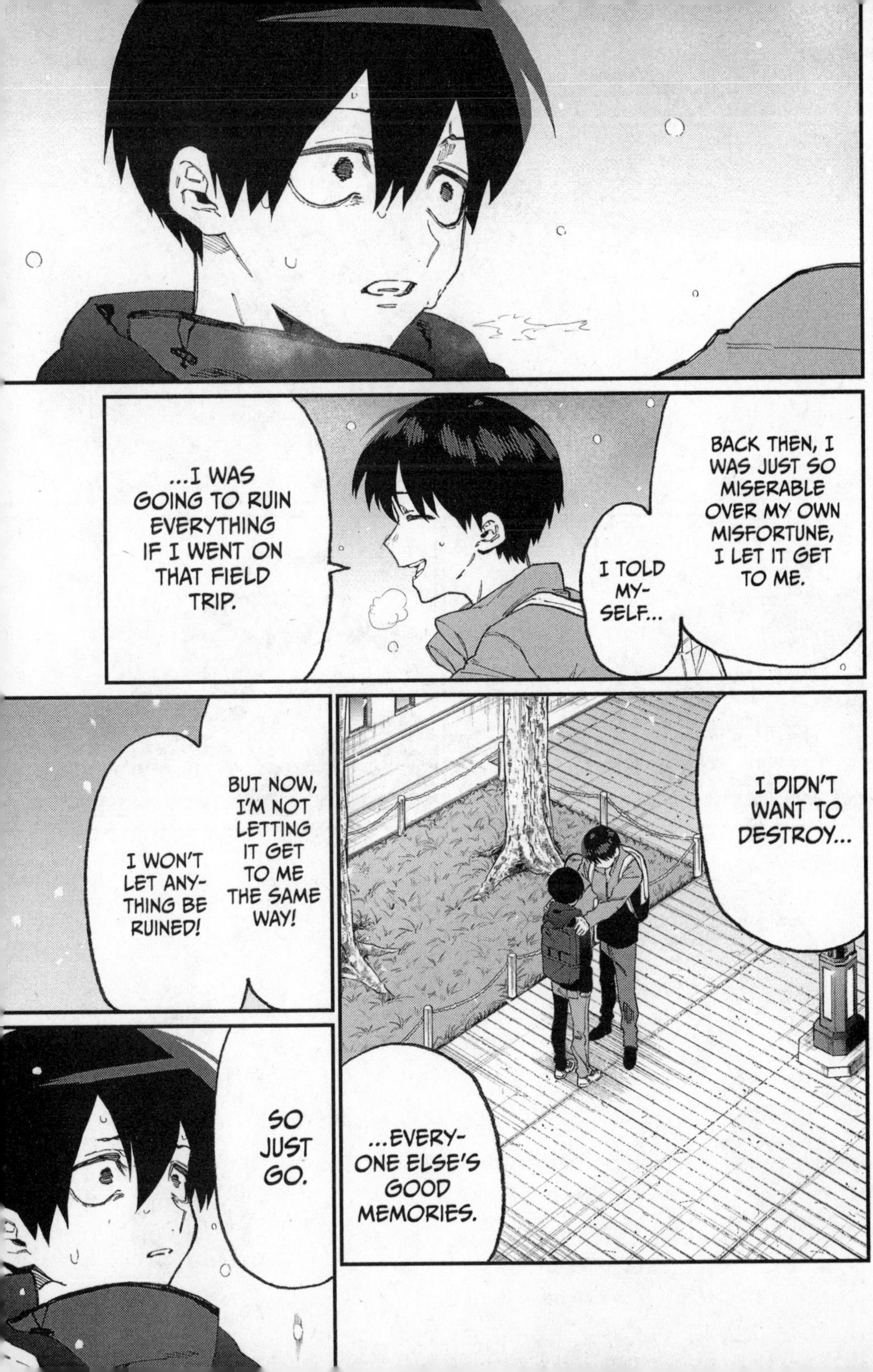
BACK THEN, I WAS JUST SO MISERABLE OVER MY OWN MISFORTUNE, I LET IT GET TO ME.
I TOLD MY-SELF...
...I WAS GOING TO RUIN EVERYTHING IF I WENT ON THAT FIELD TRIP.
I DIDN'T WANT TO DESTROY...
...EVERY-ONE ELSE'S GOOD MEMORIES.
BUT NOW, I'M NOT LETTING IT GET TO ME THE SAME WAY!
I WON'T LET ANY-THING BE RUINED!
SO JUST GO.

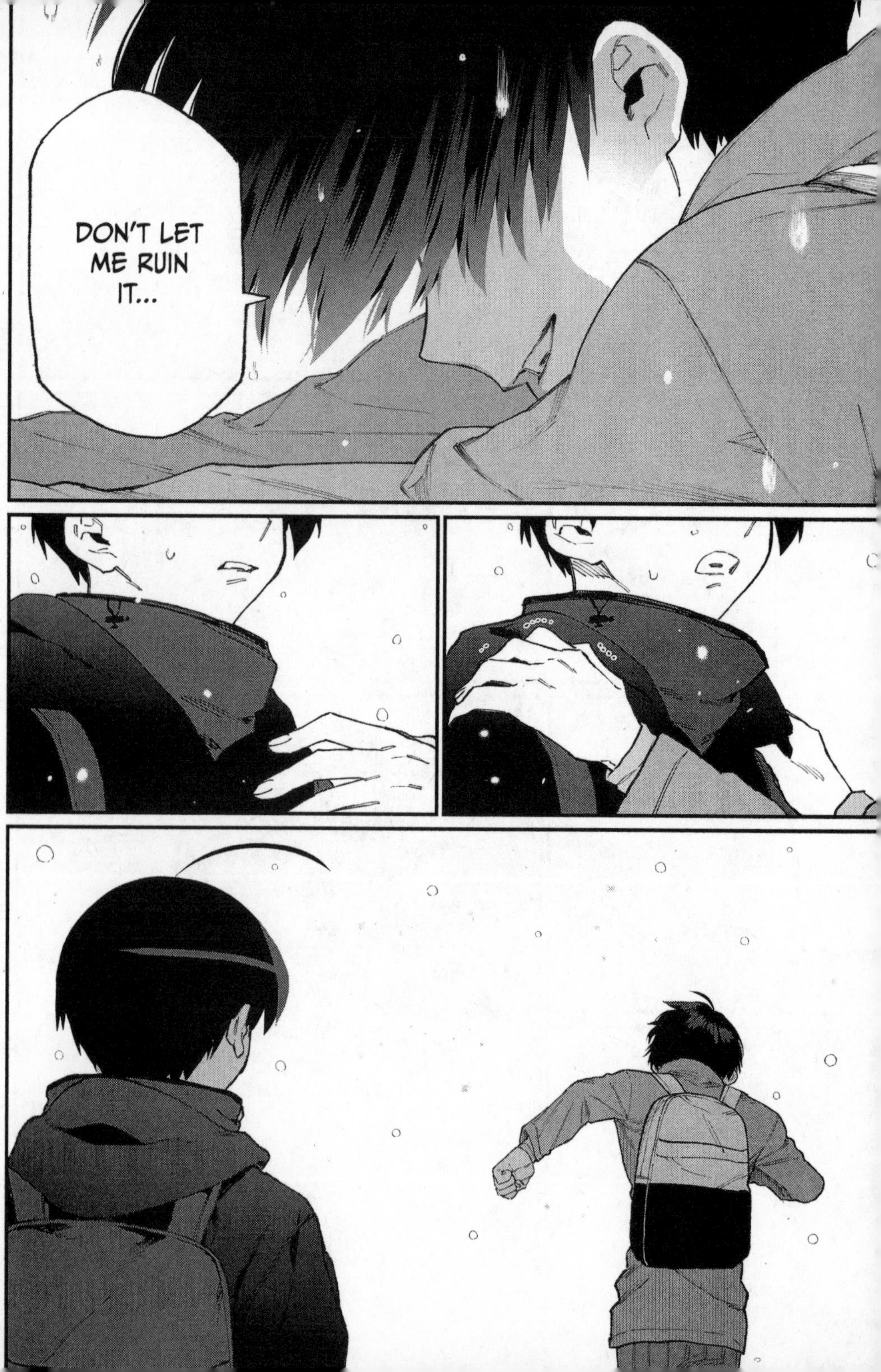
DON'T LET ME RUIN IT...

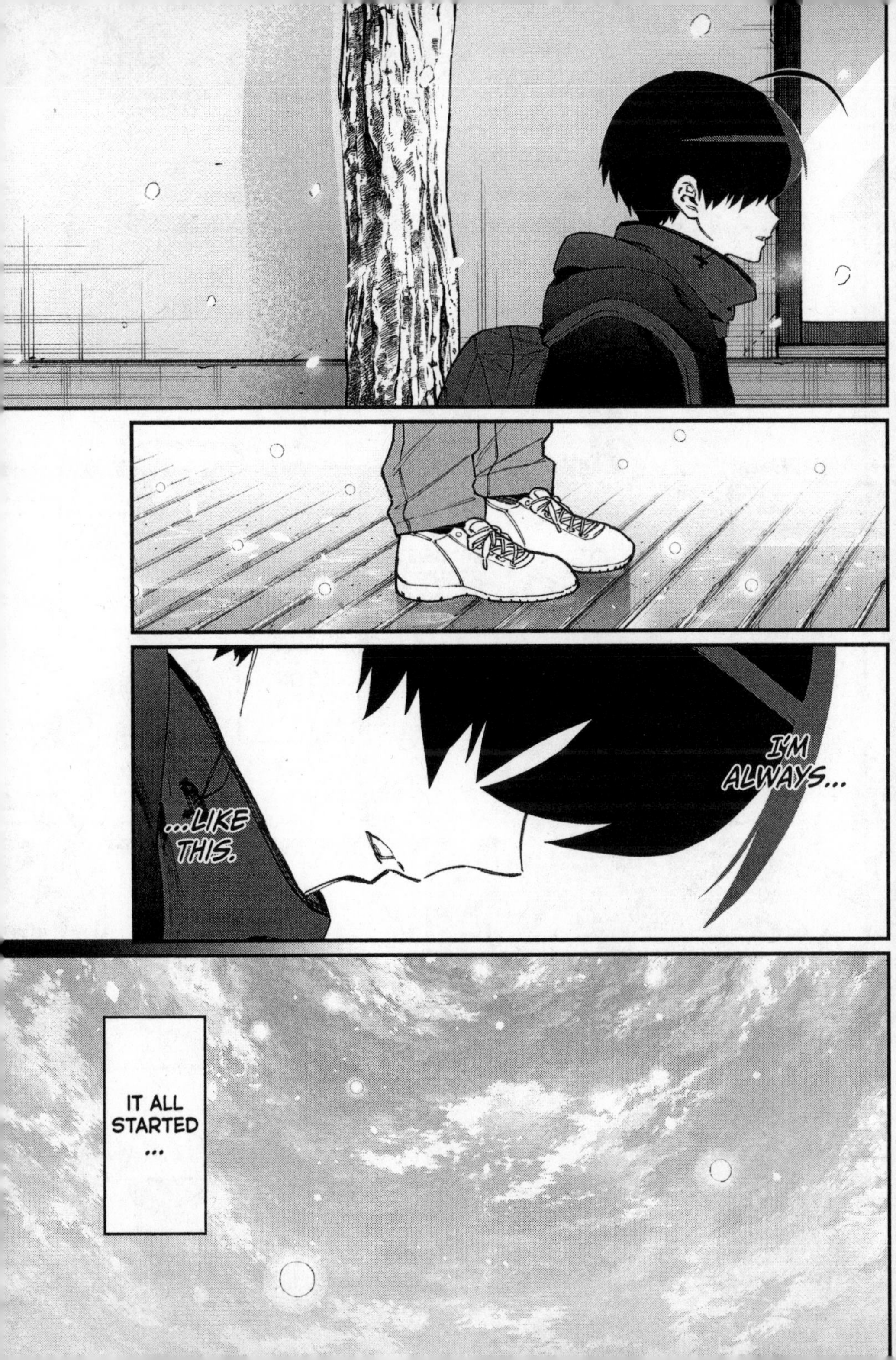
I'M ALWAYS...
...LIKE THIS.
IT ALL STARTED ...

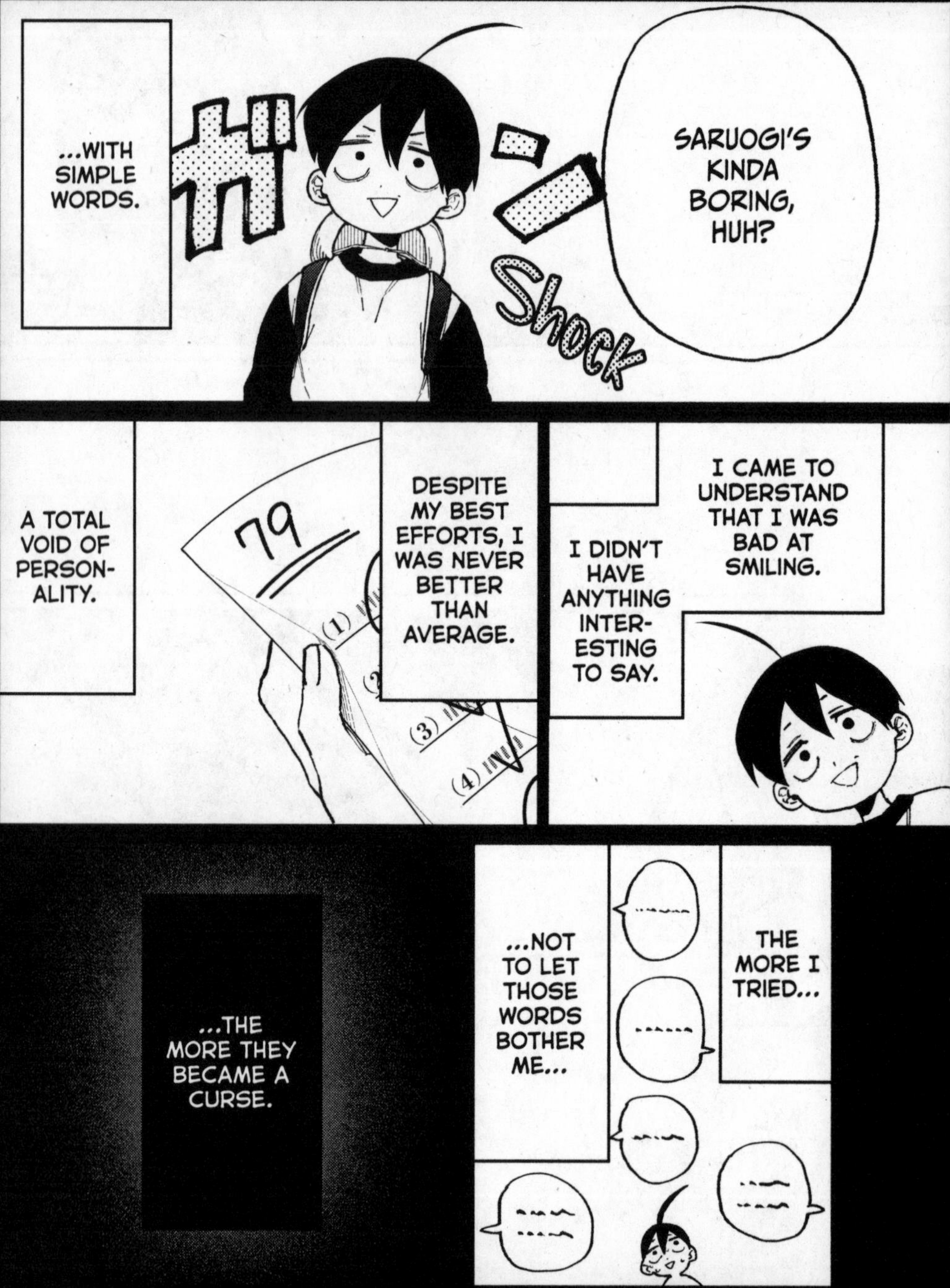
SARUOGI'S KINDA BORING, HUH?
ガー
SHOCK
...WITH SIMPLE WORDS.
I CAME TO UNDERSTAND THAT I WAS BAD AT SMILING.
I DIDN'T HAVE ANYTHING INTER-ESTING TO SAY.
DESPITE MY BEST EFFORTS, I WAS NEVER BETTER THAN AVERAGE.
79
A TOTAL VOID OF PERSON-ALITY.
THE MORE I TRIED...
...NOT TO LET THOSE WORDS BOTHER ME...
...THE MORE THEY BECAME A CURSE.

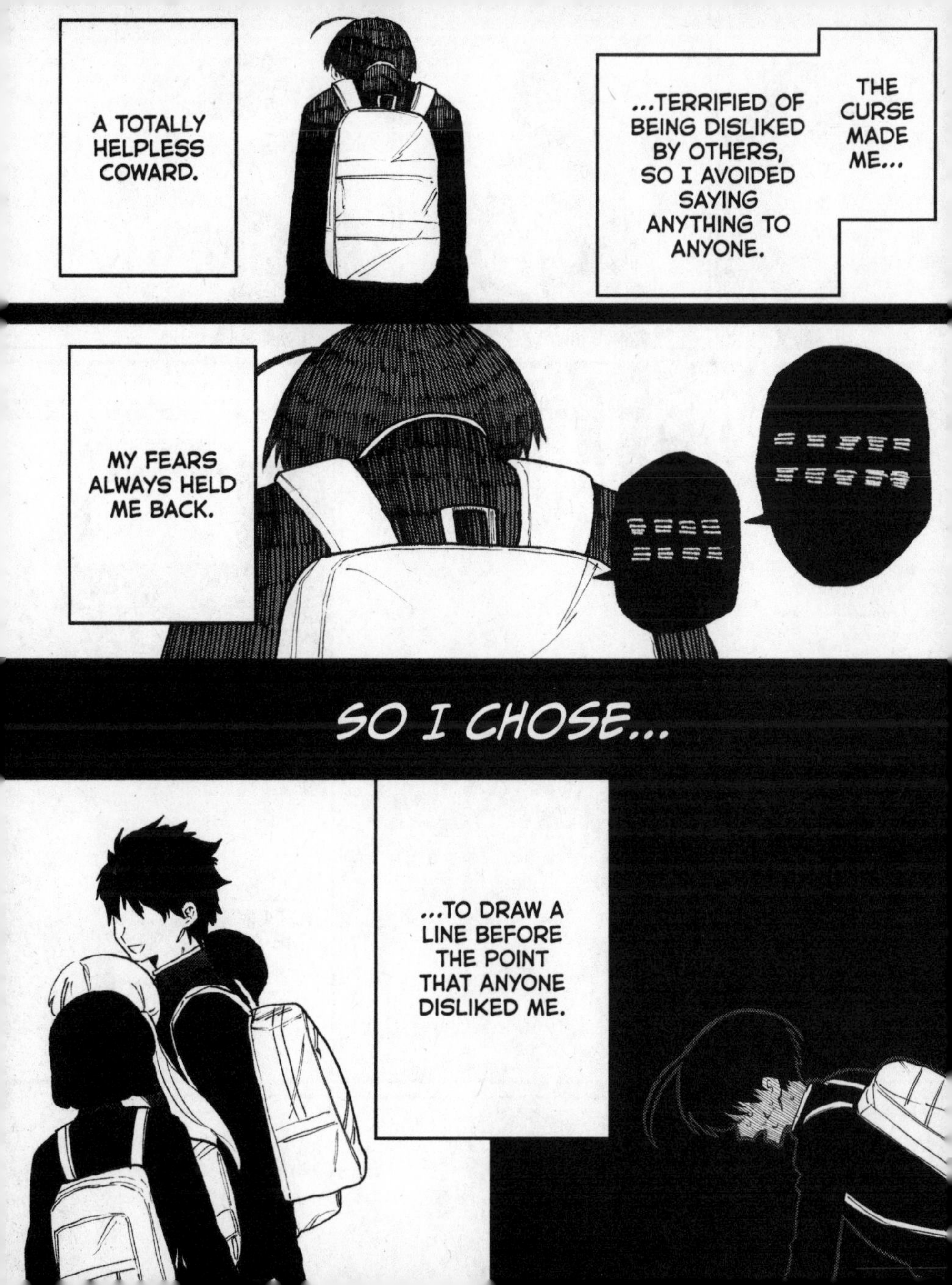
THE CURSE MADE ME...
...TERRIFIED OF BEING DISLIKED BY OTHERS, SO I AVOIDED SAYING ANYTHING TO ANYONE.
A TOTALLY HELPLESS COWARD.
MY FEARS ALWAYS HELD ME BACK.
SO I CHOSE...
...TO DRAW A LINE BEFORE THE POINT THAT ANYONE DISLIKED ME.

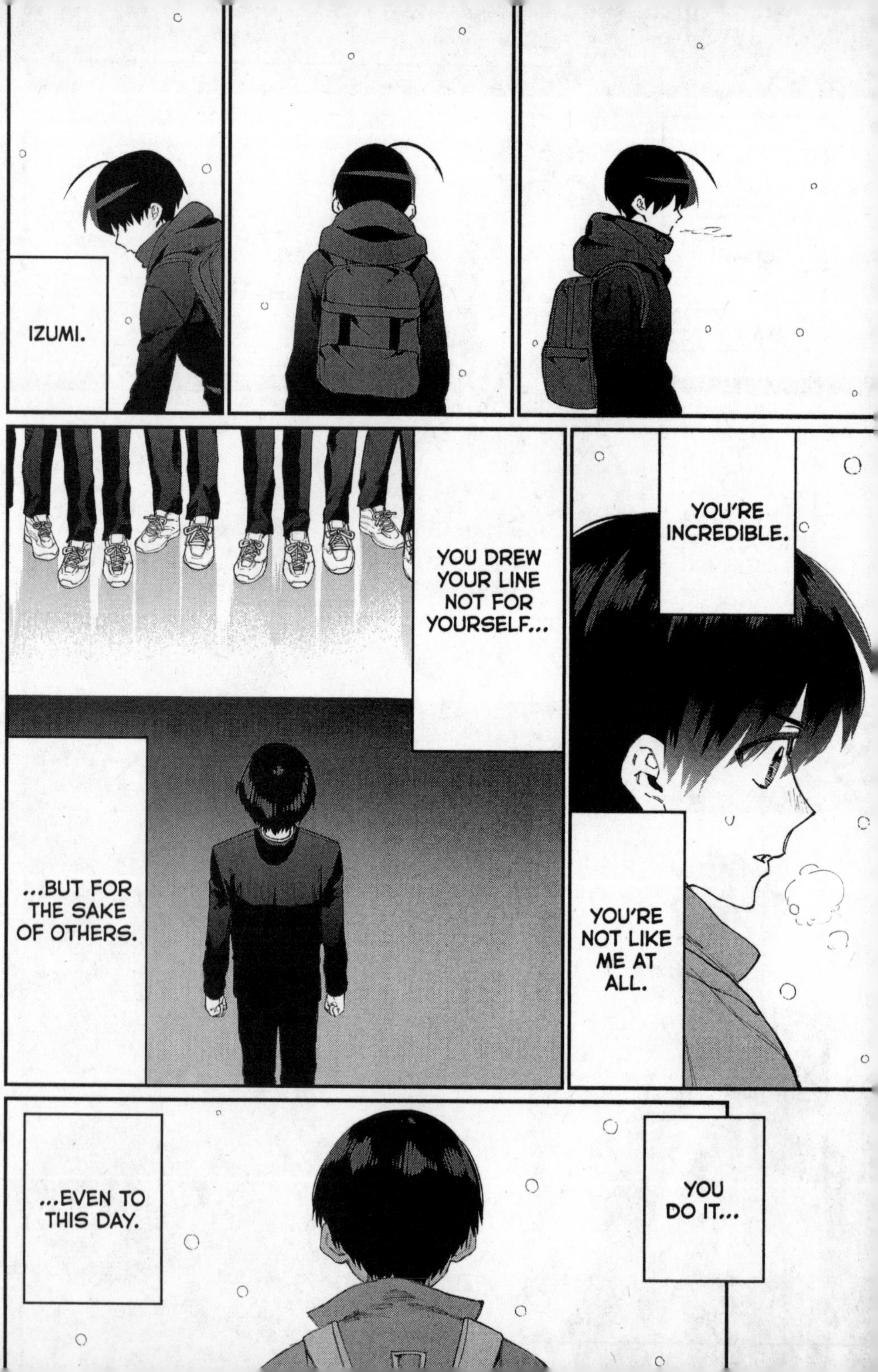
IZUMI.
YOU'RE INCREDIBLE.
YOU'RE NOT LIKE ME AT ALL.
YOU DREW YOUR LINE NOT FOR YOURSELF...
...BUT FOR THE SAKE OF OTHERS.
YOU DO IT...
...EVEN TO THIS DAY.

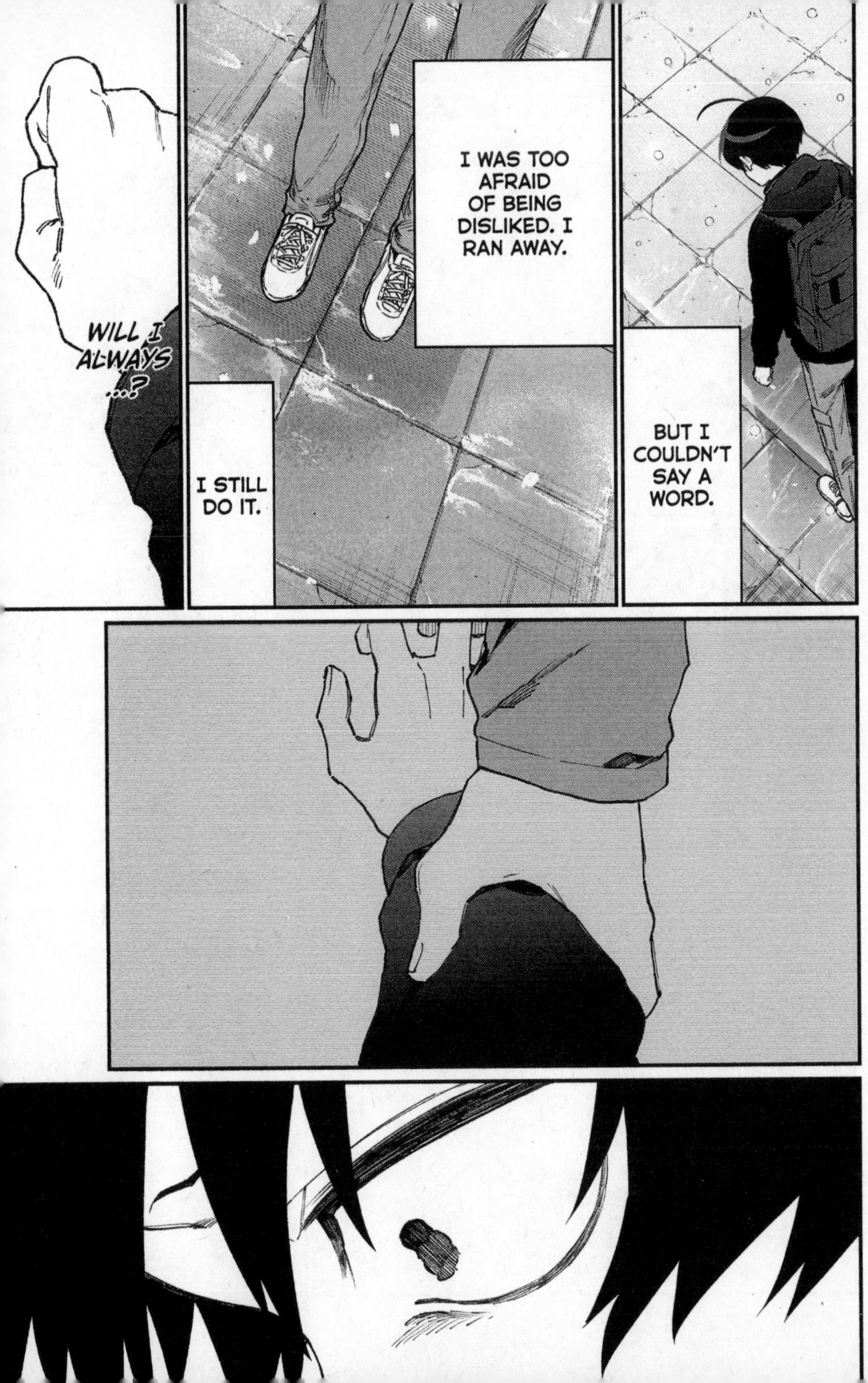
BUT I COULDN'T SAY A WORD.
I WAS TOO AFRAID OF BEING DISLIKED. I RAN AWAY.
I STILL DO IT.
WILL I ALWAYS ...?

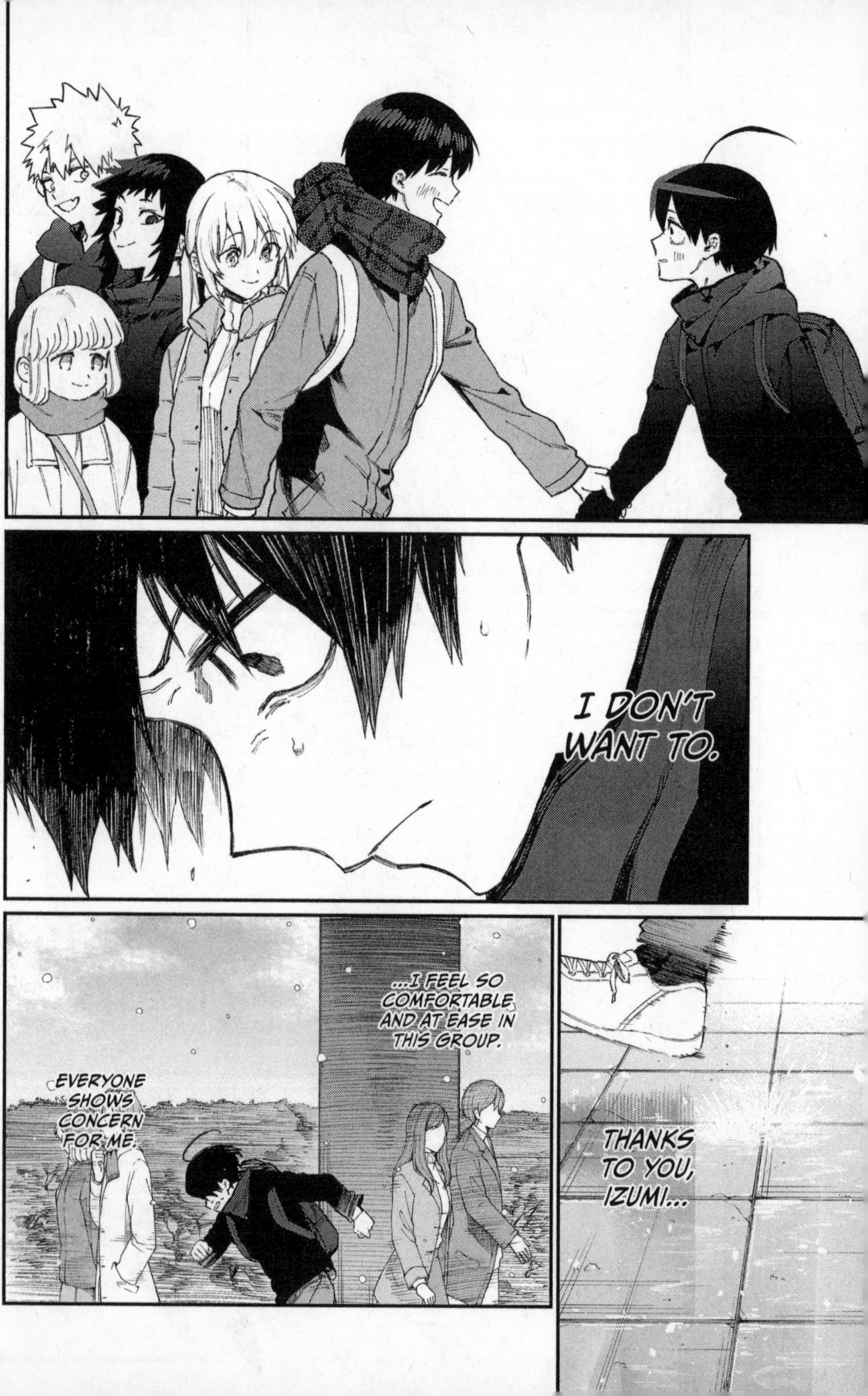
I DON'T WANT TO.
THANKS TO YOU, IZUMI...
...I FEEL SO COMFORTABLE AND AT EASE IN THIS GROUP.
EVERYONE SHOWS CONCERN FOR ME.

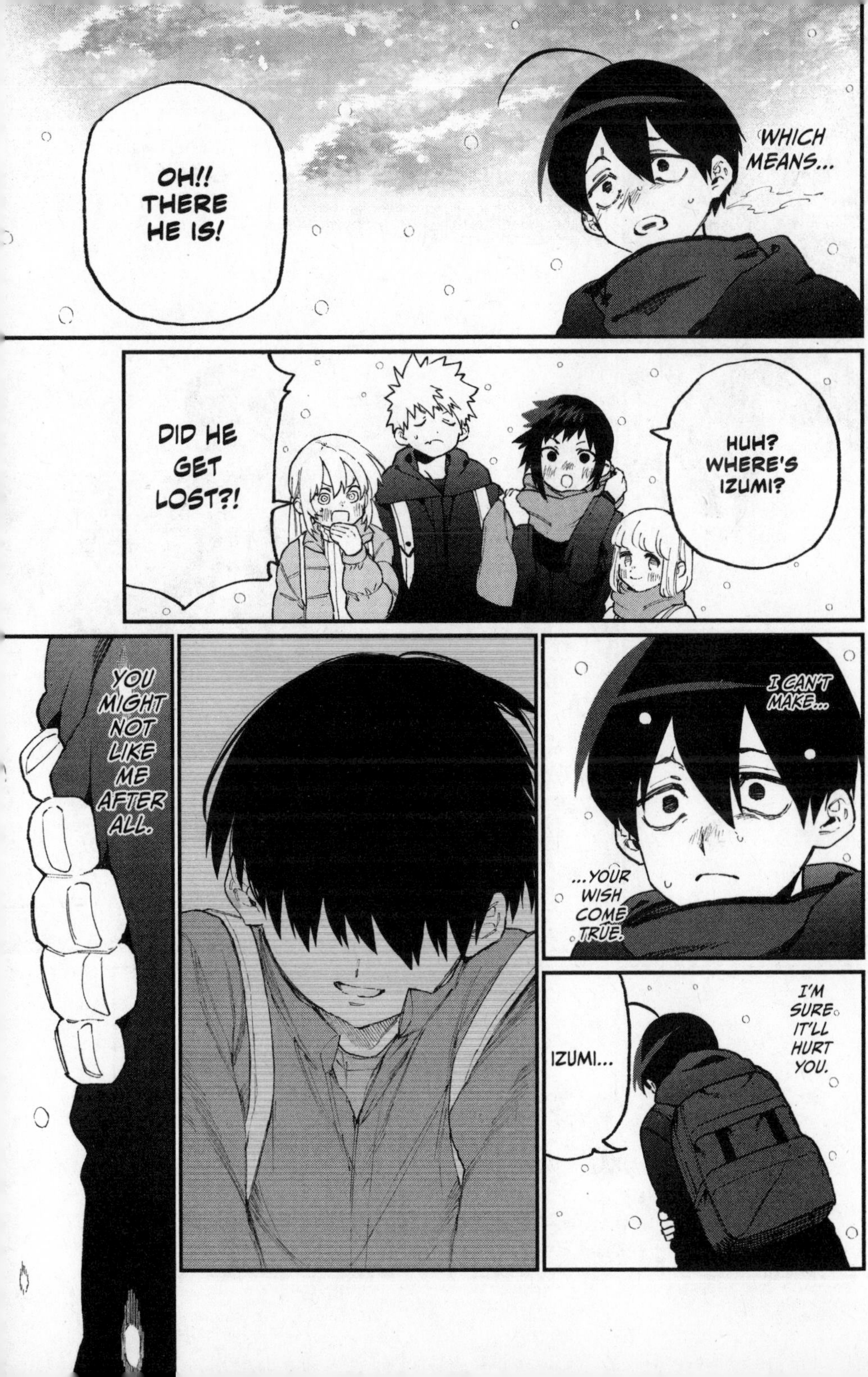
WHICH MEANS...
OH!! THERE HE IS!
HUH? WHERE'S IZUMI?
DID HE GET LOST?!
I CAN'T MAKE...
...YOUR WISH COME TRUE.
I'M SURE IT'LL HURT YOU.
IZUMI...
YOU MIGHT NOT LIKE ME AFTER ALL.

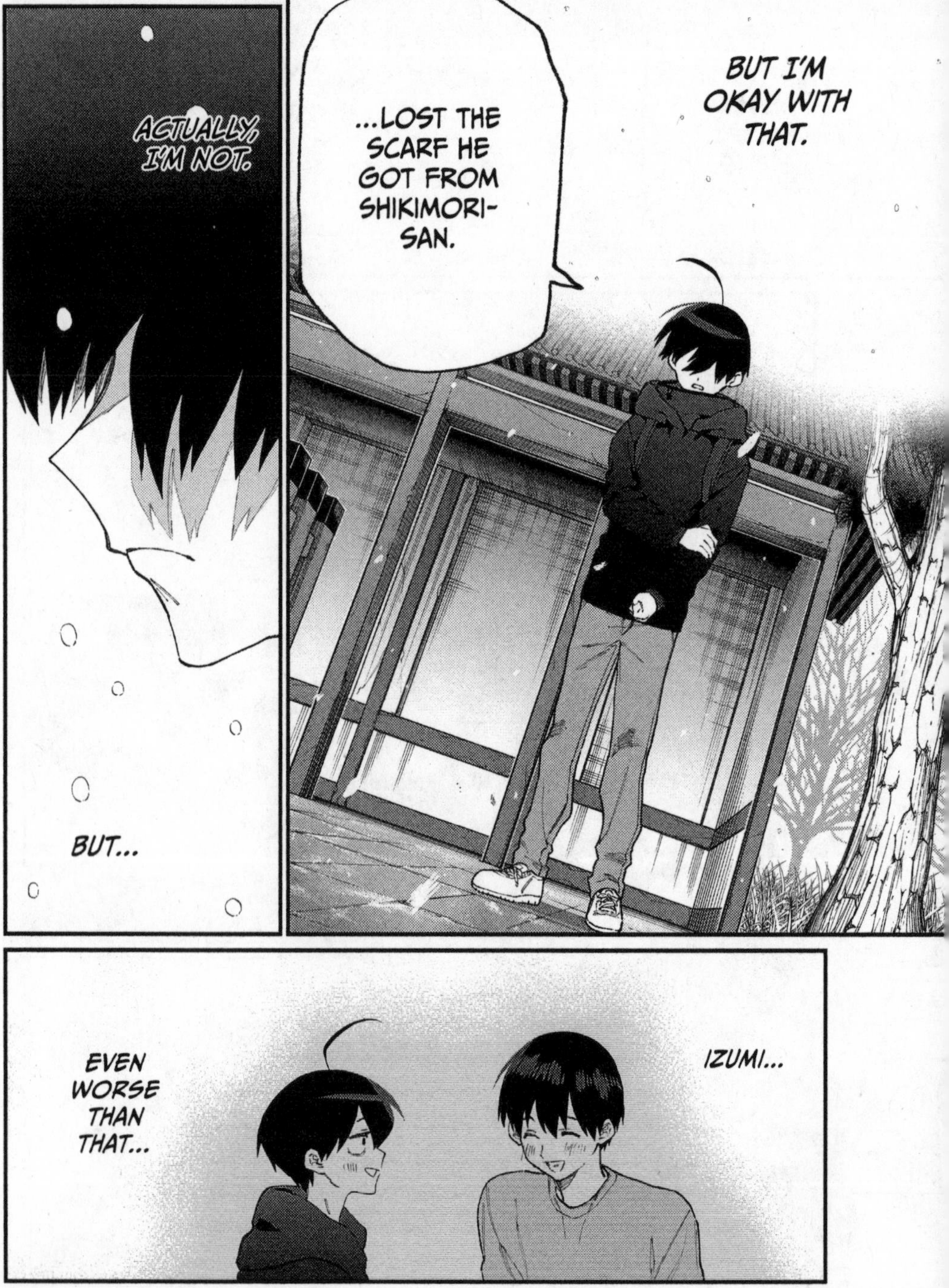
BUT I'M OKAY WITH THAT.
...LOST THE SCARF HE GOT FROM SHIKIMORI-SAN.
ACTUALLY, I'M NOT.
BUT...
IZUMI...
EVEN WORSE THAN THAT...

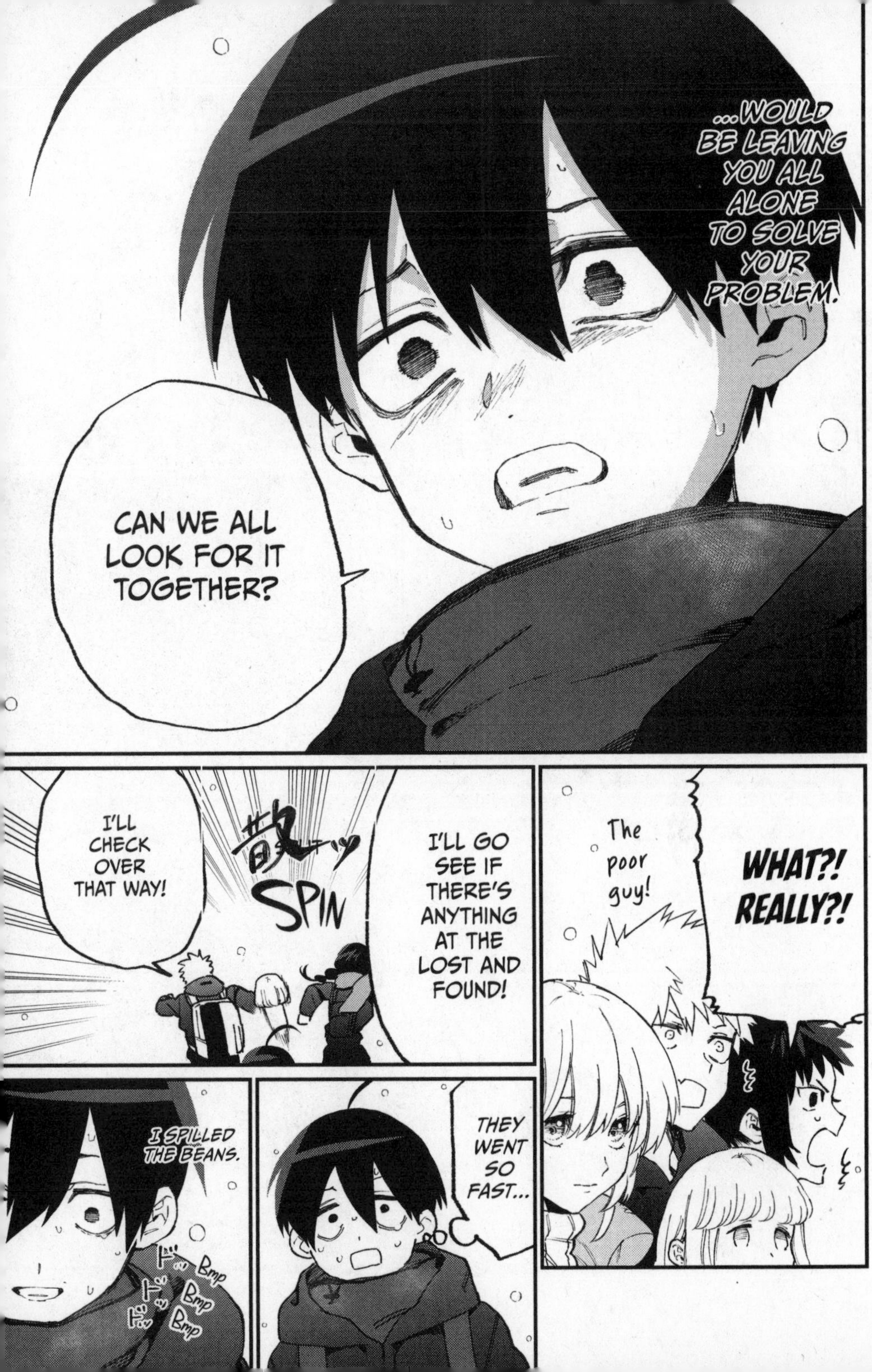

...WOULD BE LEAVING YOU ALL ALONE TO SOLVE YOUR PROBLEM.
CAN WE ALL LOOK FOR IT TOGETHER?
WHAT?! REALLY?!
The poor guy!
I'LL GO SEE IF THERE'S ANYTHING AT THE LOST AND FOUND!
SPIN
I'LL CHECK OVER THAT WAY!
THEY WENT SO FAST...
I SPILLED THE BEANS.
Bmp
Bmp
Bmp

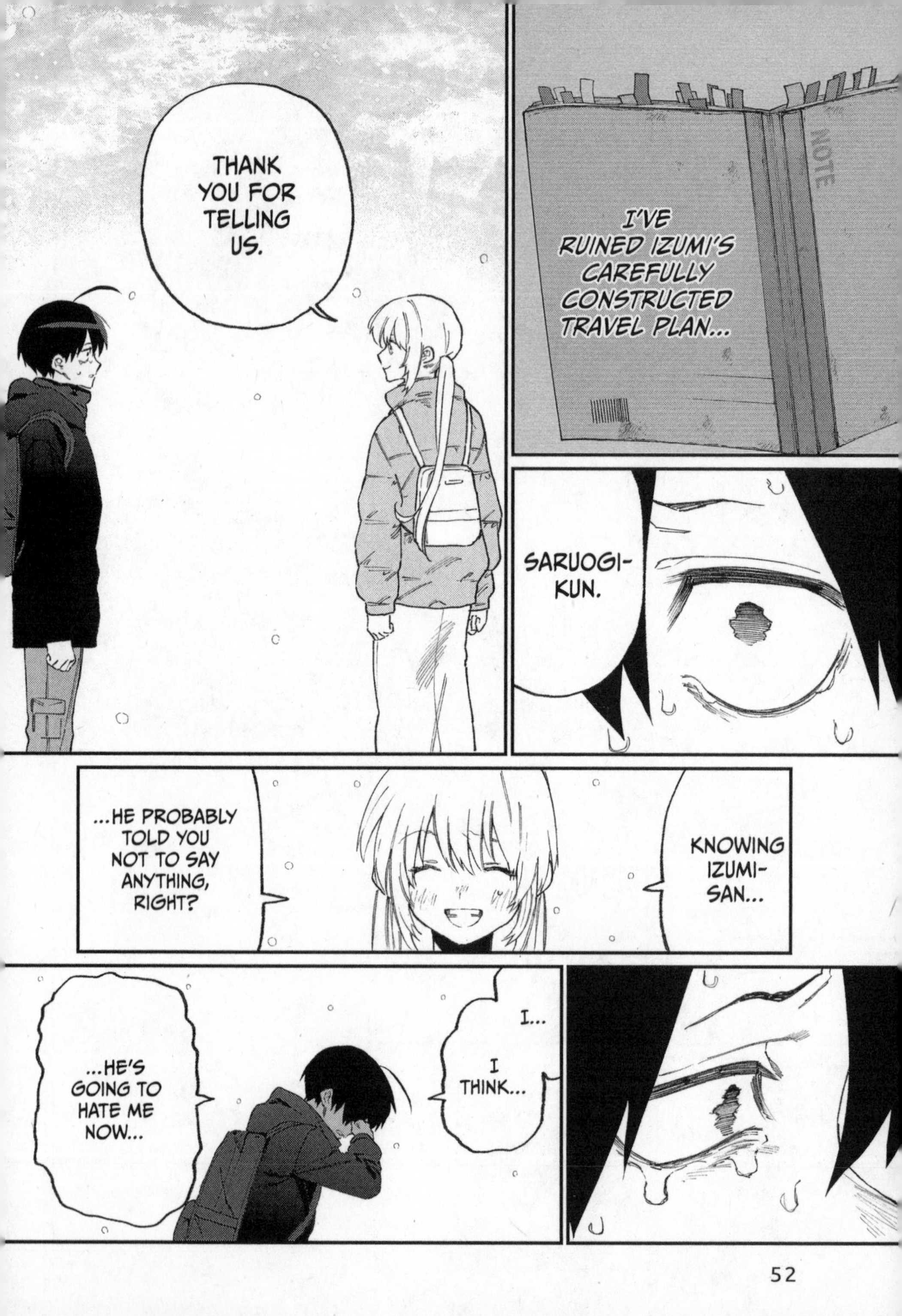
NOTE
I'VE RUINED IZUMI'S CAREFULLY CONSTRUCTED TRAVEL PLAN...
SARUOGI-KUN.
THANK YOU FOR TELLING US.
KNOWING IZUMI-SAN...
...HE PROBABLY TOLD YOU NOT TO SAY ANYTHING, RIGHT?
I...
I THINK...
...HE'S GOING TO HATE ME NOW...

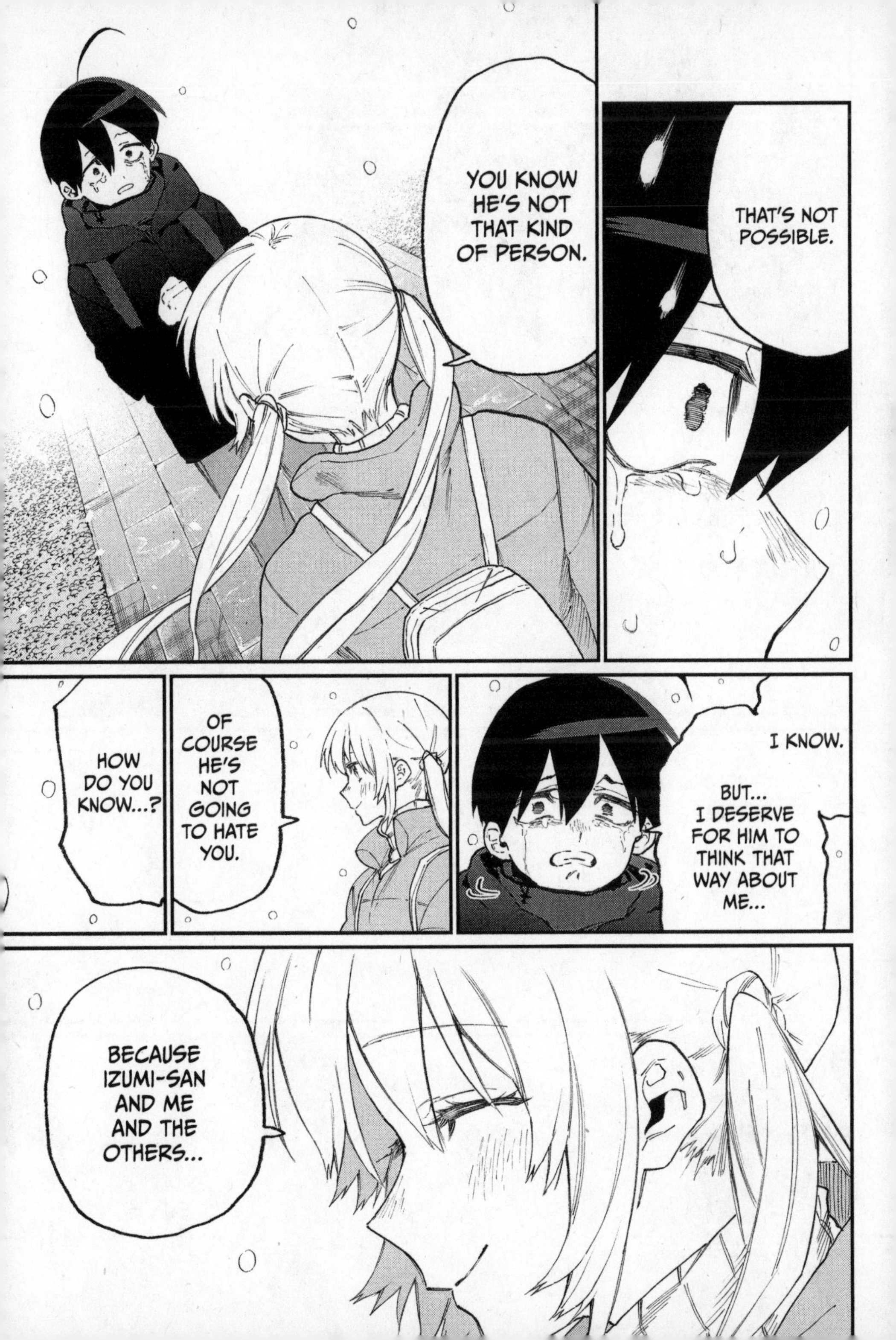
THAT'S NOT POSSIBLE.
YOU KNOW HE'S NOT THAT KIND OF PERSON.
I KNOW.
BUT... I DESERVE FOR HIM TO THINK THAT WAY ABOUT ME...
OF COURSE HE'S NOT GOING TO HATE YOU.
HOW DO YOU KNOW...?
BECAUSE IZUMI-SAN AND ME AND THE OTHERS...

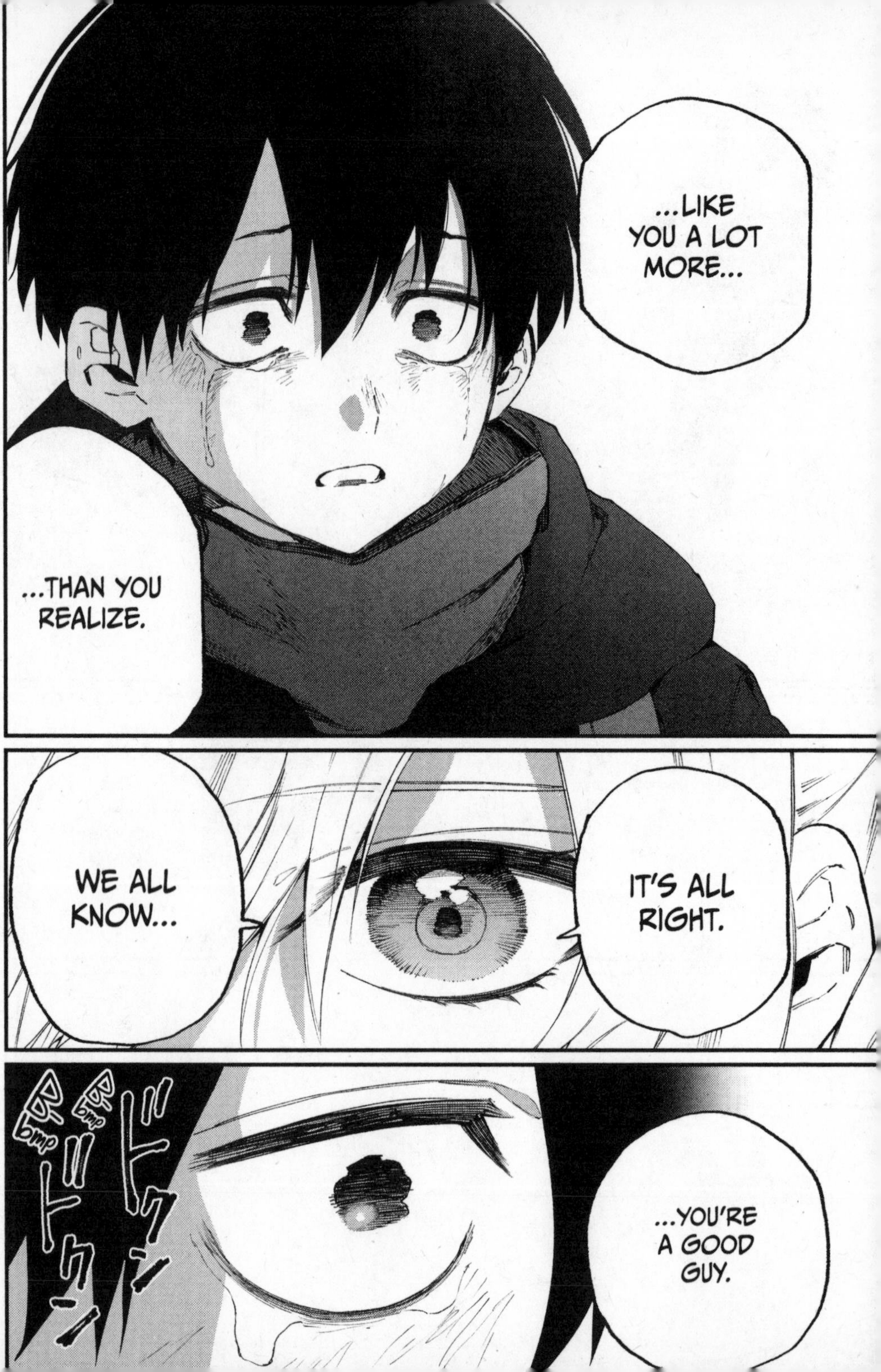
...LIKE YOU A LOT MORE...
...THAN YOU REALIZE.
IT'S ALL RIGHT.
WE ALL KNOW...
...YOU'RE A GOOD GUY.
ドクン
B-bmp
ドクン
B-bmp

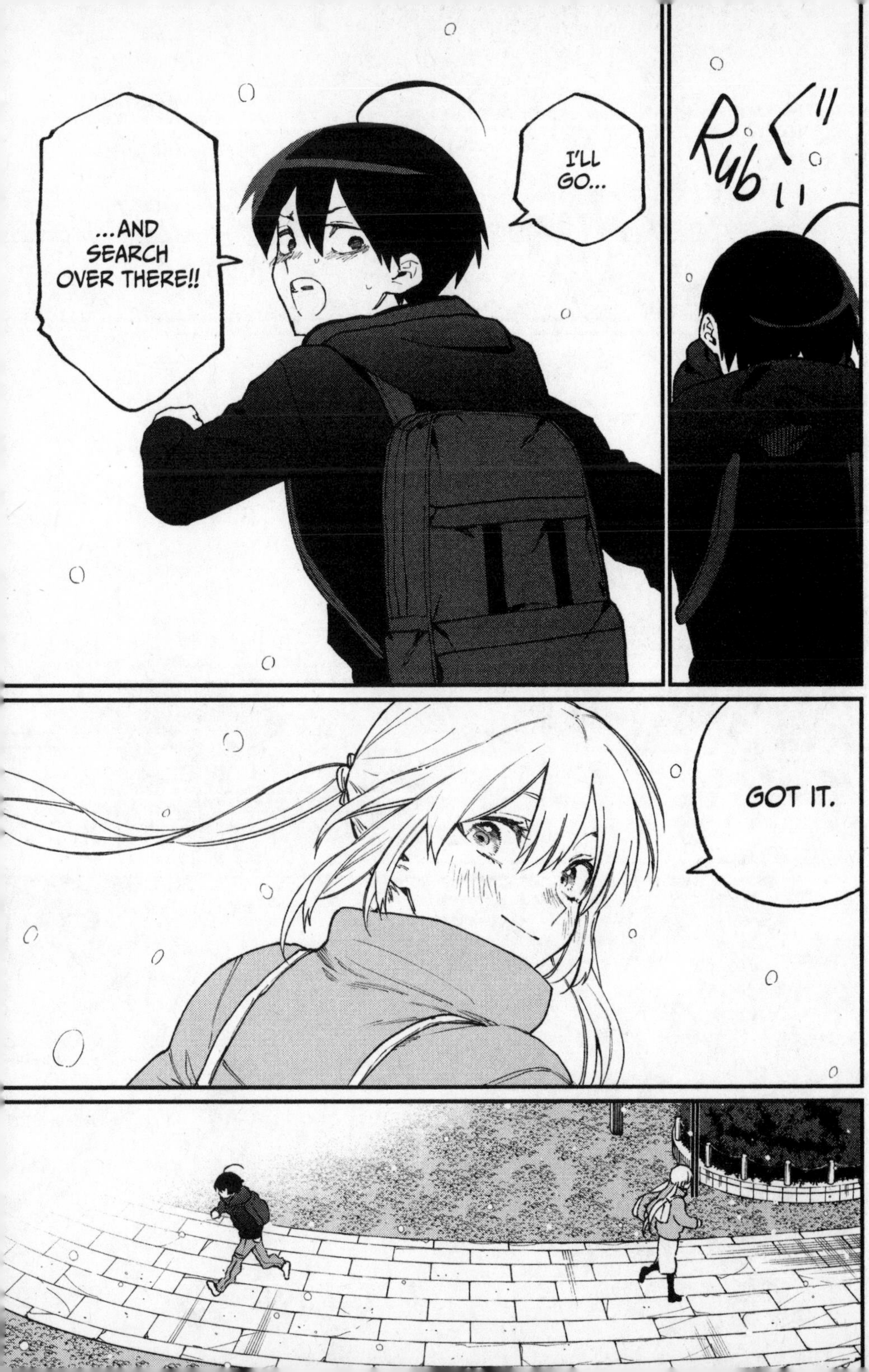
Rub
I'LL GO...
...AND SEARCH OVER THERE!!
GOT IT.

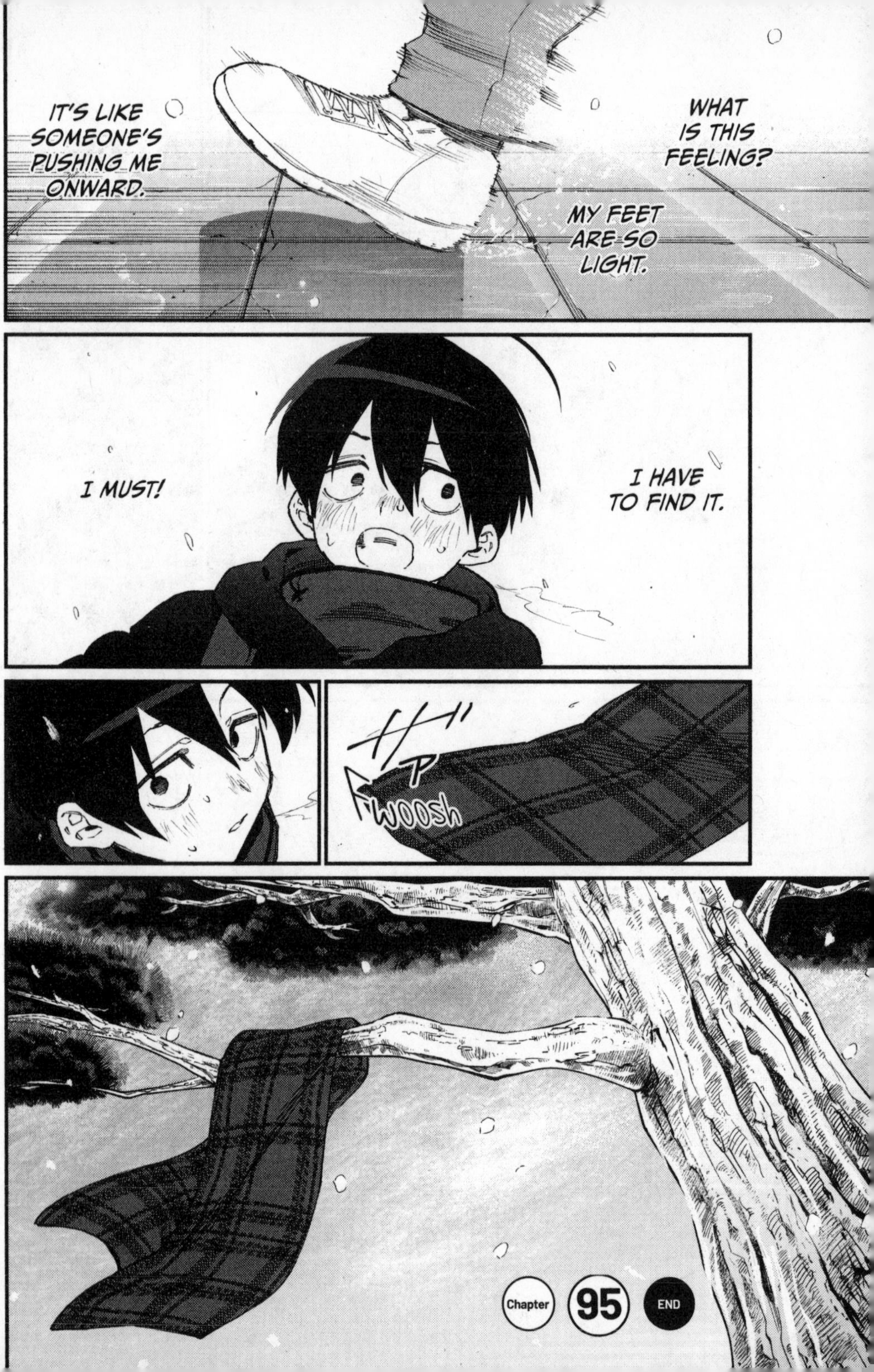
WHAT IS THIS FEELING?
MY FEET ARE SO LIGHT.
IT'S LIKE SOMEONE'S PUSHING ME ONWARD.
I HAVE TO FIND IT.
I MUST!
FWOOSH
Chapter 95 END

SHIKIMORI'S
not just a cutie

SHiKiMORi'S
not just a cutie

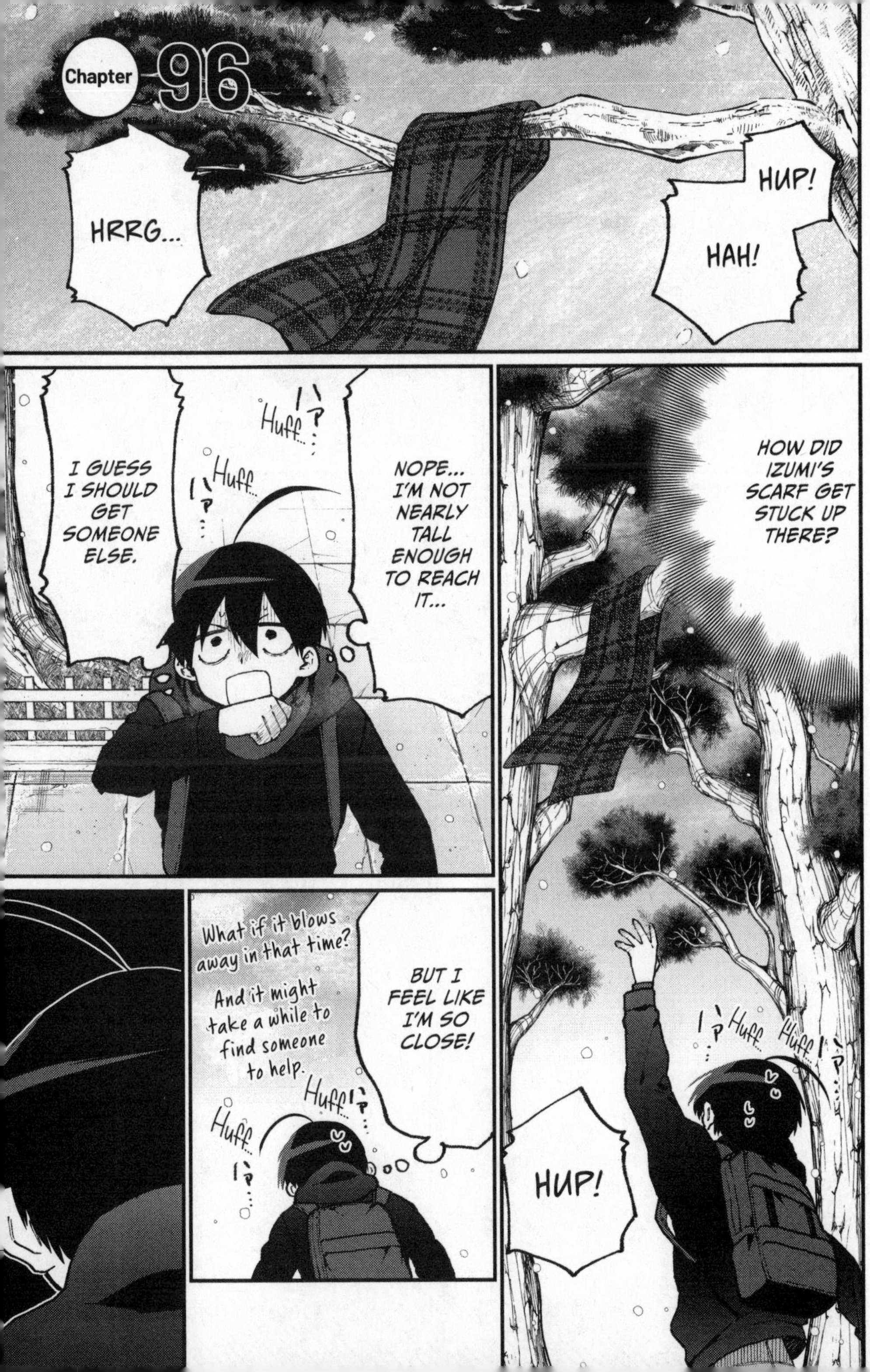
Chapter 96
HUP!
HAH!
HRRG...
HOW DID IZUMI'S SCARF GET STUCK UP THERE?
Huff...
Huff...
HUP!
NOPE... I'M NOT NEARLY TALL ENOUGH TO REACH IT...
Huff...
Huff...
I GUESS I SHOULD GET SOMEONE ELSE.
BUT I FEEL LIKE I'M SO CLOSE!
What if it blows away in that time?
And it might take a while to find someone to help.
Huff...
Huff...

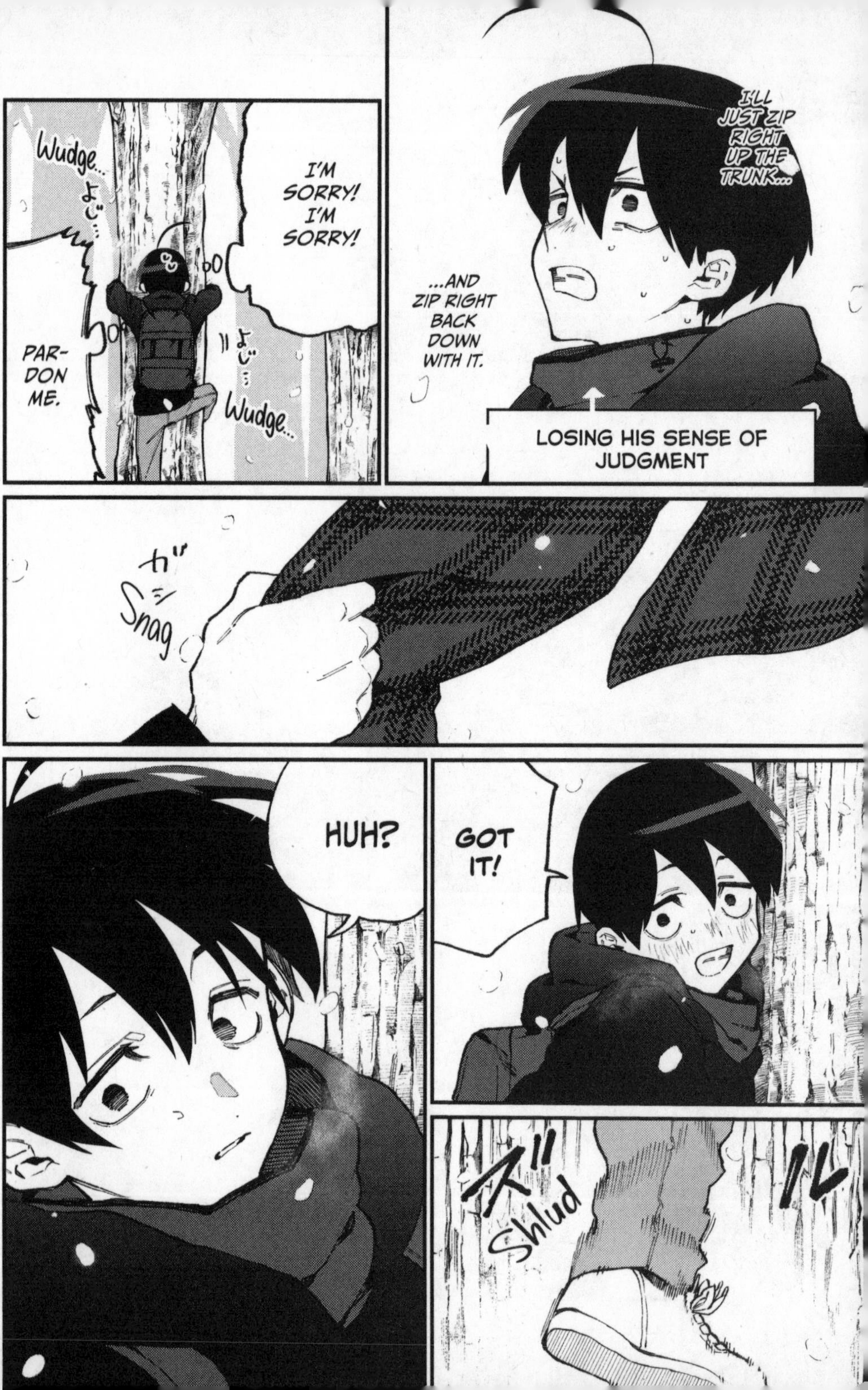
I'LL JUST ZIP RIGHT UP THE TRUNK...
...AND ZIP RIGHT BACK DOWN WITH IT.
LOSING HIS SENSE OF JUDGMENT
I'M SORRY! I'M SORRY!
Wudge... よじ…
よじ… Wudge...
PAR-DON ME.
ガシ Snag
GOT IT!
ズル Shlud
HUH?

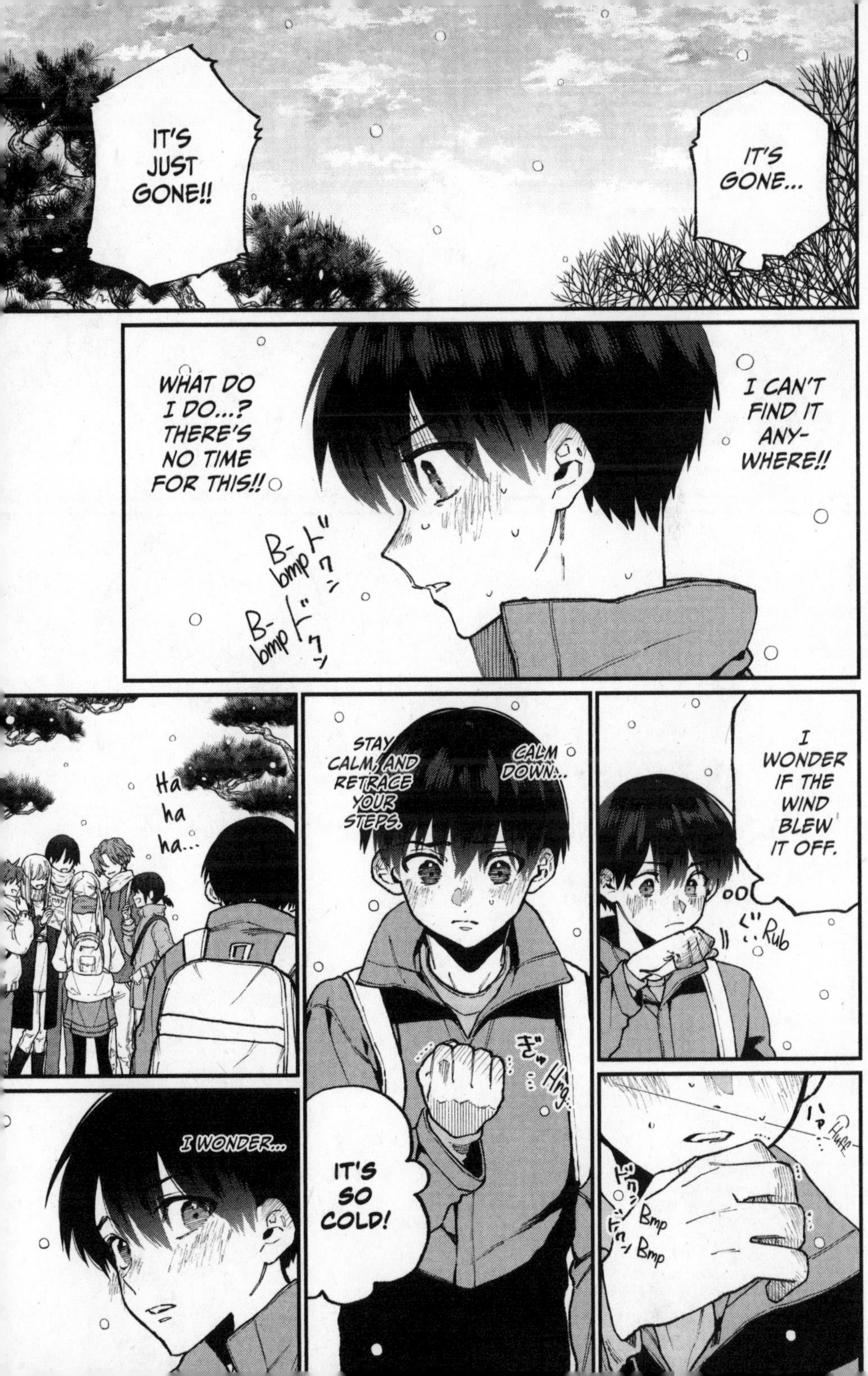

IT'S GONE...
IT'S JUST GONE!!
I CAN'T FIND IT ANYWHERE!!
WHAT DO I DO...? THERE'S NO TIME FOR THIS!!
B-bmp
B-bmp
I WONDER IF THE WIND BLEW IT OFF.
Rub
Huff
Bmp
Bmp
CALM DOWN...
STAY CALM, AND RETRACE YOUR STEPS.
Hrng
IT'S SO COLD!
Ha ha ha...
I WONDER...

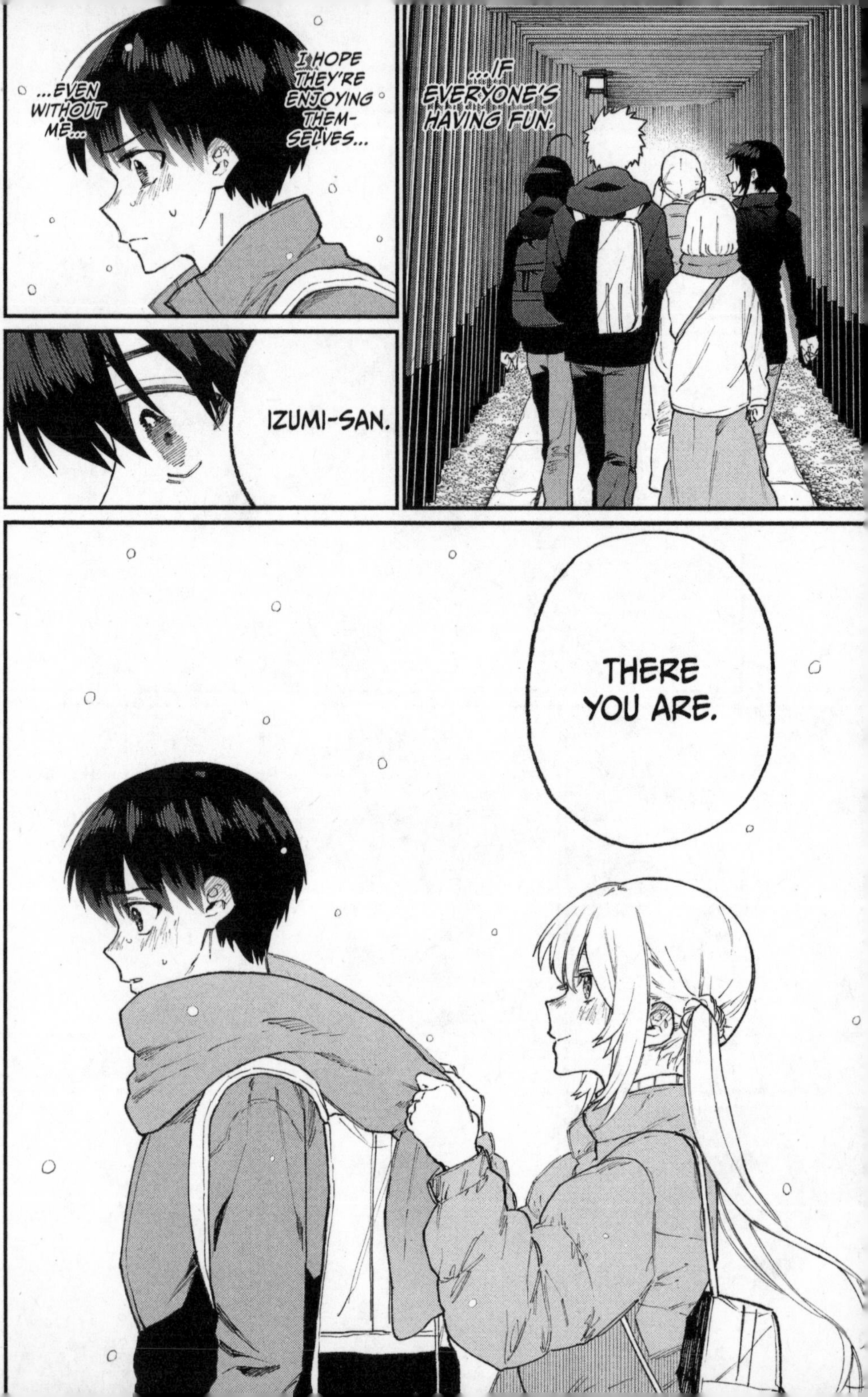
...IF EVERYONE'S HAVING FUN.
I HOPE THEY'RE ENJOYING THEM-SELVES...
...EVEN WITHOUT ME...
IZUMI-SAN.
THERE YOU ARE.

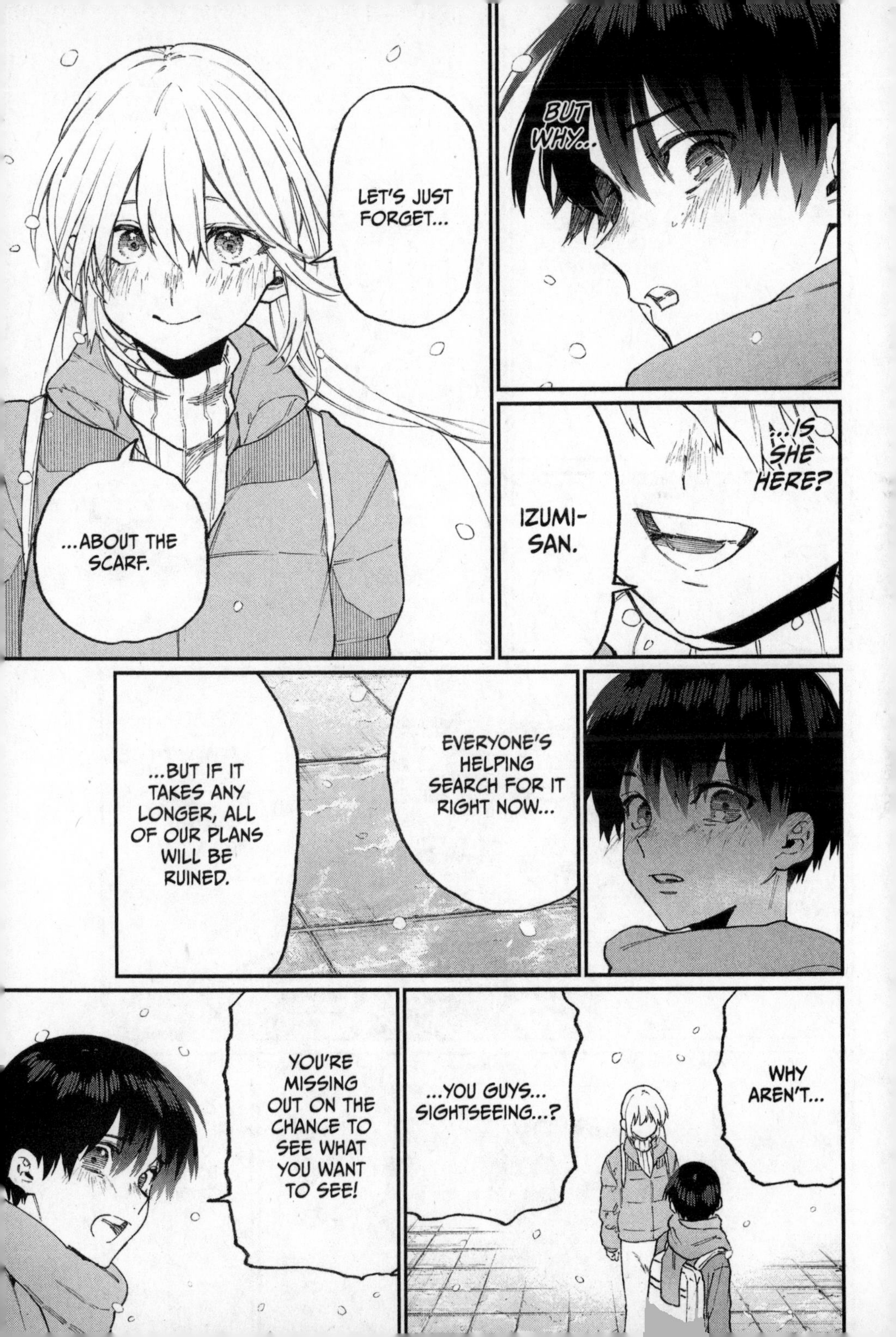
BUT WHY...
...IS SHE HERE?
IZUMI-SAN.
LET'S JUST FORGET...
...ABOUT THE SCARF.
EVERYONE'S HELPING SEARCH FOR IT RIGHT NOW...
...BUT IF IT TAKES ANY LONGER, ALL OF OUR PLANS WILL BE RUINED.
WHY AREN'T...
...YOU GUYS... SIGHTSEEING...?
YOU'RE MISSING OUT ON THE CHANCE TO SEE WHAT YOU WANT TO SEE!

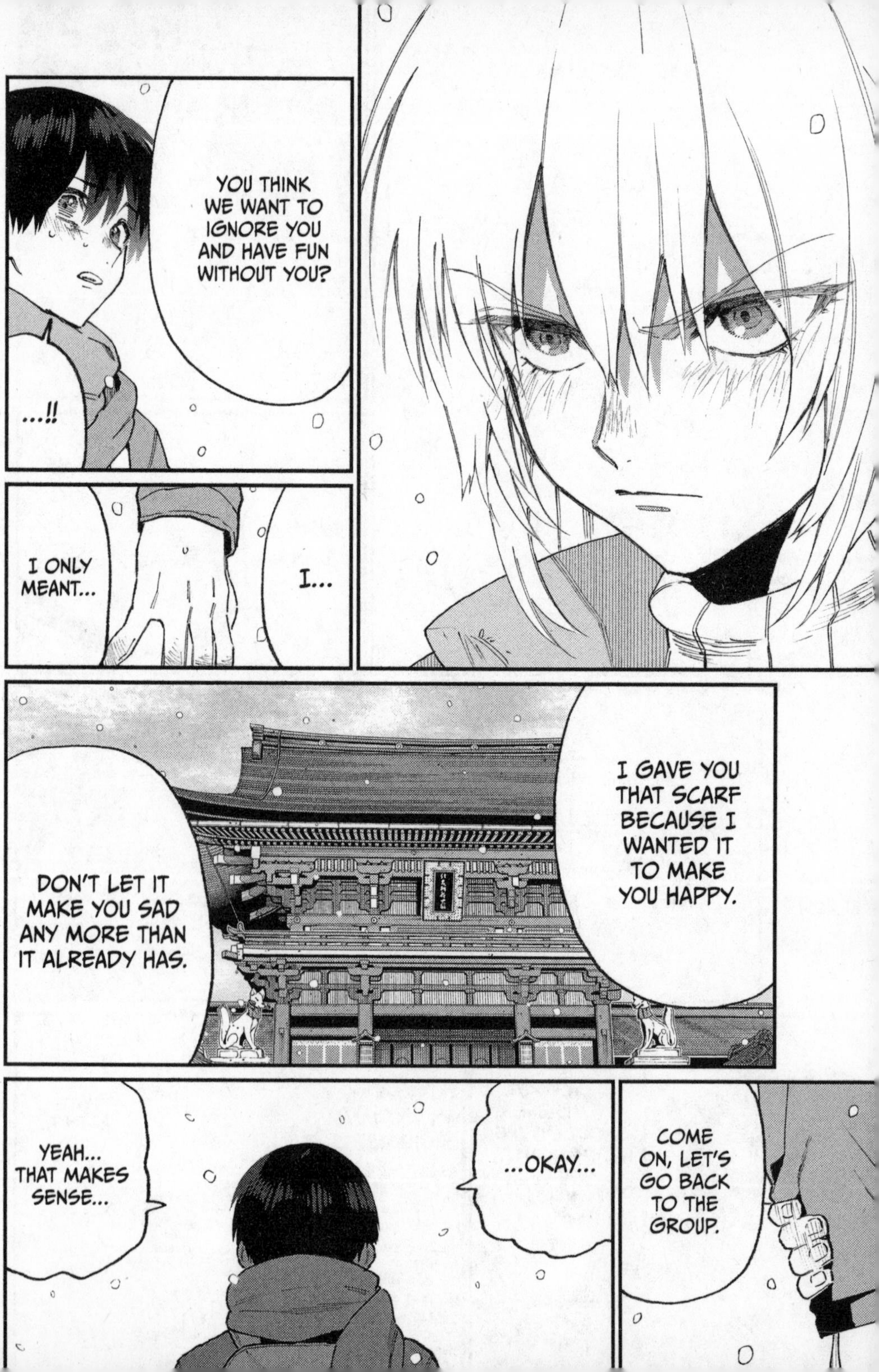
YOU THINK WE WANT TO IGNORE YOU AND HAVE FUN WITHOUT YOU?
...!!
I...
I ONLY MEANT...
I GAVE YOU THAT SCARF BECAUSE I WANTED IT TO MAKE YOU HAPPY.
DON'T LET IT MAKE YOU SAD ANY MORE THAN IT ALREADY HAS.
COME ON, LET'S GO BACK TO THE GROUP.
...OKAY...
YEAH... THAT MAKES SENSE...

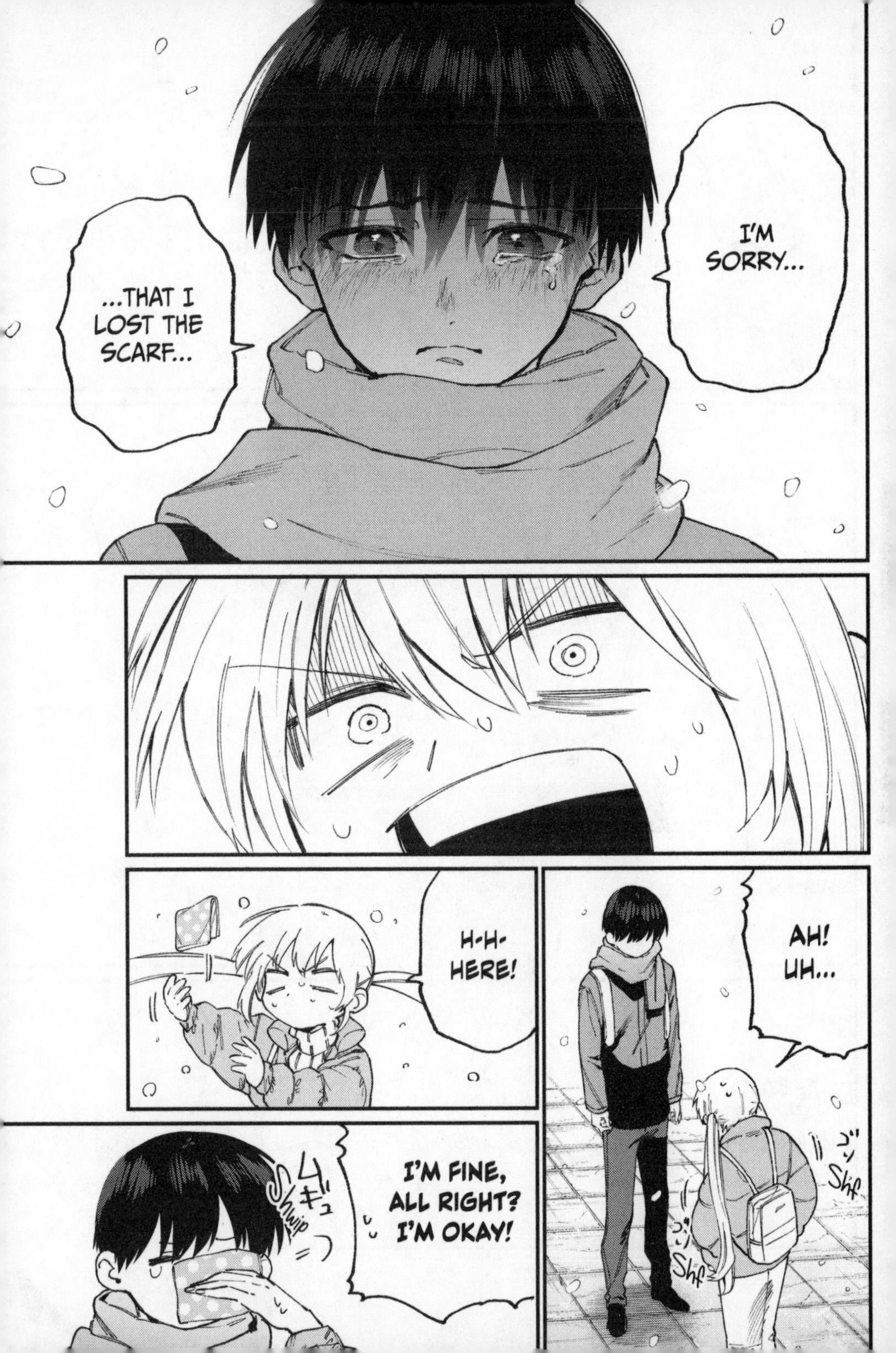
I'M SORRY...
...THAT I LOST THE SCARF...
AH! UH...
ゴソ
Shf
ゴソ
Shf
H-H-HERE!
I'M FINE, ALL RIGHT? I'M OKAY!
ムギュ
Shwip

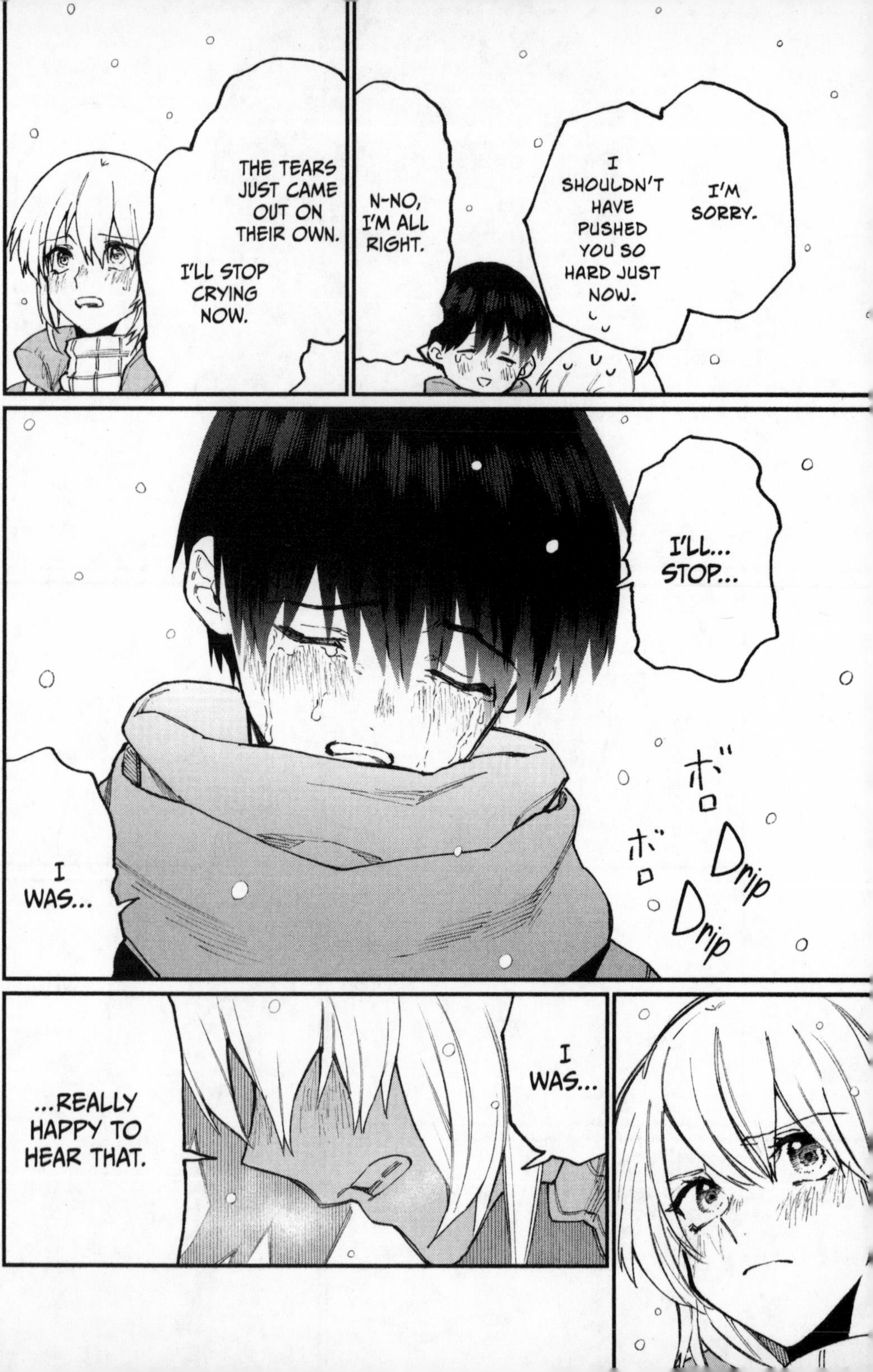
I'M SORRY.
I SHOULDN'T HAVE PUSHED YOU SO HARD JUST NOW.
N-NO, I'M ALL RIGHT.
THE TEARS JUST CAME OUT ON THEIR OWN.
I'LL STOP CRYING NOW.
I'LL... STOP...
ボロ
Drip
ボロ
Drip
I WAS...
I WAS...
...REALLY HAPPY TO HEAR THAT.

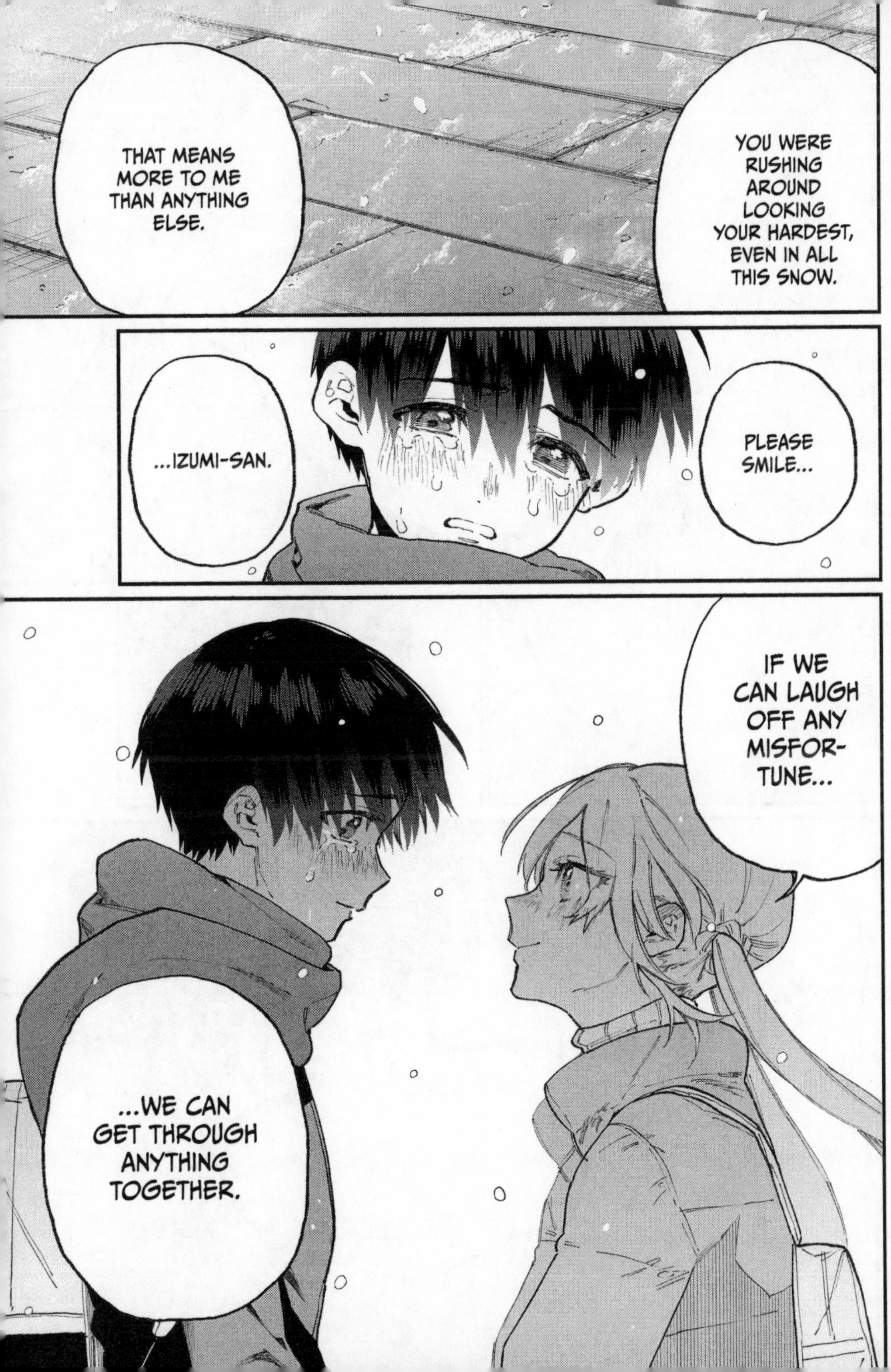
YOU WERE RUSHING AROUND LOOKING YOUR HARDEST, EVEN IN ALL THIS SNOW.
THAT MEANS MORE TO ME THAN ANYTHING ELSE.
PLEASE SMILE...
...IZUMI-SAN.
IF WE CAN LAUGH OFF ANY MISFOR-TUNE...
...WE CAN GET THROUGH ANYTHING TOGETHER.

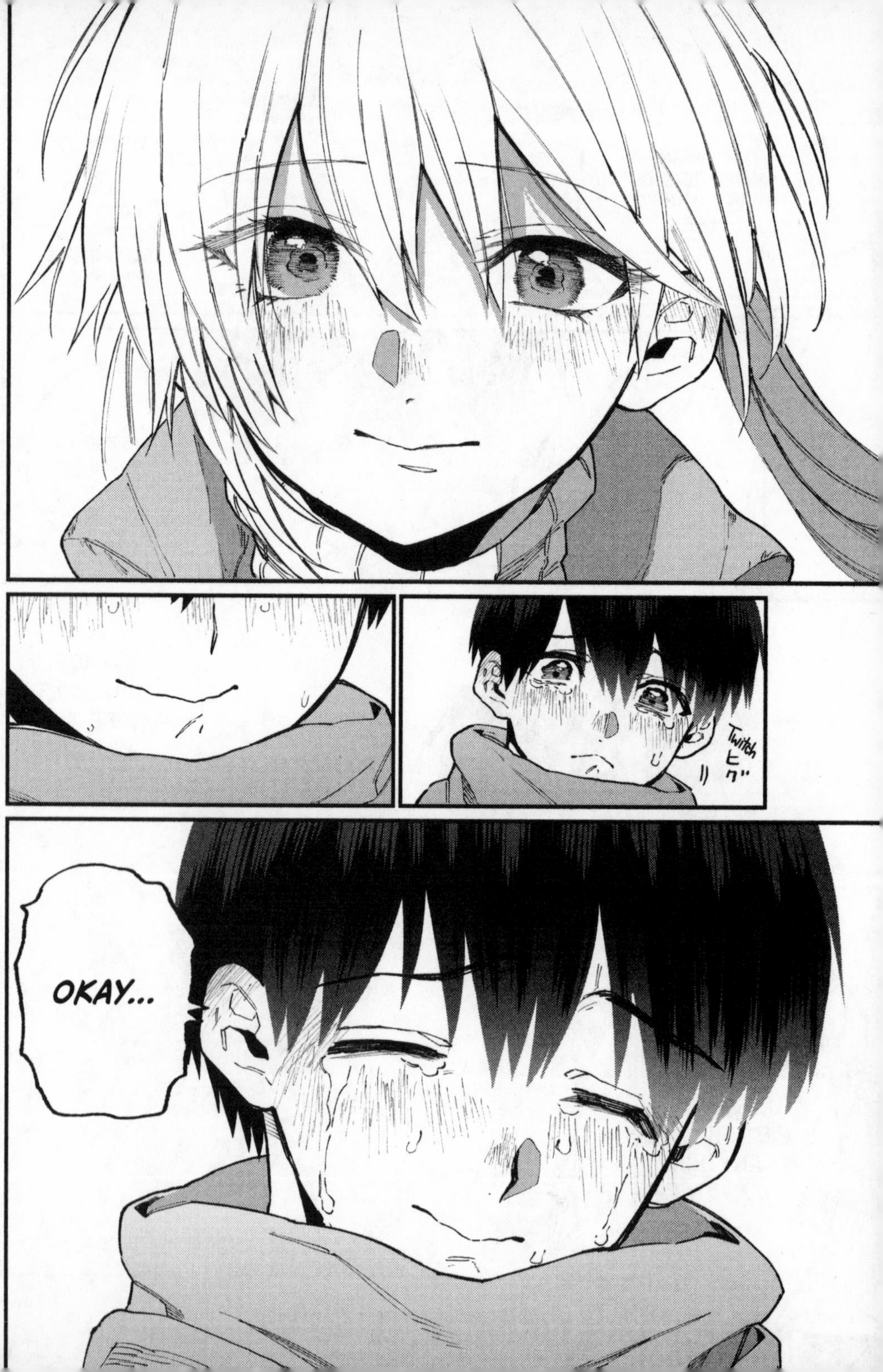
Twitch
ピク
OKAY...

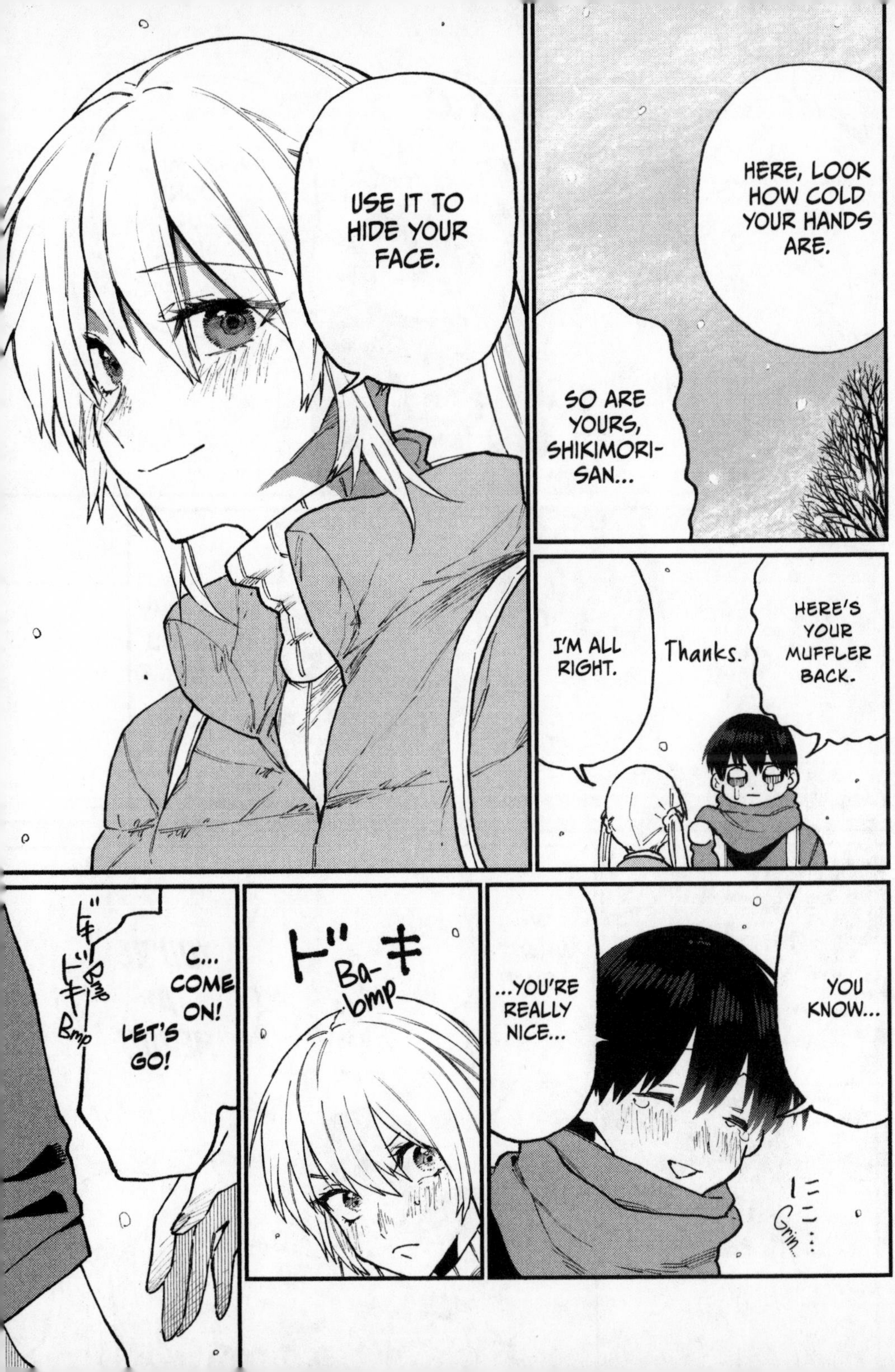
HERE, LOOK HOW COLD YOUR HANDS ARE.
SO ARE YOURS, SHIKIMORI-SAN...
HERE'S YOUR MUFFLER BACK.
Thanks.
I'M ALL RIGHT.
USE IT TO HIDE YOUR FACE.
YOU KNOW...
...YOU'RE REALLY NICE...
ニコ...
Grin...
ドキ
Ba-bmp
ドキドキ
Bmp Bmp
C... COME ON! LET'S GO!

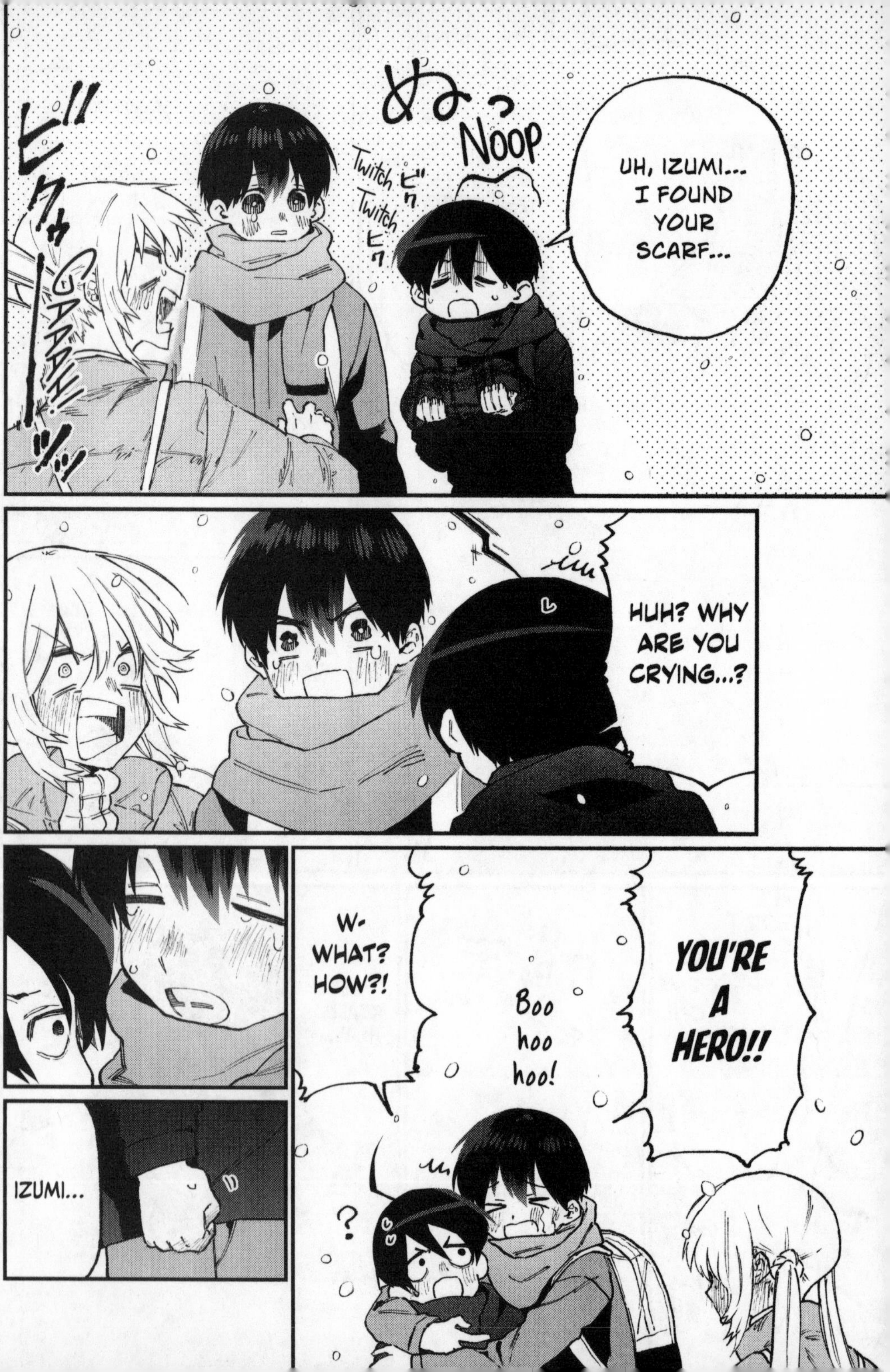
UH, IZUMI... I FOUND YOUR SCARF...
ぬっ
NOOP
Twitch ビク
Twitch ビク
GAAAH!!
HUH? WHY ARE YOU CRYING...?
YOU'RE A HERO!!
Boo hoo hoo!
W-WHAT? HOW?!
?
IZUMI...

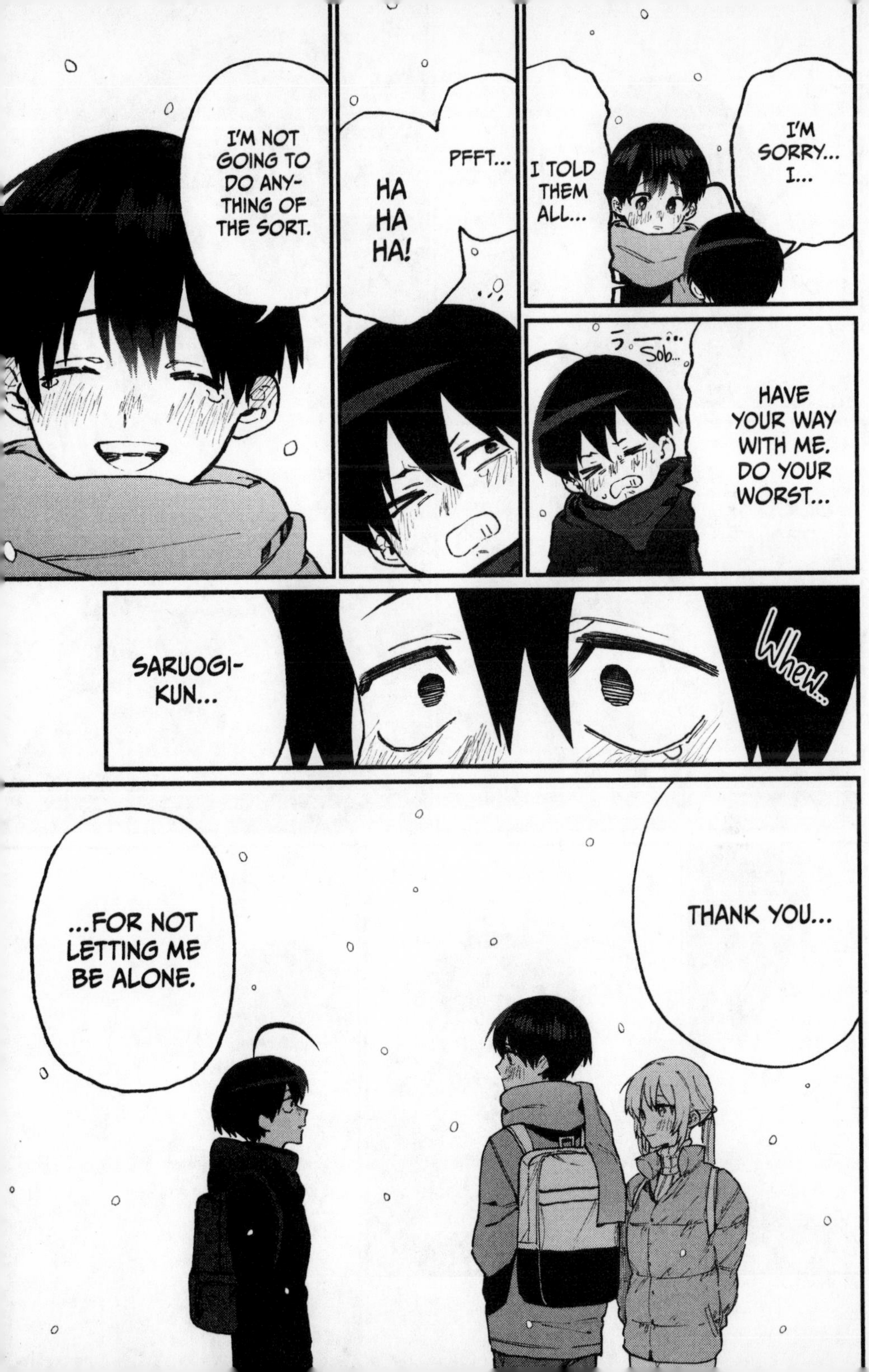
I'M SORRY... I...
I TOLD THEM ALL...
Sob...
HAVE YOUR WAY WITH ME. DO YOUR WORST...
PFFT...
HA HA HA!
I'M NOT GOING TO DO ANY-THING OF THE SORT.
Whew...
SARUOGI-KUN...
THANK YOU...
...FOR NOT LETTING ME BE ALONE.

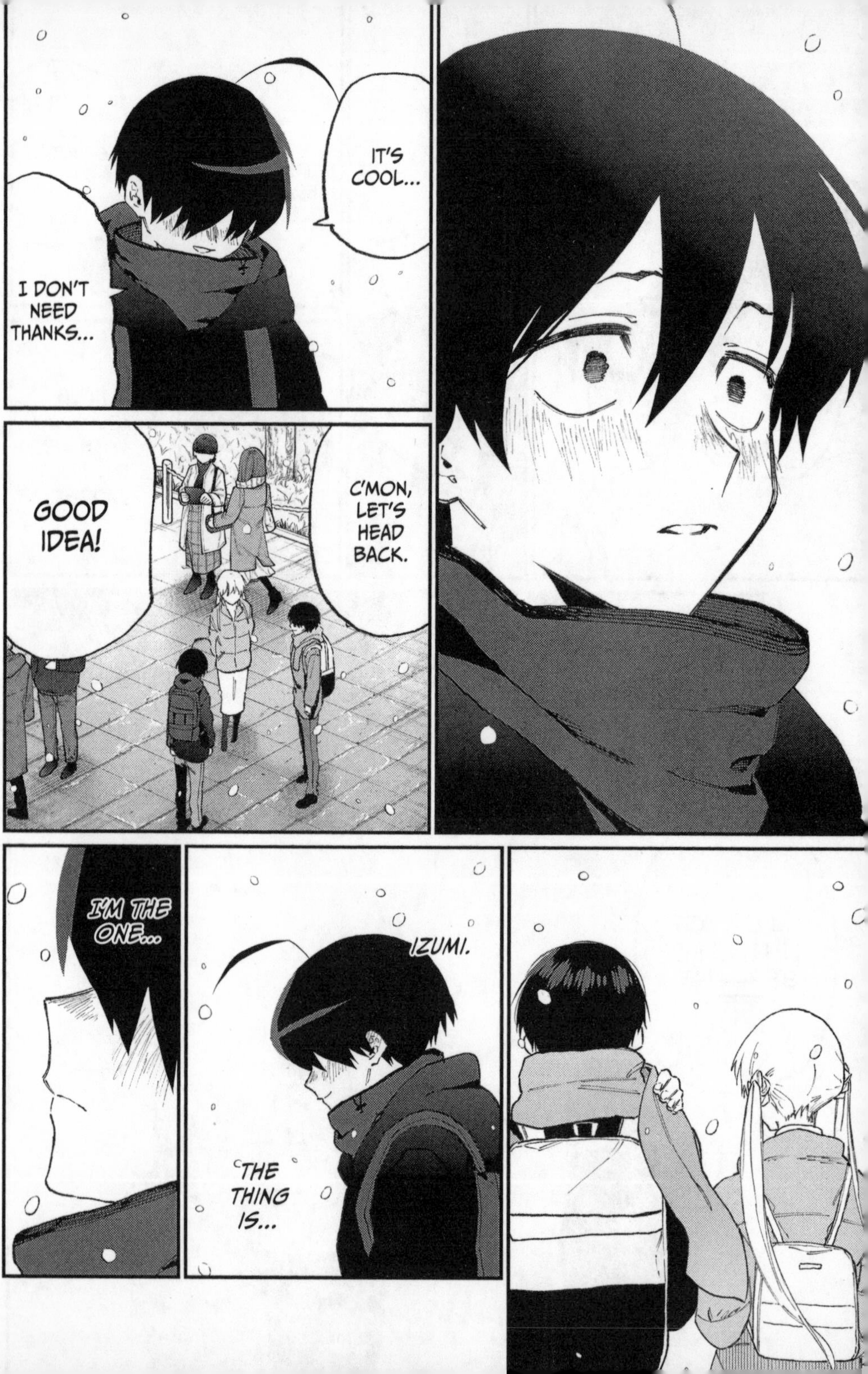
IT'S COOL...
I DON'T NEED THANKS...
C'MON, LET'S HEAD BACK.
GOOD IDEA!
IZUMI.
THE THING IS...
I'M THE ONE...

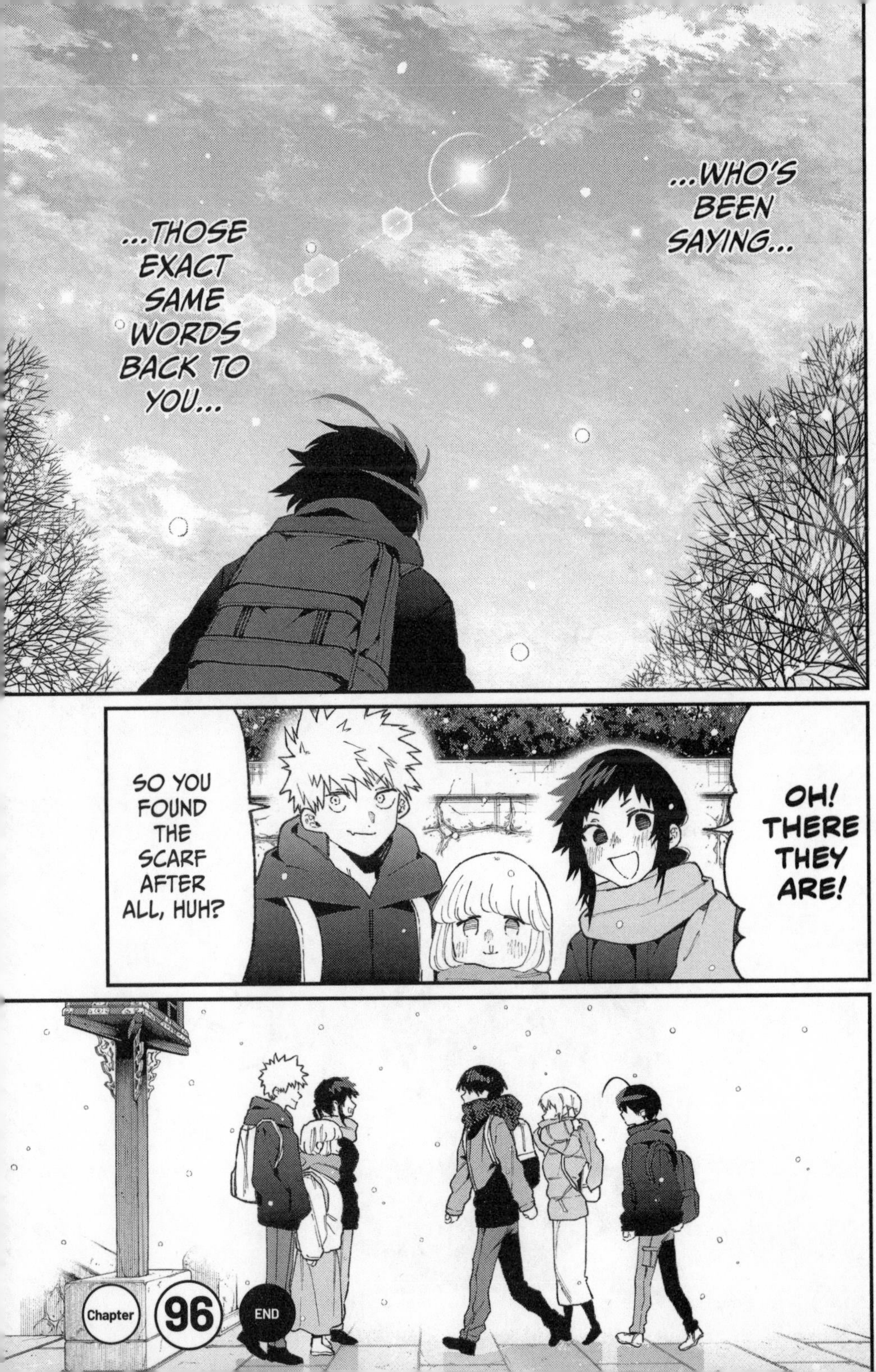
...WHO'S BEEN SAYING...
...THOSE EXACT SAME WORDS BACK TO YOU...
OH! THERE THEY ARE!
SO YOU FOUND THE SCARF AFTER ALL, HUH?
Chapter 96 END

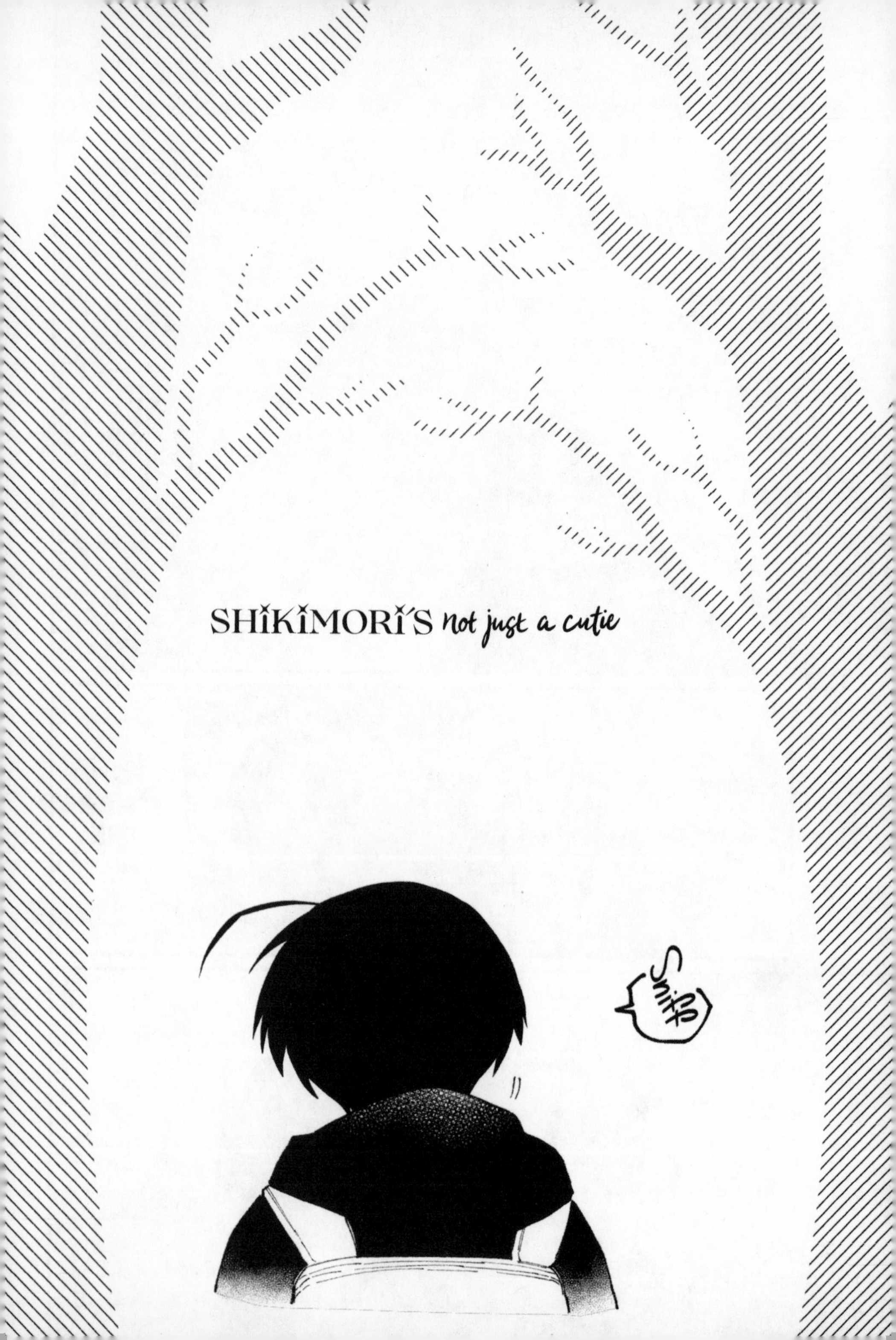
SHIKIMORI'S not just a cutie
Sniff

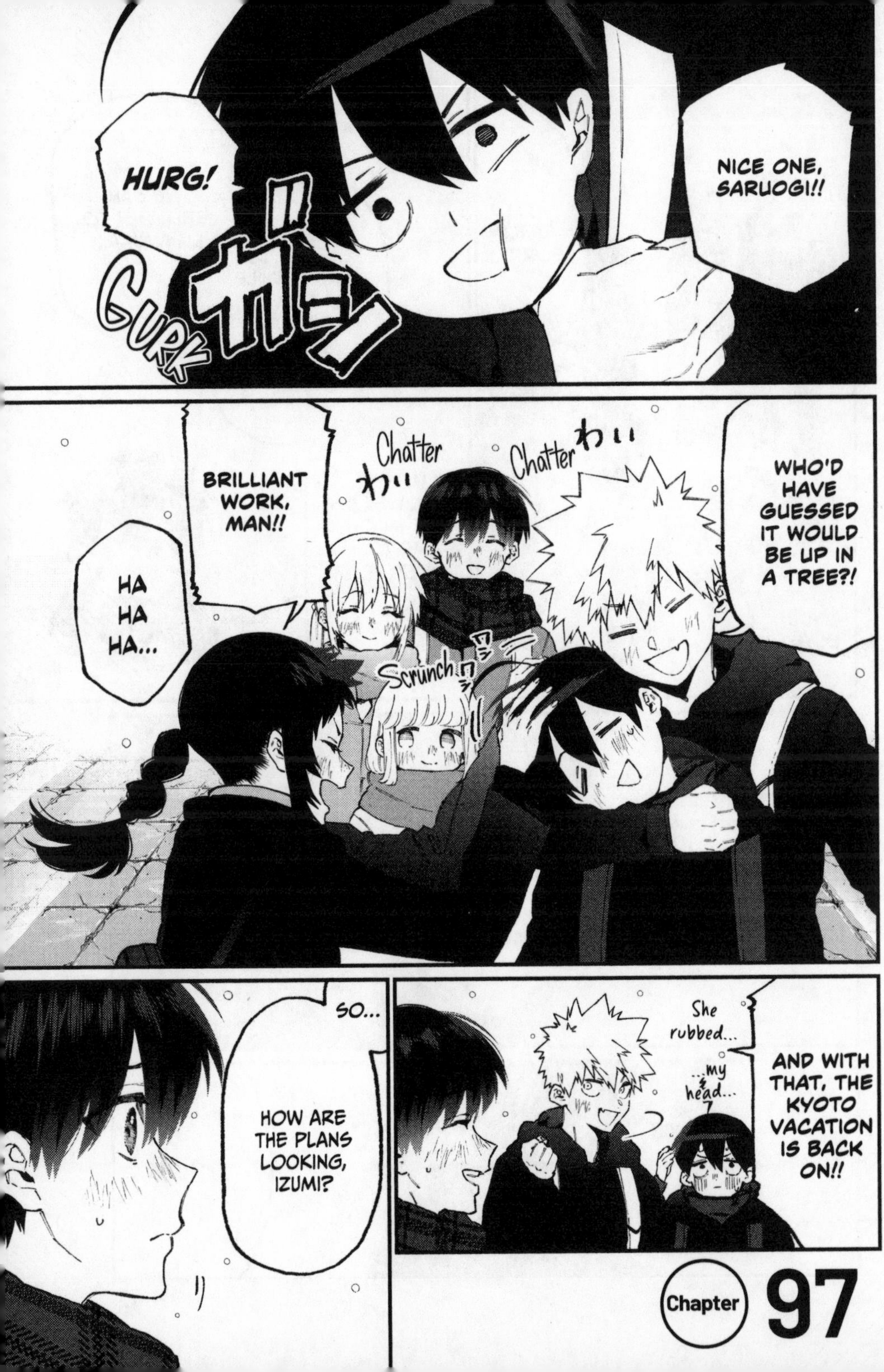
NICE ONE, SARUOGI!!
HURG!
GURK
WHO'D HAVE GUESSED IT WOULD BE UP IN A TREE?!
Chatter
Chatter
Scrunch
BRILLIANT WORK, MAN!!
HA HA HA...
AND WITH THAT, THE KYOTO VACATION IS BACK ON!!
She rubbed...
...my head...
SO...
HOW ARE THE PLANS LOOKING, IZUMI?

Chapter 97

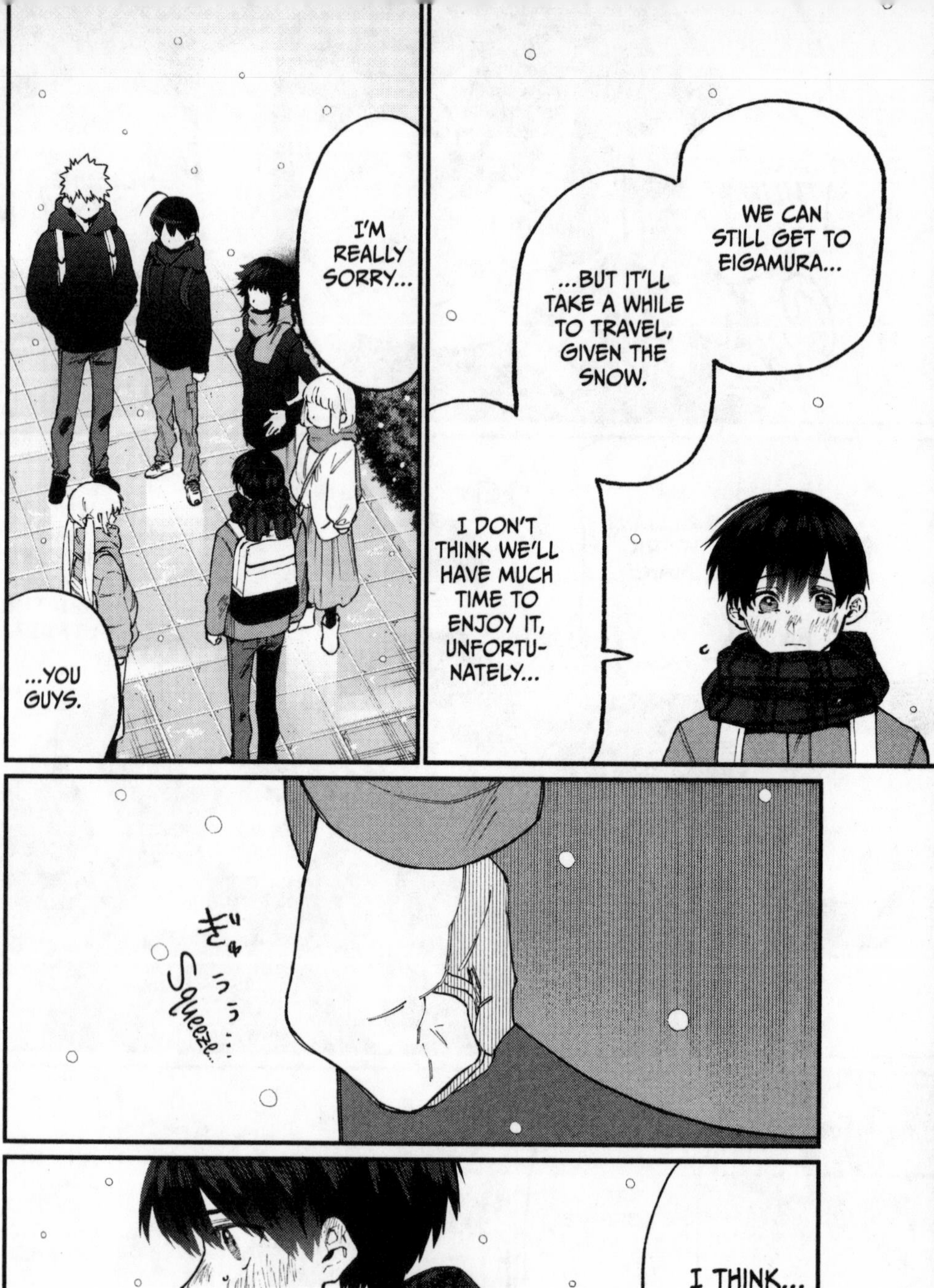

WE CAN STILL GET TO EIGAMURA...
...BUT IT'LL TAKE A WHILE TO TRAVEL, GIVEN THE SNOW.
I DON'T THINK WE'LL HAVE MUCH TIME TO ENJOY IT, UNFORTUNATELY...
I'M REALLY SORRY...
...YOU GUYS.
Squeeze...
I THINK...

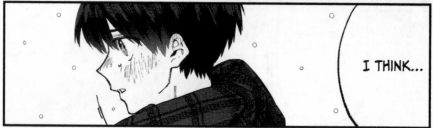

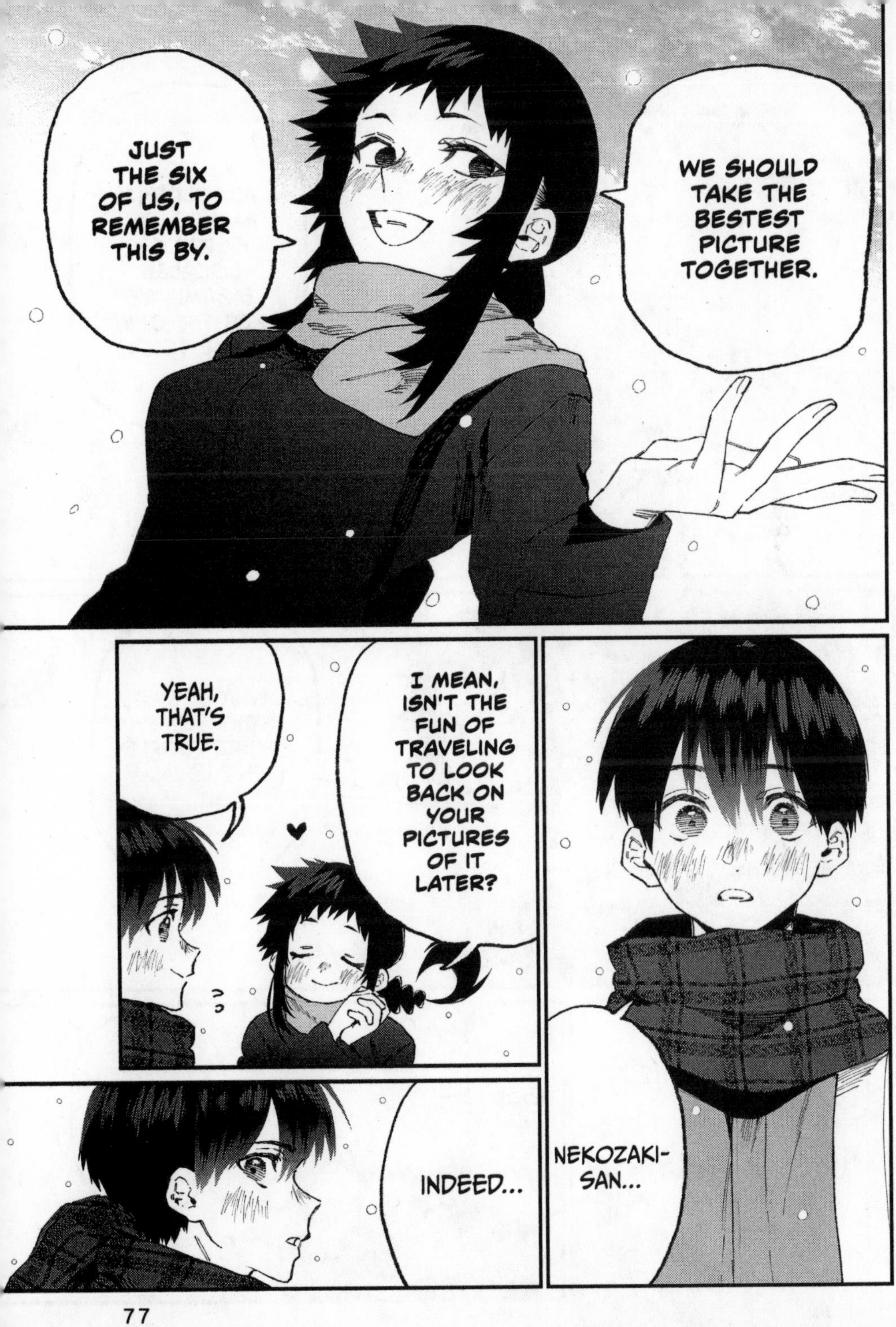
WE SHOULD TAKE THE BESTEST PICTURE TOGETHER.
JUST THE SIX OF US, TO REMEMBER THIS BY.
NEKOZAKI-SAN...
I MEAN, ISN'T THE FUN OF TRAVELING TO LOOK BACK ON YOUR PICTURES OF IT LATER?
YEAH, THAT'S TRUE.
INDEED...

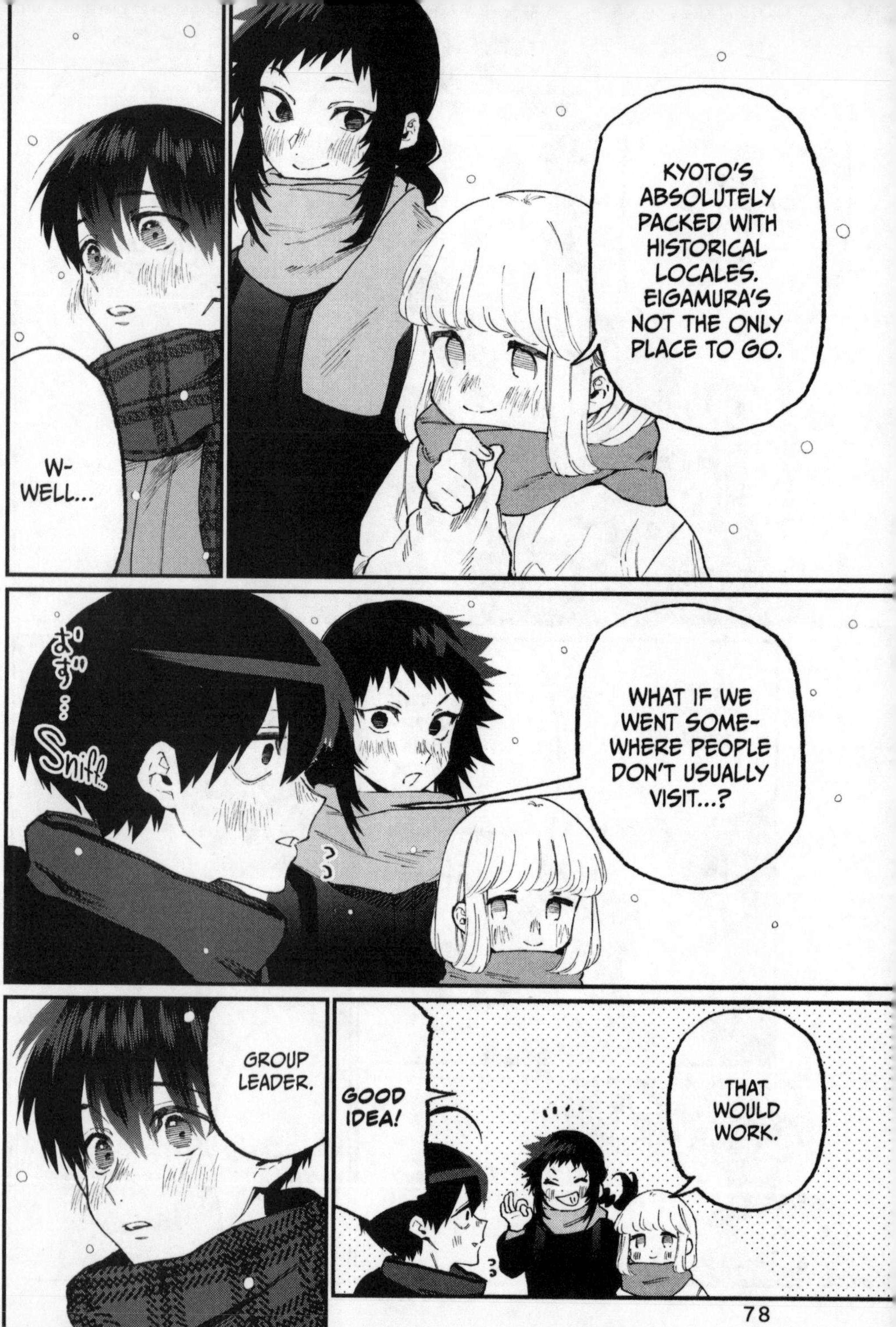
KYOTO'S ABSOLUTELY PACKED WITH HISTORICAL LOCALES. EIGAMURA'S NOT THE ONLY PLACE TO GO.
W-WELL...
WHAT IF WE WENT SOME-WHERE PEOPLE DON'T USUALLY VISIT...?
むず…
Sniff...
THAT WOULD WORK.
GOOD IDEA!
GROUP LEADER.

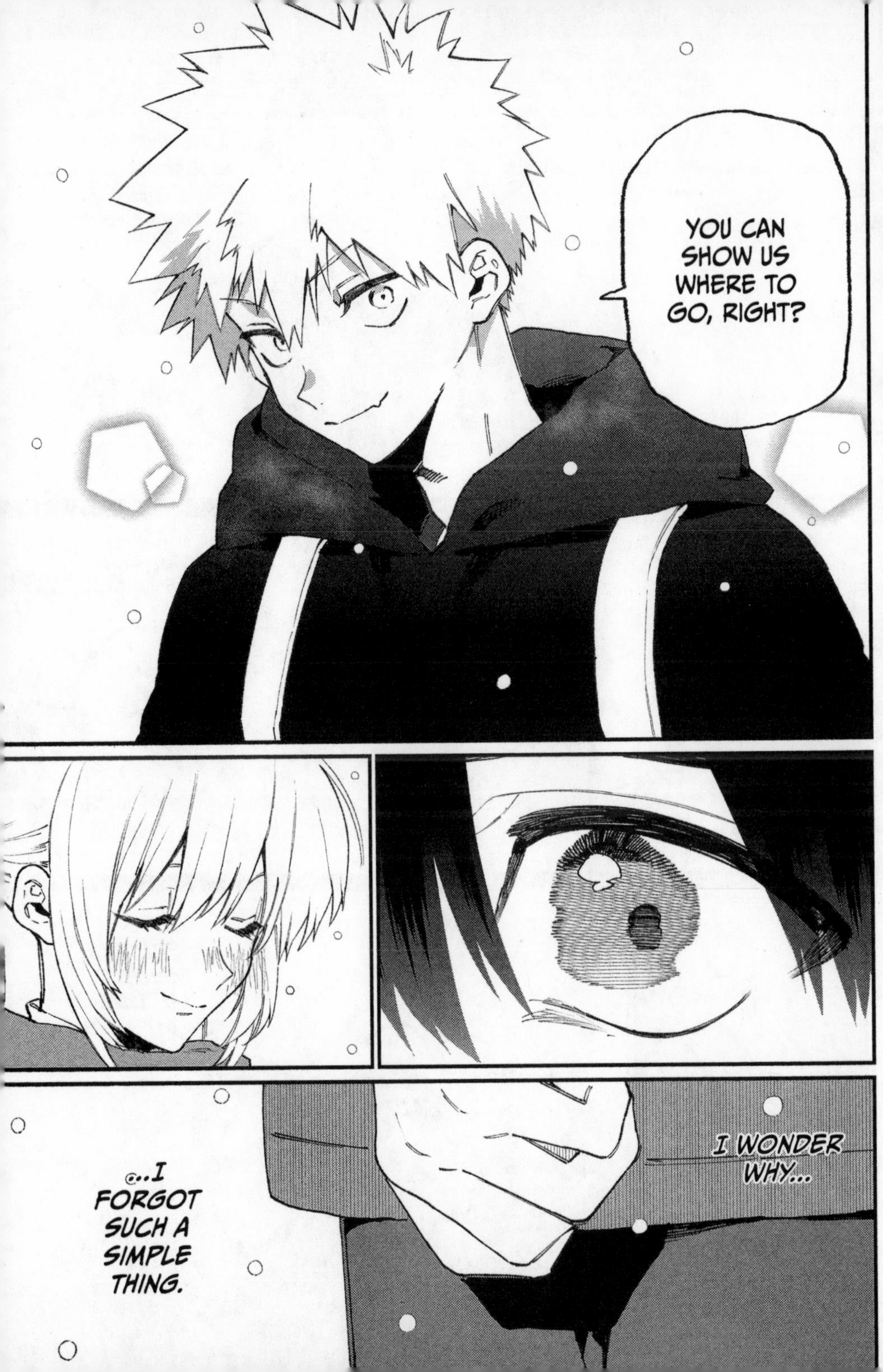
YOU CAN SHOW US WHERE TO GO, RIGHT?
I WONDER WHY...
...I FORGOT SUCH A SIMPLE THING.

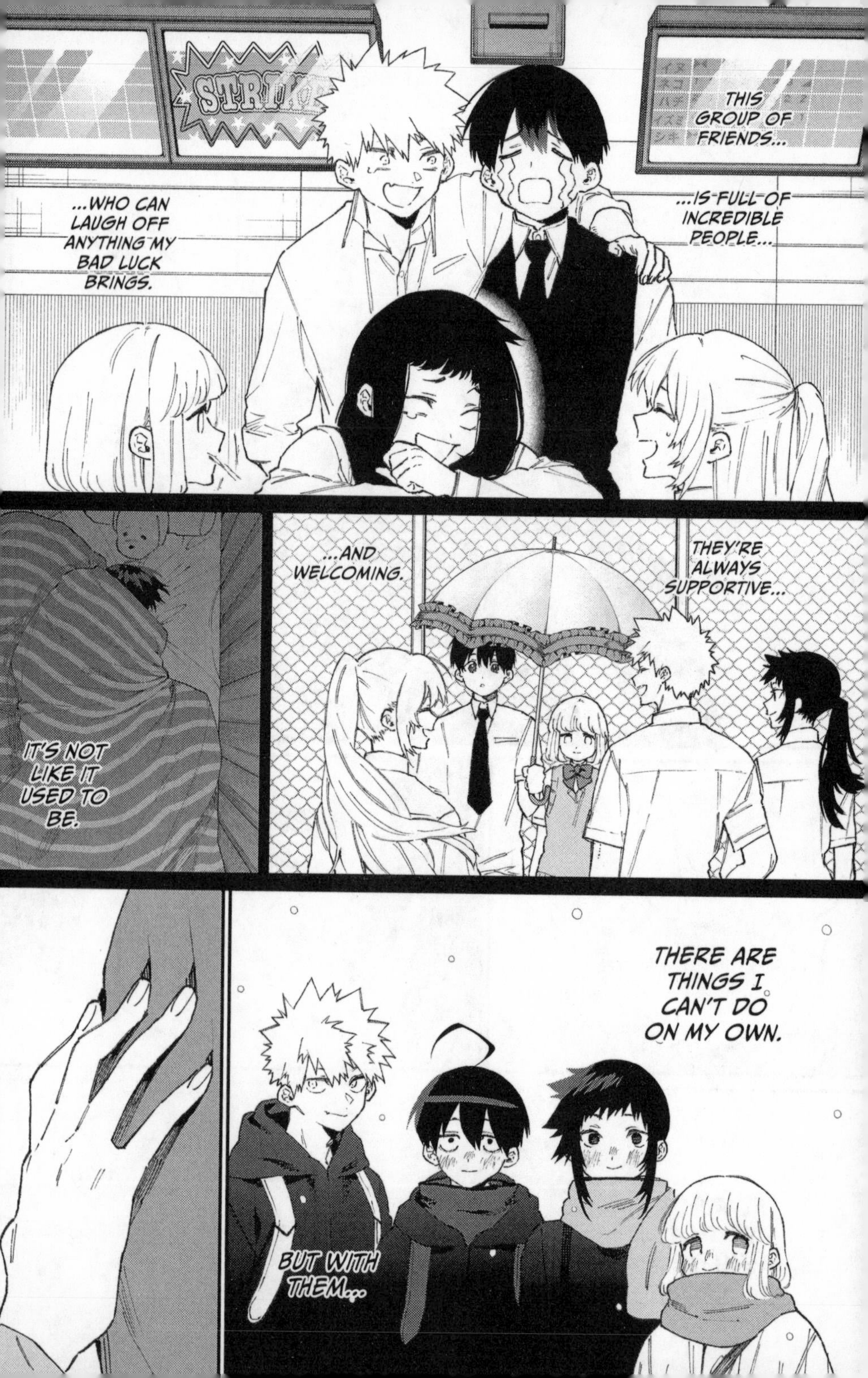
THIS GROUP OF FRIENDS...
...IS FULL OF INCREDIBLE PEOPLE...
...WHO CAN LAUGH OFF ANYTHING MY BAD LUCK BRINGS.
THEY'RE ALWAYS SUPPORTIVE...
...AND WELCOMING.
IT'S NOT LIKE IT USED TO BE.
THERE ARE THINGS I CAN'T DO ON MY OWN.
BUT WITH THEM...

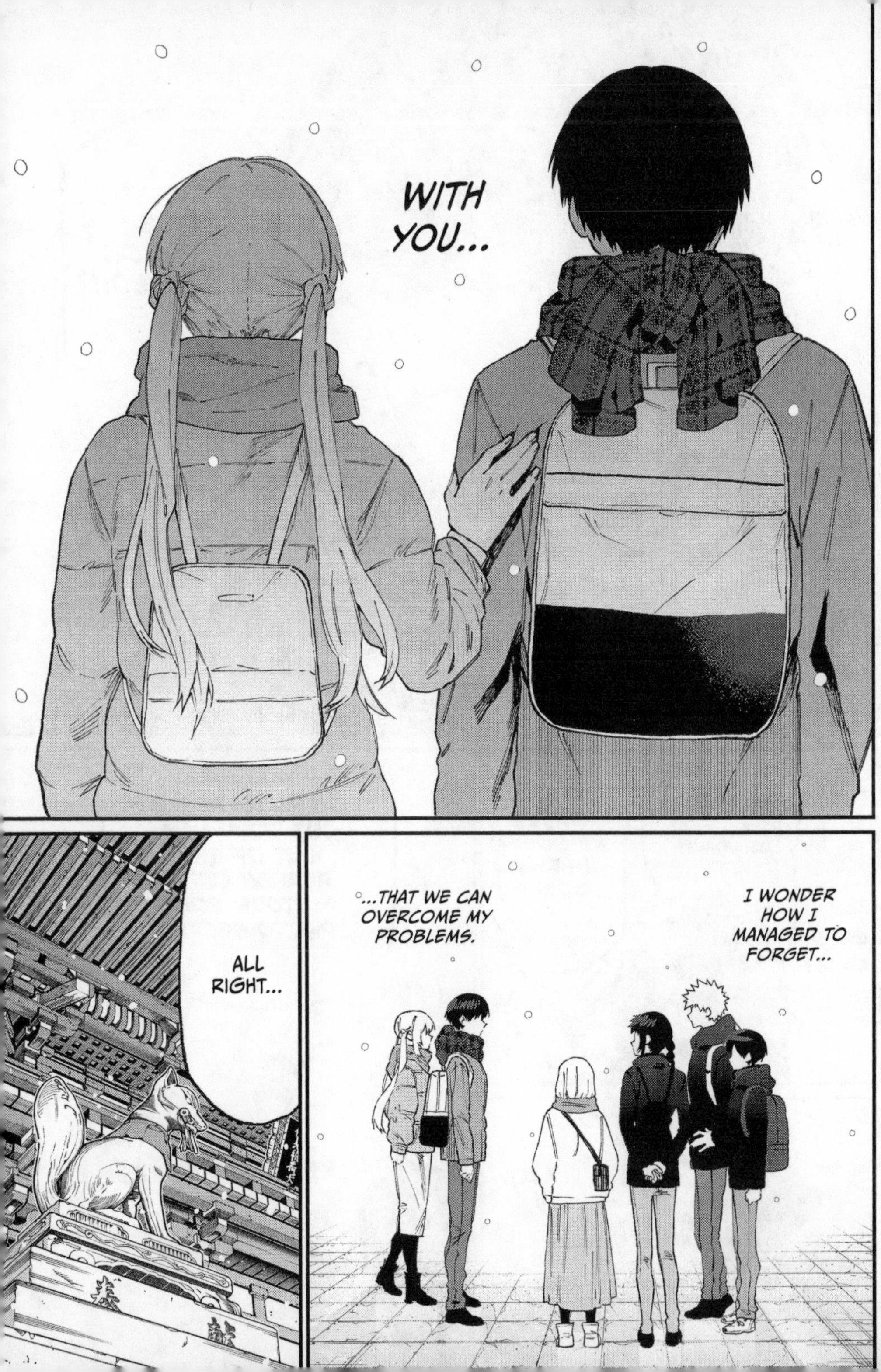

WITH YOU...
I WONDER HOW I MANAGED TO FORGET...
...THAT WE CAN OVERCOME MY PROBLEMS.
ALL RIGHT...

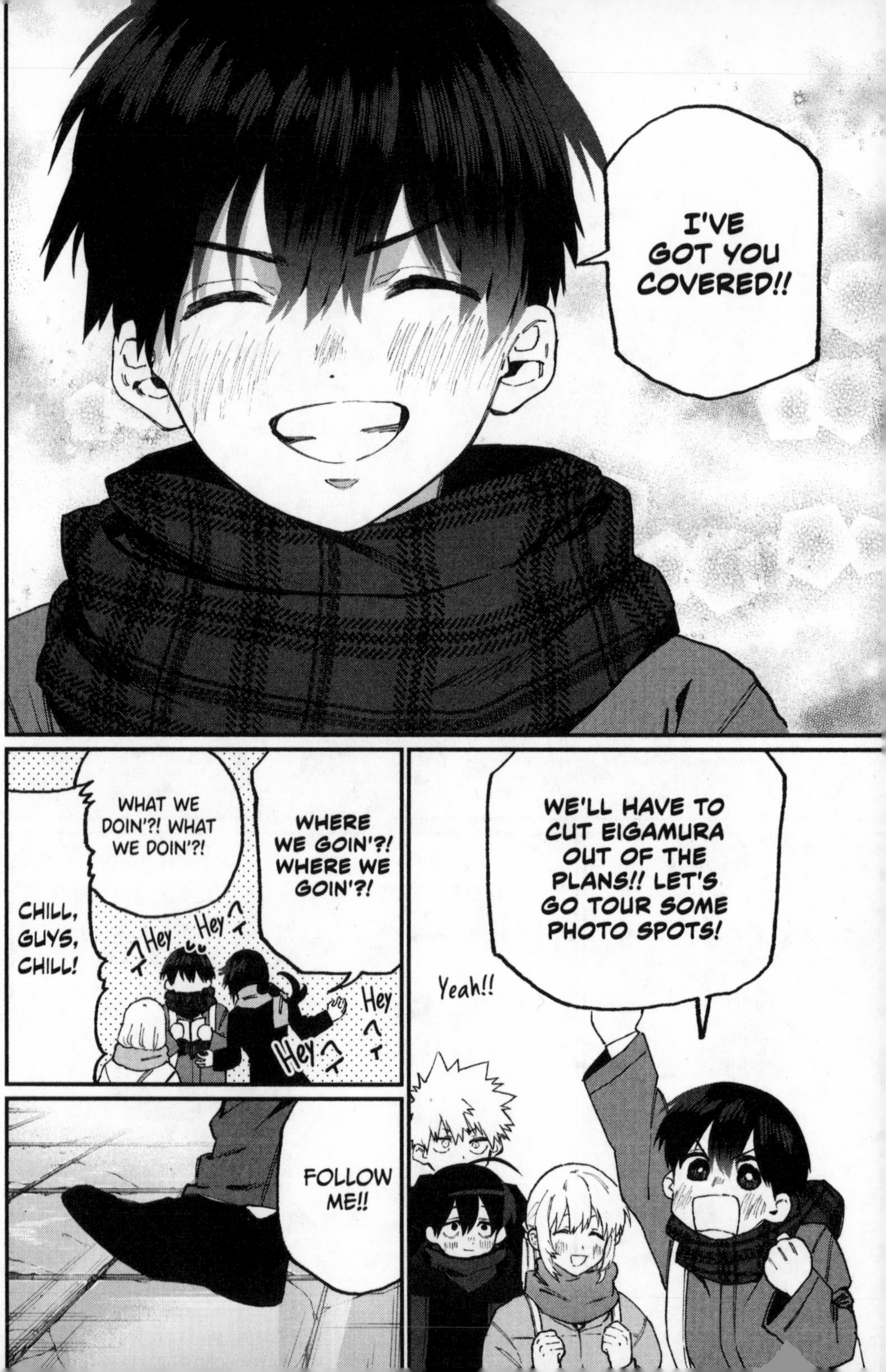
I'VE GOT YOU COVERED!!
WE'LL HAVE TO CUT EIGAMURA OUT OF THE PLANS!! LET'S GO TOUR SOME PHOTO SPOTS!
Yeah!!
WHERE WE GOIN'?! WHERE WE GOIN'?!
WHAT WE DOIN'?! WHAT WE DOIN'?!
Hey
Hey
Hey
Hey
CHILL, GUYS, CHILL!
FOLLOW ME!!

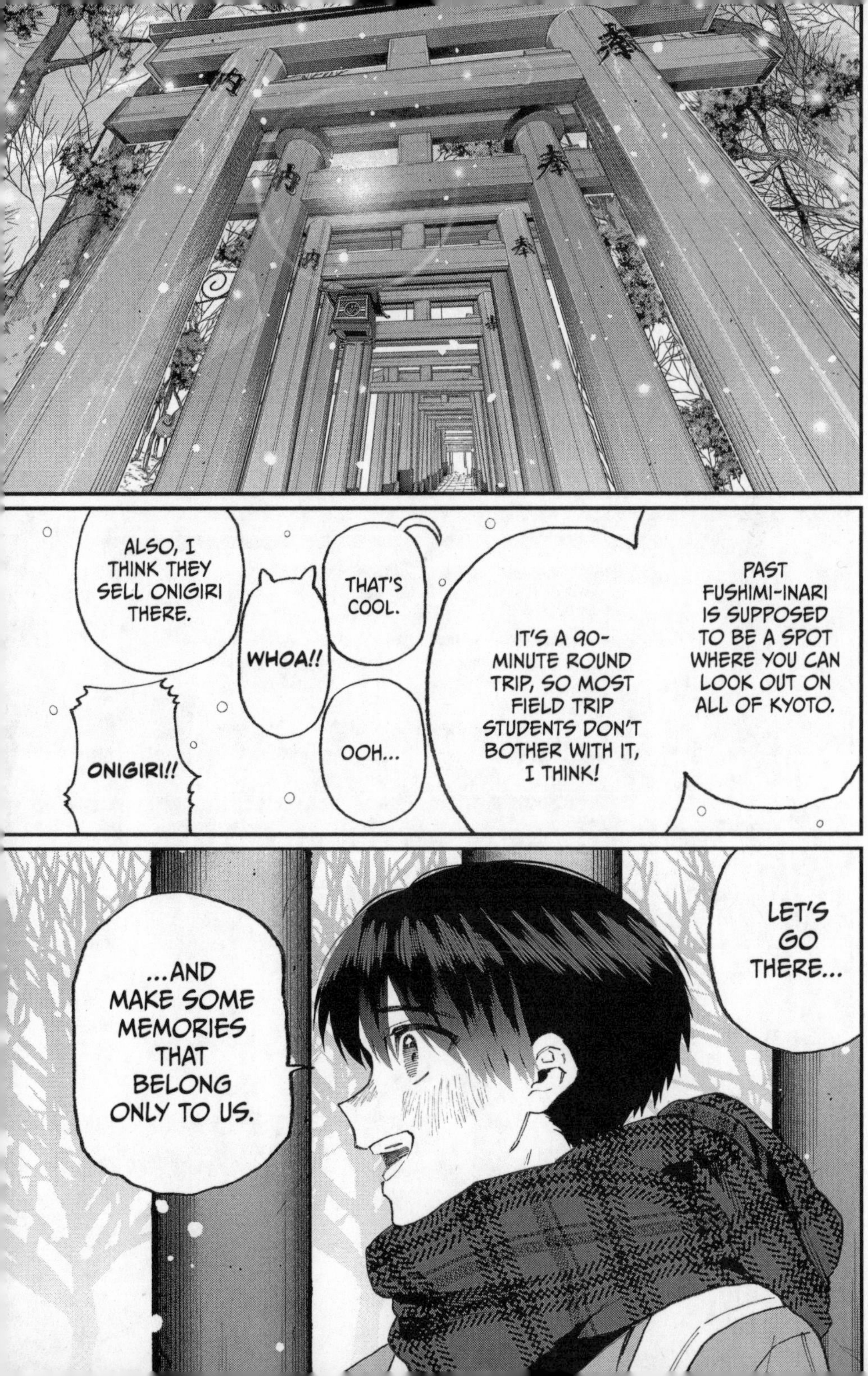
PAST FUSHIMI-INARI IS SUPPOSED TO BE A SPOT WHERE YOU CAN LOOK OUT ON ALL OF KYOTO.
IT'S A 90-MINUTE ROUND TRIP, SO MOST FIELD TRIP STUDENTS DON'T BOTHER WITH IT, I THINK!
THAT'S COOL.
OOH...
WHOA!!
ALSO, I THINK THEY SELL ONIGIRI THERE.
ONIGIRI!!
LET'S GO THERE...
...AND MAKE SOME MEMORIES THAT BELONG ONLY TO US.

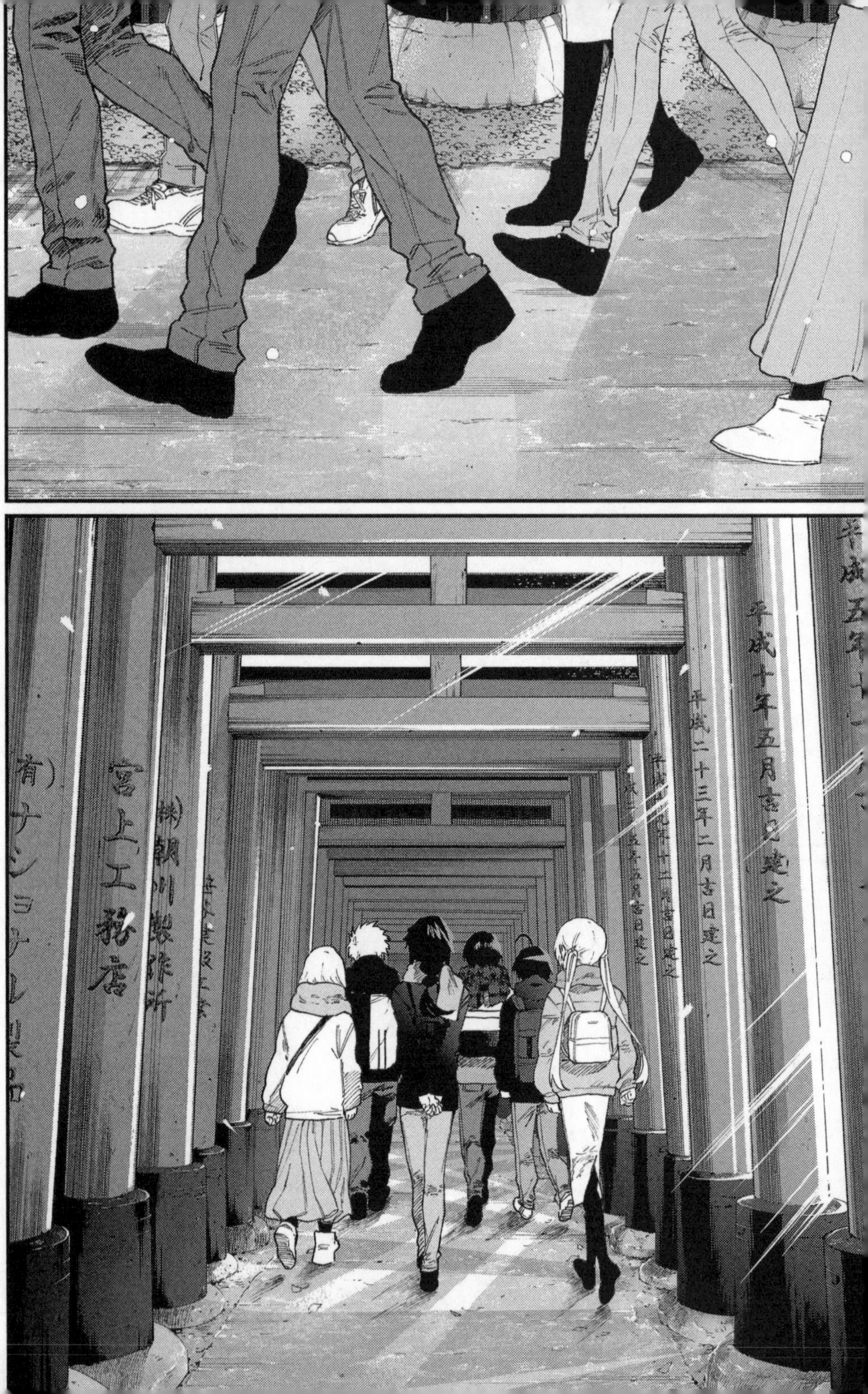
平成十年五月吉日建之
平成二十三年二月吉日建之
宮上工務店

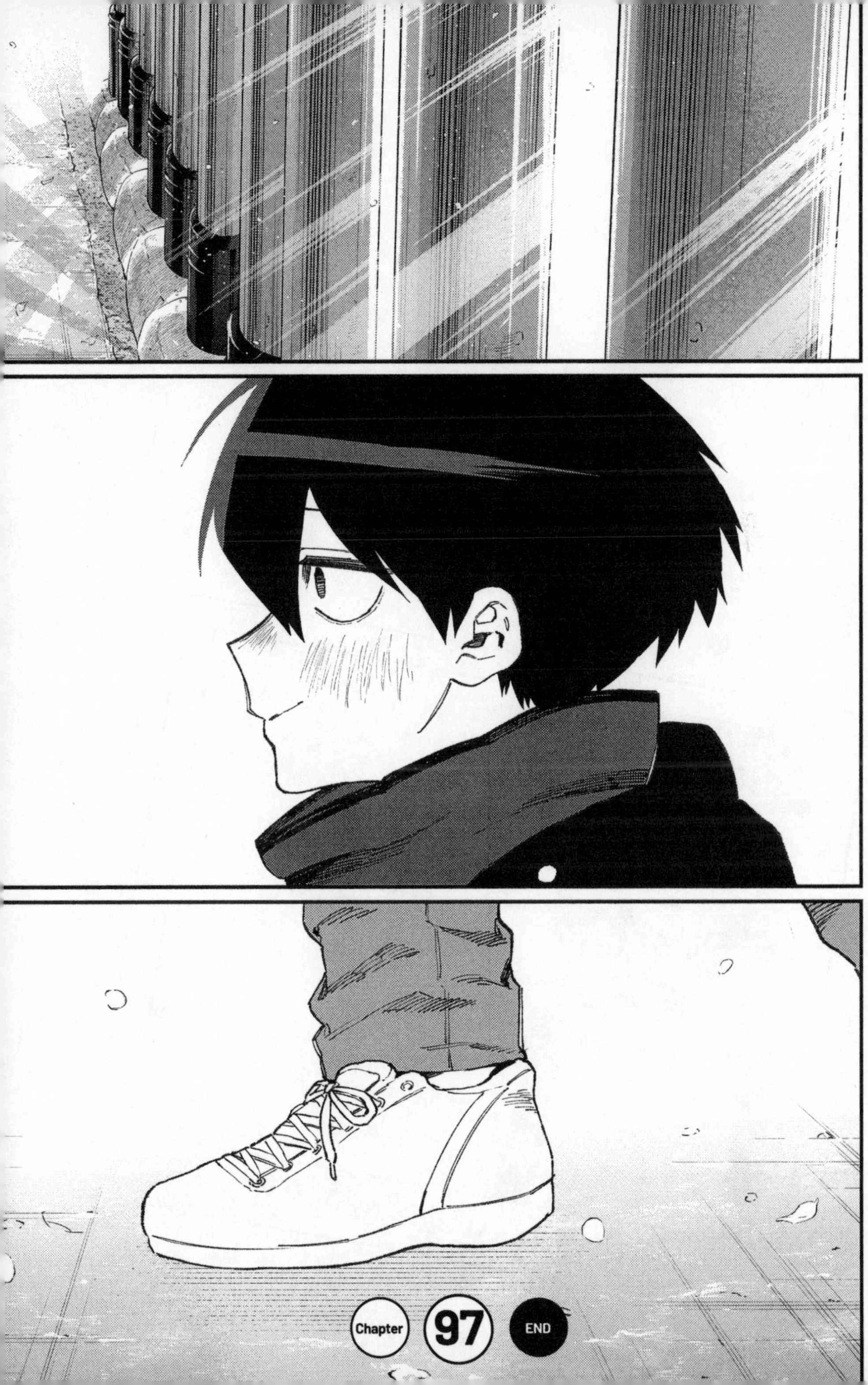
Chapter 97 END

SHIKIMORI'S not just a cutie

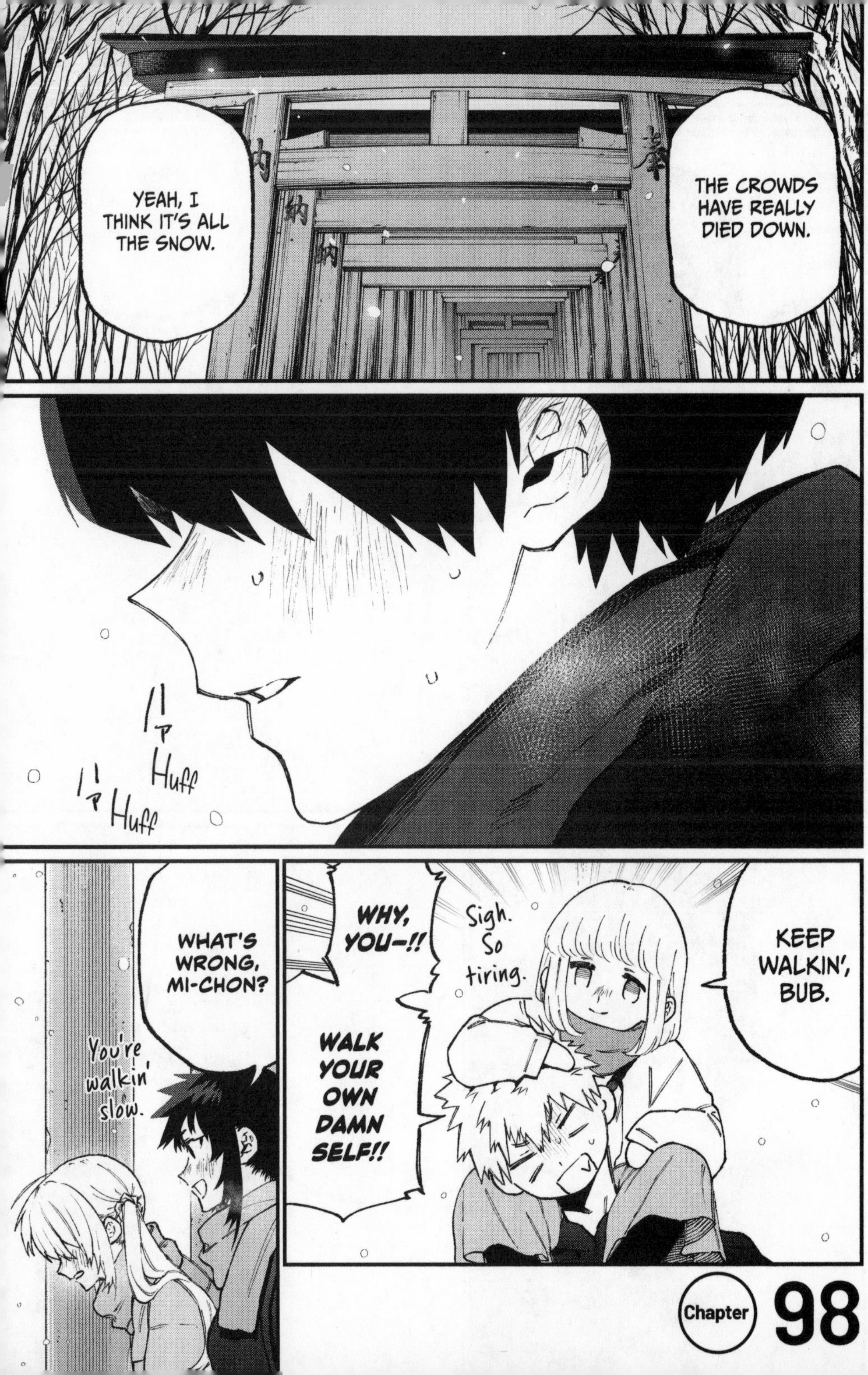
THE CROWDS HAVE REALLY DIED DOWN.
YEAH, I THINK IT'S ALL THE SNOW.
Huff
Huff
KEEP WALKIN', BUB.
Sigh. So tiring.
WHY, YOU-!!
WALK YOUR OWN DAMN SELF!!
WHAT'S WRONG, MI-CHON?
You're walkin' slow.

Chapter 98

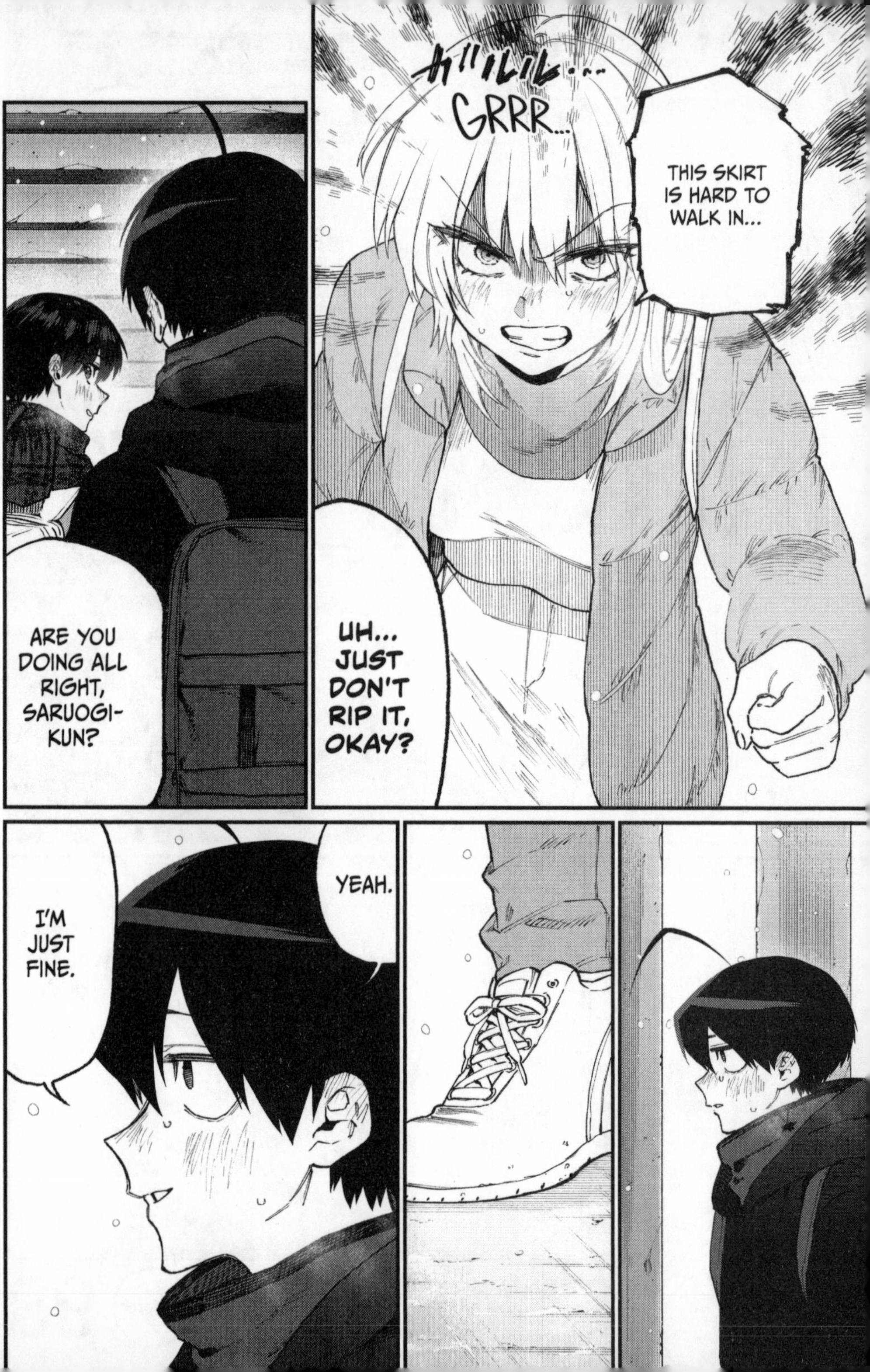
ガルルル...
GRRR...
THIS SKIRT IS HARD TO WALK IN...
UH... JUST DON'T RIP IT, OKAY?
ARE YOU DOING ALL RIGHT, SARUOGI-KUN?
YEAH.
I'M JUST FINE.

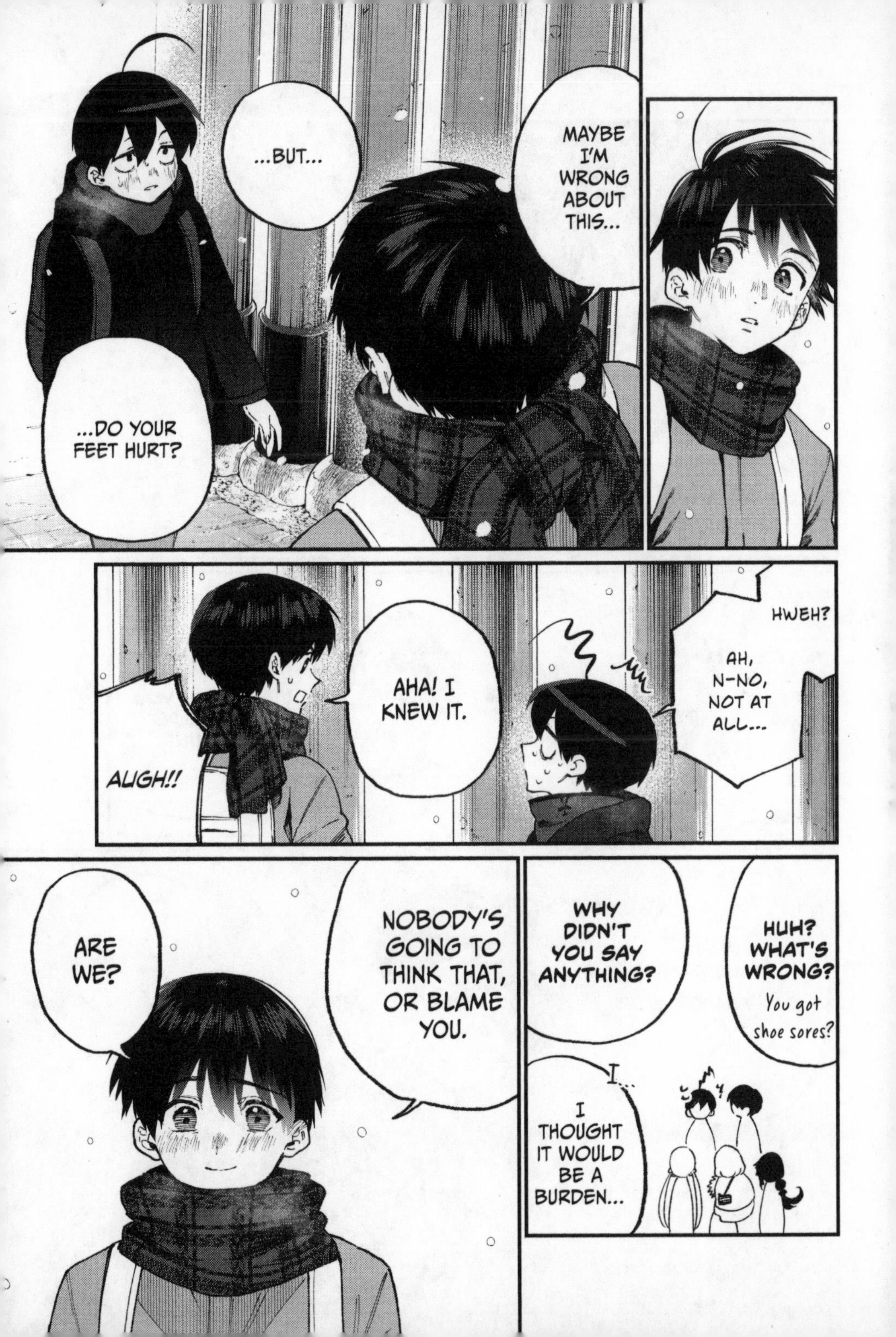
MAYBE I'M WRONG ABOUT THIS...
...BUT...
...DO YOUR FEET HURT?
HWEH?
AH, N-NO, NOT AT ALL...
AHA! I KNEW IT.
AUGH!!
HUH? WHAT'S WRONG?
You got shoe sores?
WHY DIDN'T YOU SAY ANYTHING?
I...
I THOUGHT IT WOULD BE A BURDEN...
NOBODY'S GOING TO THINK THAT, OR BLAME YOU.
ARE WE?

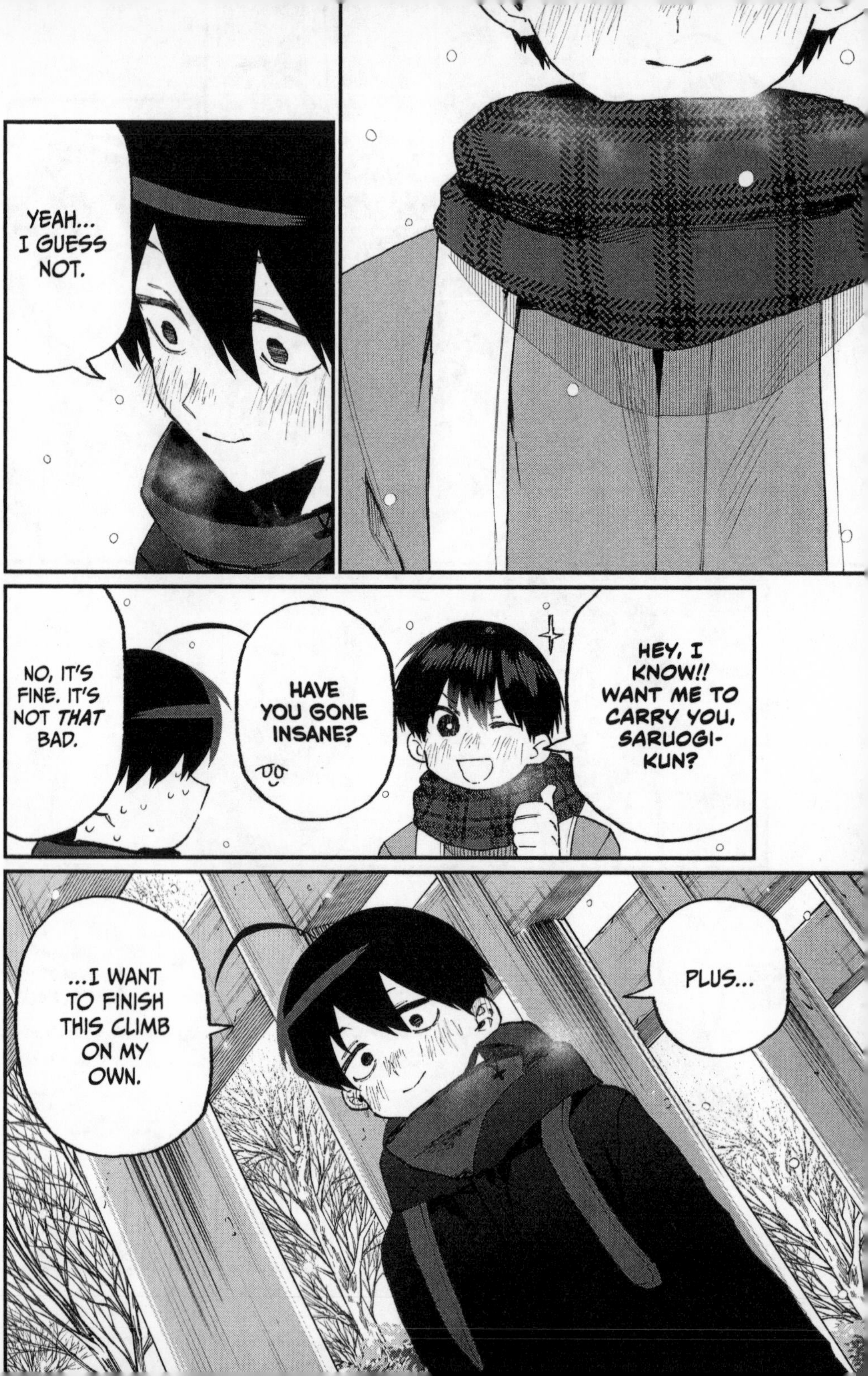
YEAH... I GUESS NOT.
HEY, I KNOW!! WANT ME TO CARRY YOU, SARUOGI-KUN?
HAVE YOU GONE INSANE?
NO, IT'S FINE. IT'S NOT *THAT* BAD.
PLUS...
...I WANT TO FINISH THIS CLIMB ON MY OWN.

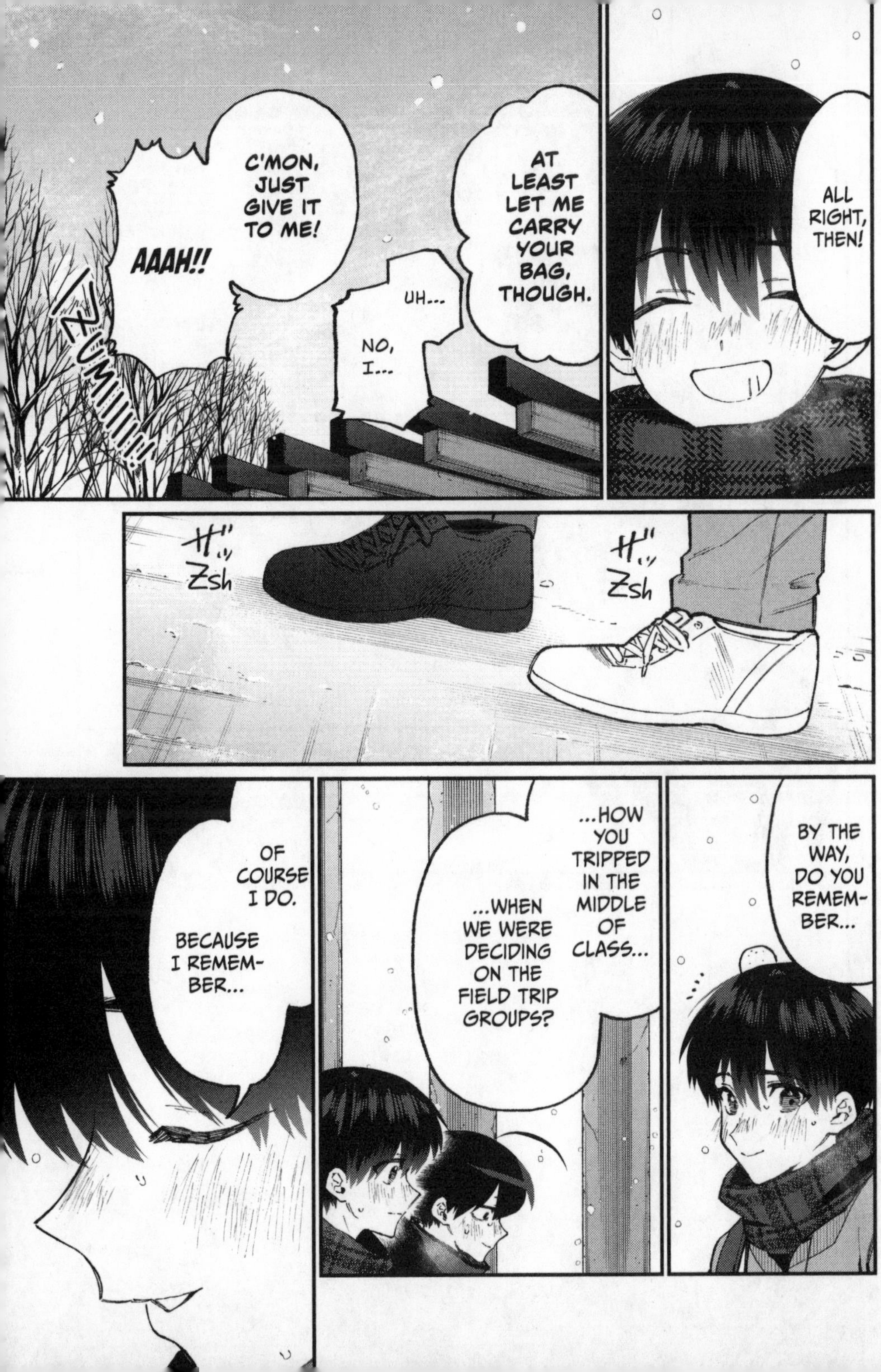
ALL RIGHT, THEN!
AT LEAST LET ME CARRY YOUR BAG, THOUGH.
UH...
NO, I...
C'MON, JUST GIVE IT TO ME!
AAAH!!
IZUMIIIII!!
ザッ Zsh
ザッ Zsh
BY THE WAY, DO YOU REMEMBER...
...HOW YOU TRIPPED IN THE MIDDLE OF CLASS...
...WHEN WE WERE DECIDING ON THE FIELD TRIP GROUPS?
OF COURSE I DO.
BECAUSE I REMEMBER...

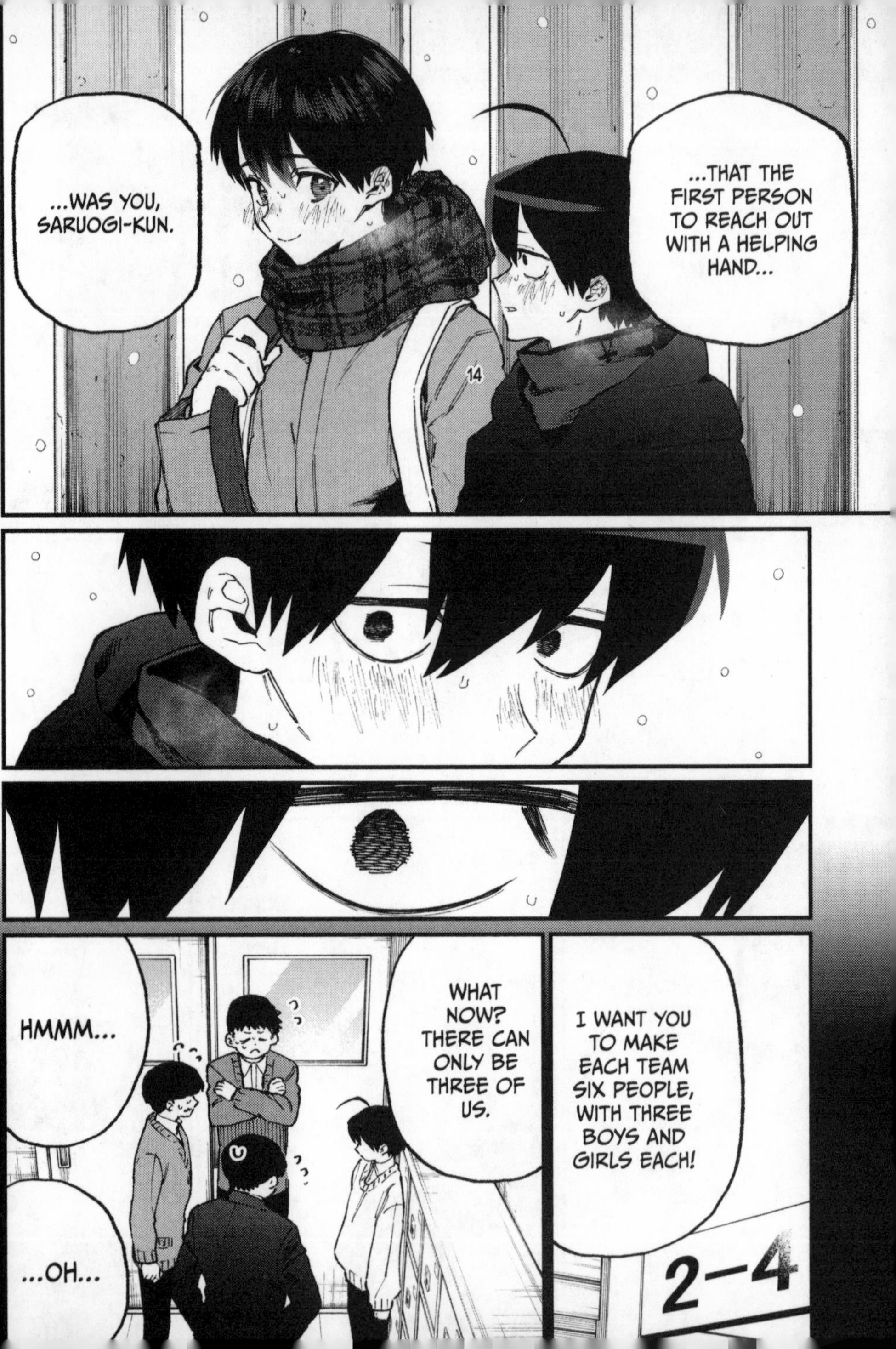
...THAT THE FIRST PERSON TO REACH OUT WITH A HELPING HAND...
...WAS YOU, SARUOGI-KUN.
14
I WANT YOU TO MAKE EACH TEAM SIX PEOPLE, WITH THREE BOYS AND GIRLS EACH!
2-4
WHAT NOW? THERE CAN ONLY BE THREE OF US.
HMMM...
...OH...

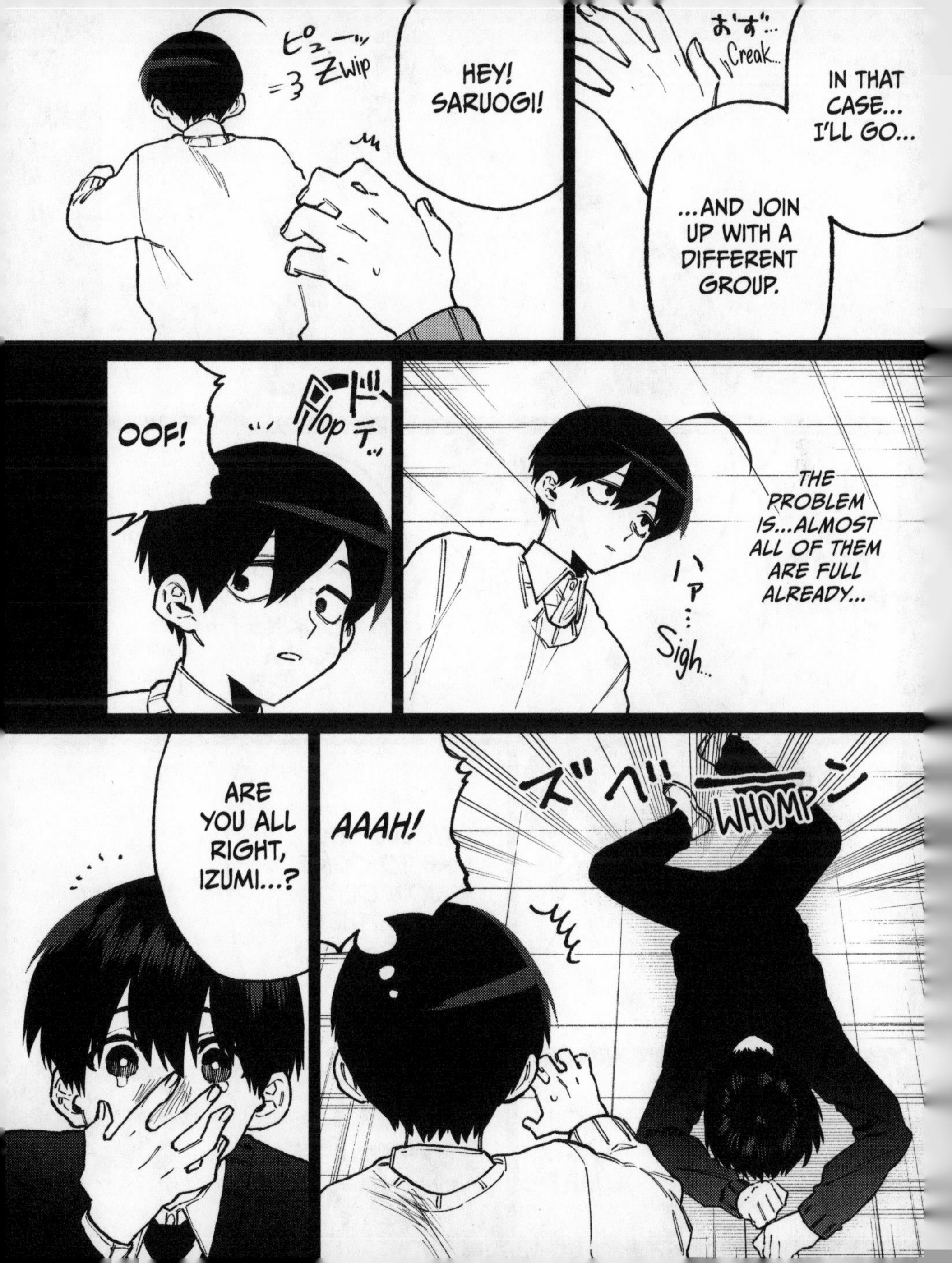
おず…
Creak...
IN THAT CASE... I'LL GO...
...AND JOIN UP WITH A DIFFERENT GROUP.
ピューッ
Zwip
HEY! SARUOGI!
THE PROBLEM IS...ALMOST ALL OF THEM ARE FULL ALREADY...
ハァ…
Sigh...
ドテッ
Flop
OOF!
ズベーン
WHOMP
AAAH!
ARE YOU ALL RIGHT, IZUMI...?

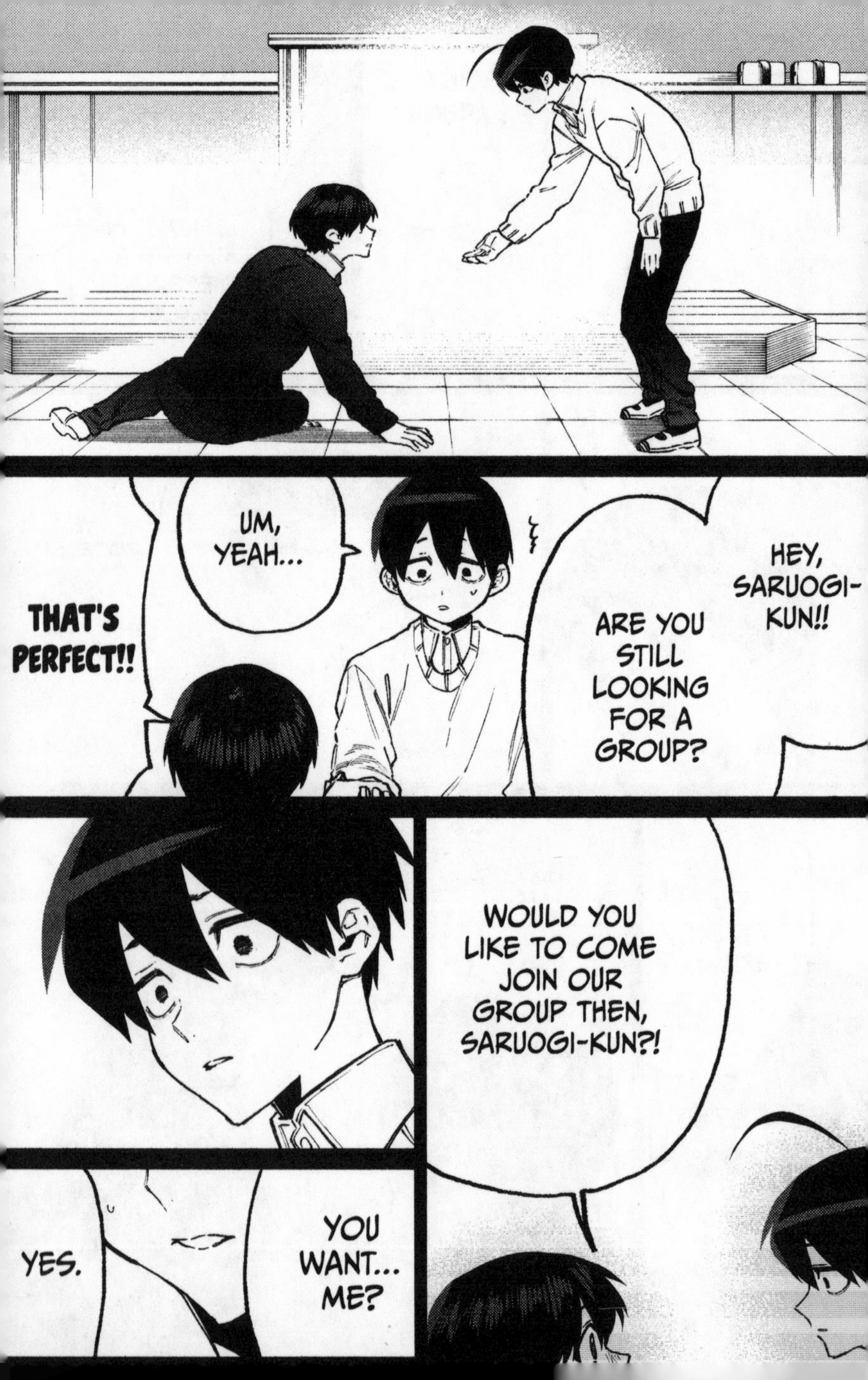
HEY, SARUOGI-KUN!! ARE YOU STILL LOOKING FOR A GROUP?
UM, YEAH...
THAT'S PERFECT!!
WOULD YOU LIKE TO COME JOIN OUR GROUP THEN, SARUOGI-KUN?!
YOU WANT... ME?
YES.

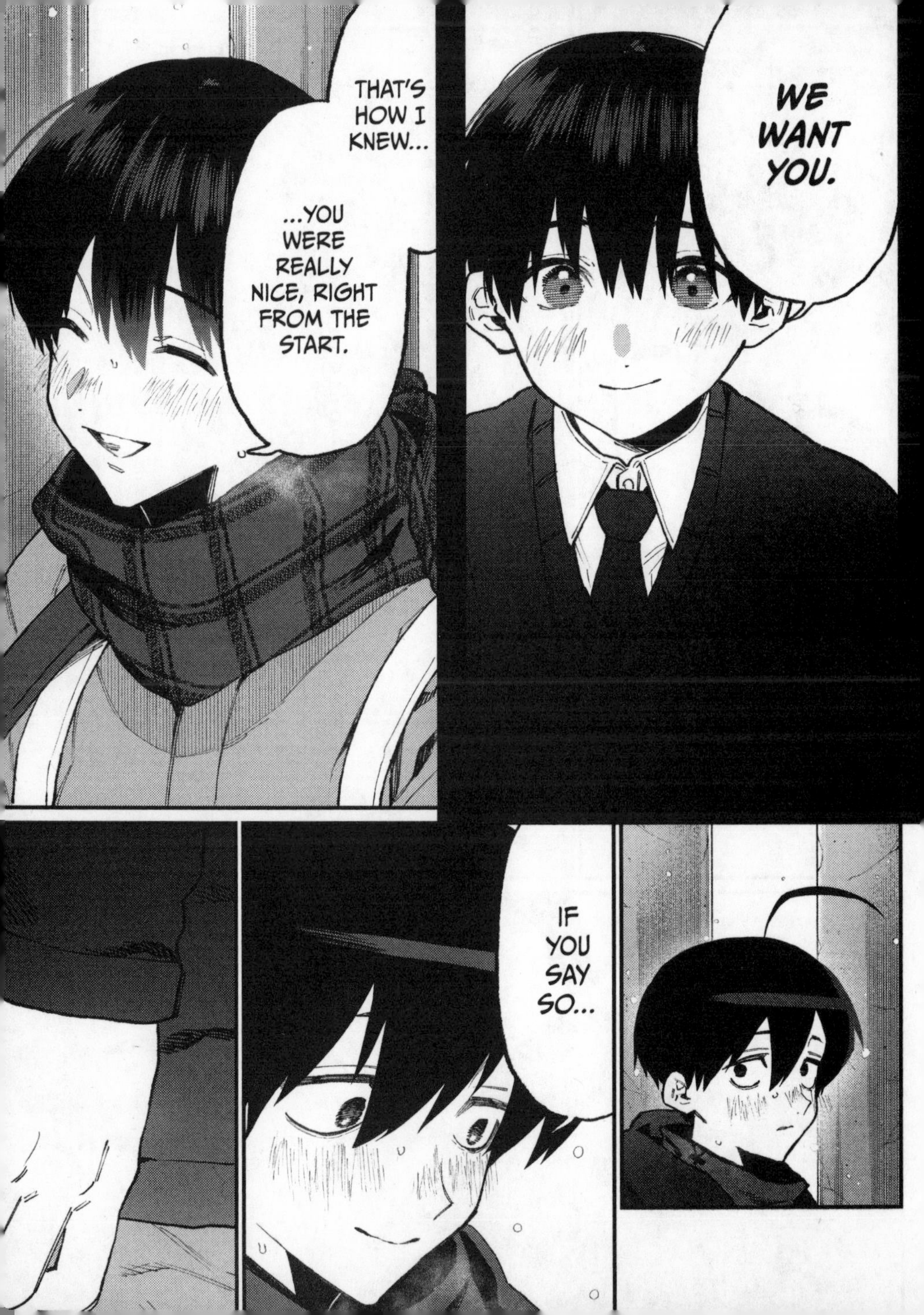
WE WANT YOU.
THAT'S HOW I KNEW...
...YOU WERE REALLY NICE, RIGHT FROM THE START.
IF YOU SAY SO...

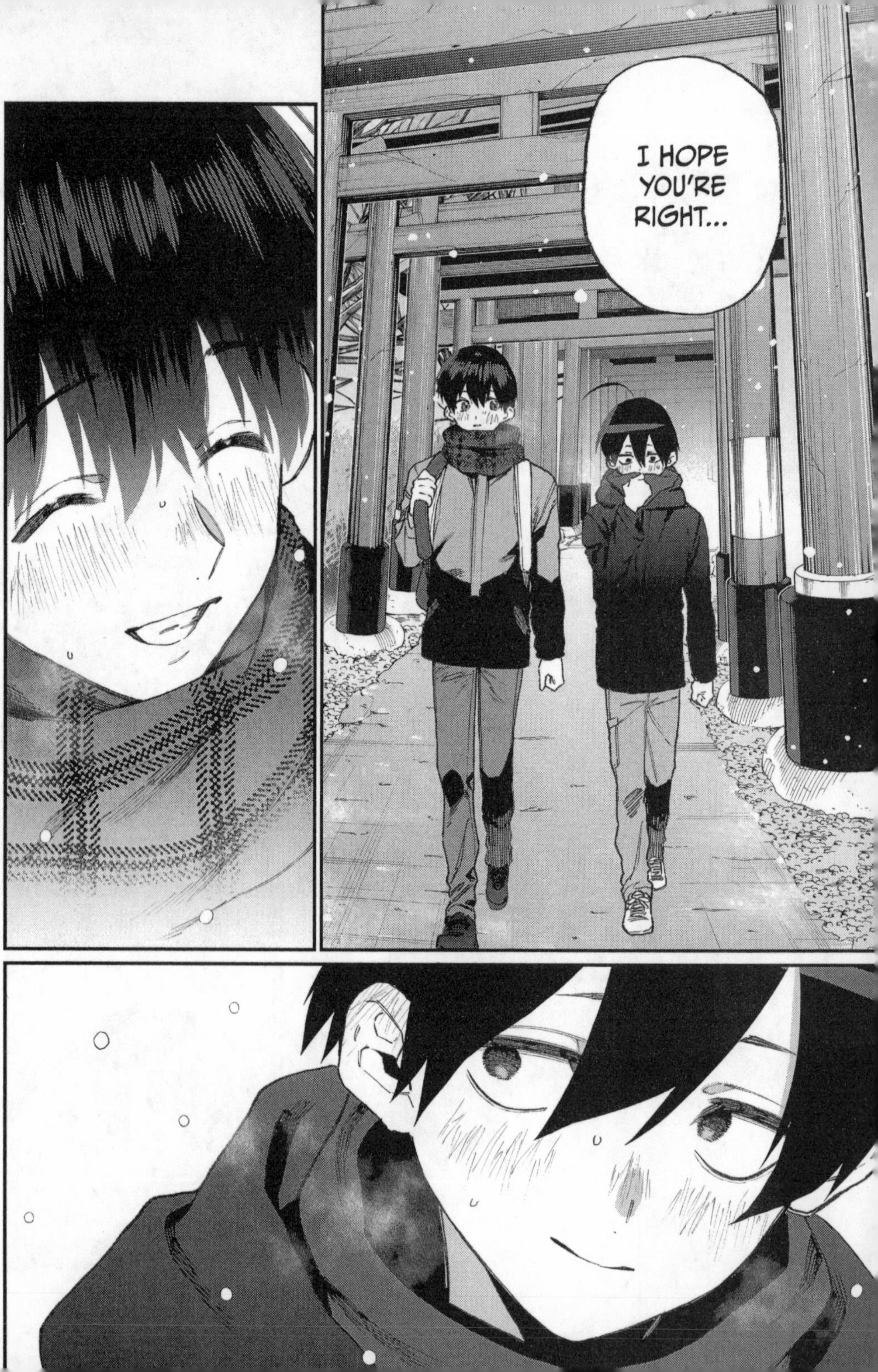
I HOPE YOU'RE RIGHT...

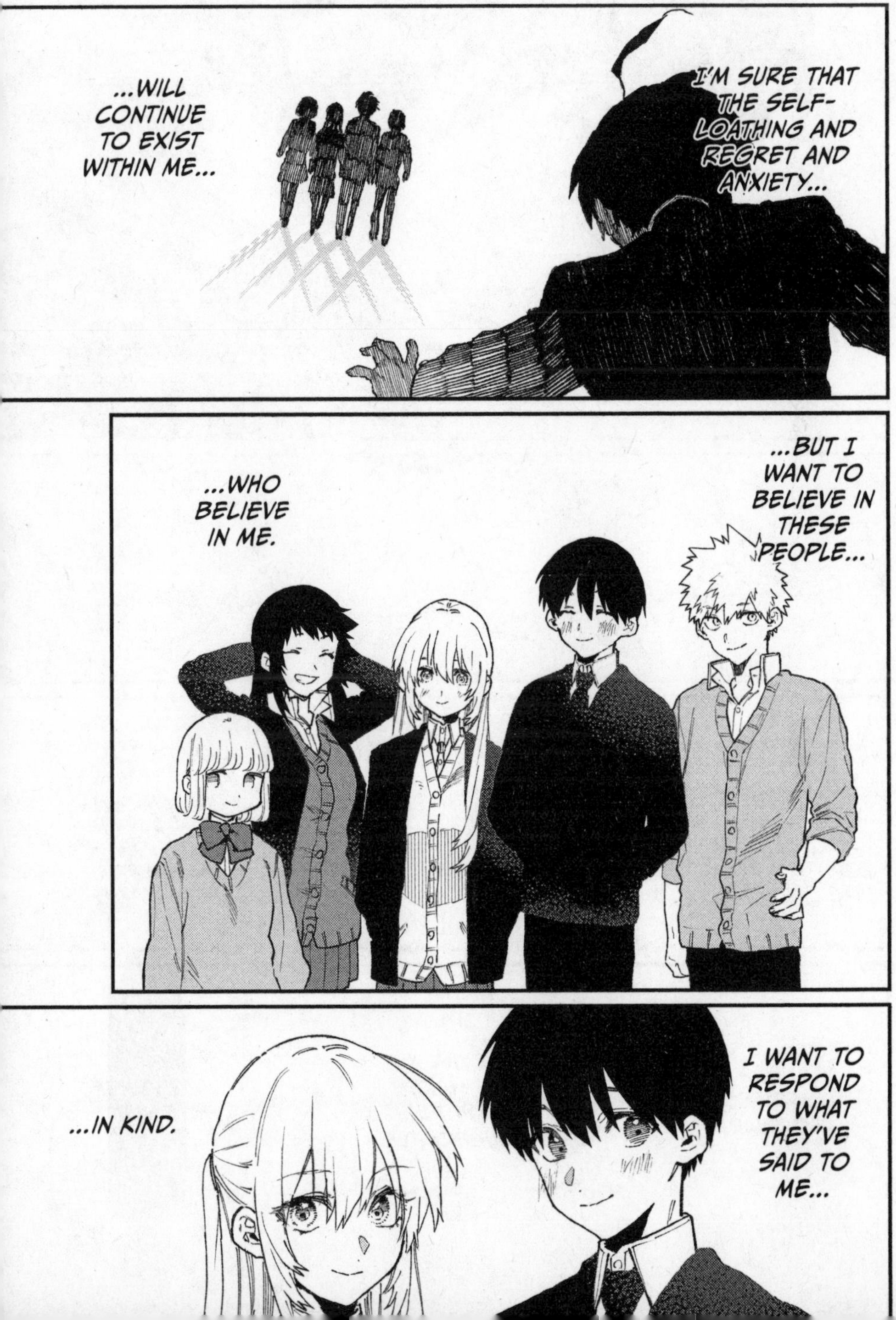
I'M SURE THAT THE SELF-LOATHING AND REGRET AND ANXIETY...
...WILL CONTINUE TO EXIST WITHIN ME...
...BUT I WANT TO BELIEVE IN THESE PEOPLE...
...WHO BELIEVE IN ME.
I WANT TO RESPOND TO WHAT THEY'VE SAID TO ME...
...IN KIND.

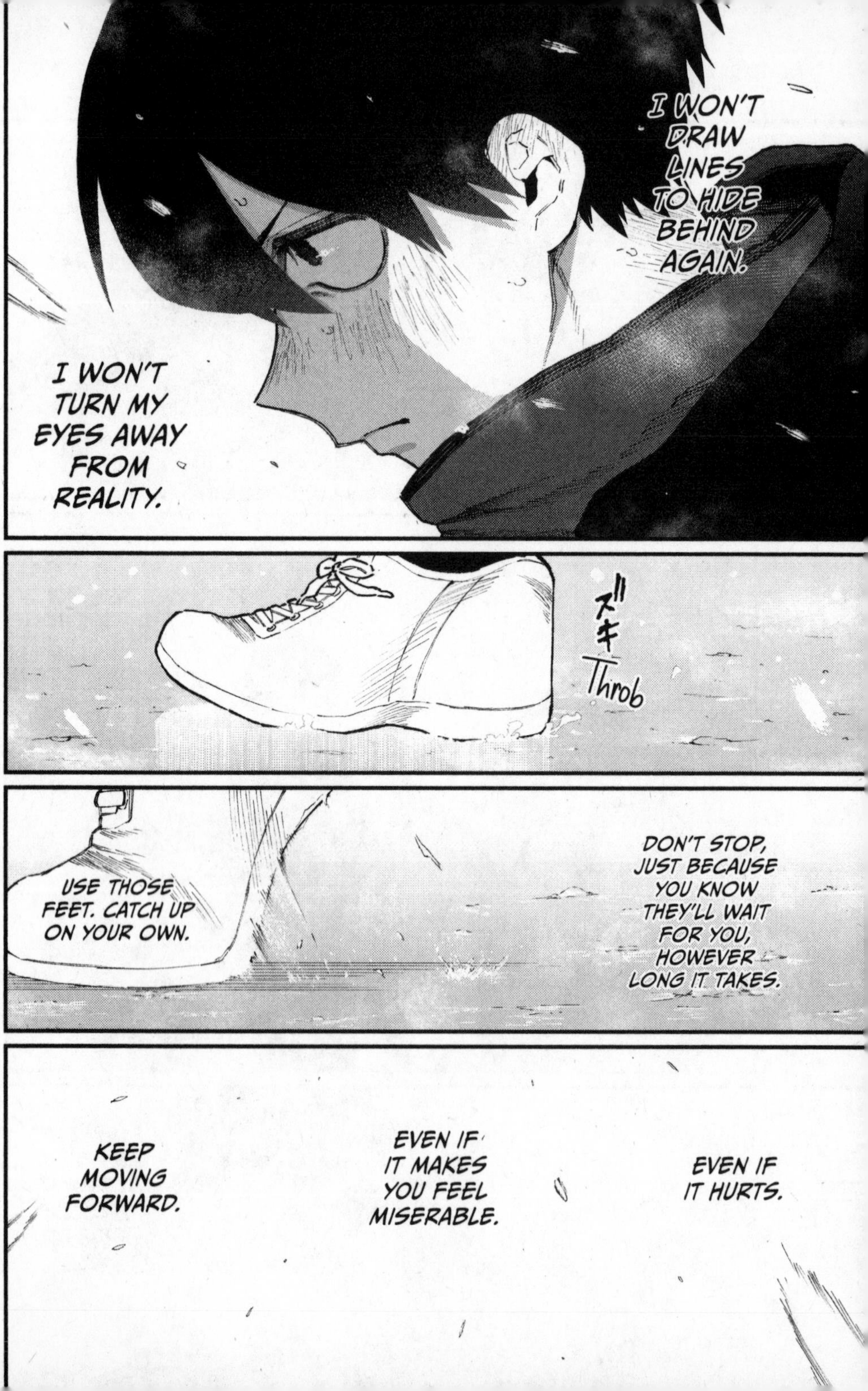
I WON'T DRAW LINES TO HIDE BEHIND AGAIN.
I WON'T TURN MY EYES AWAY FROM REALITY.
ズキ
Throb
DON'T STOP, JUST BECAUSE YOU KNOW THEY'LL WAIT FOR YOU, HOWEVER LONG IT TAKES.
USE THOSE FEET. CATCH UP ON YOUR OWN.
EVEN IF IT HURTS.
EVEN IF IT MAKES YOU FEEL MISERABLE.
KEEP MOVING FORWARD.

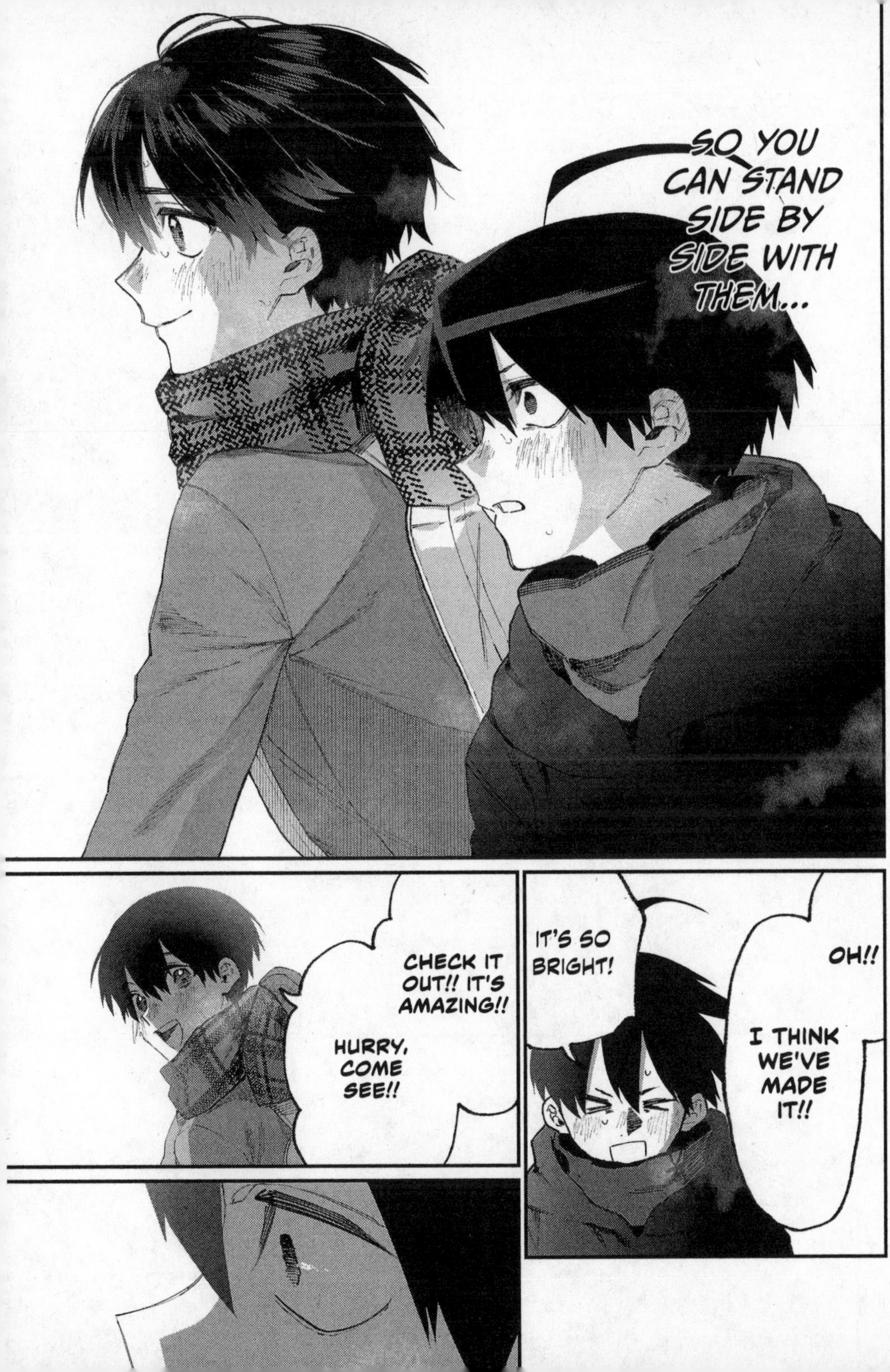
SO YOU CAN STAND SIDE BY SIDE WITH THEM...
OH!!
I THINK WE'VE MADE IT!!
IT'S SO BRIGHT!
CHECK IT OUT!! IT'S AMAZING!!
HURRY, COME SEE!!

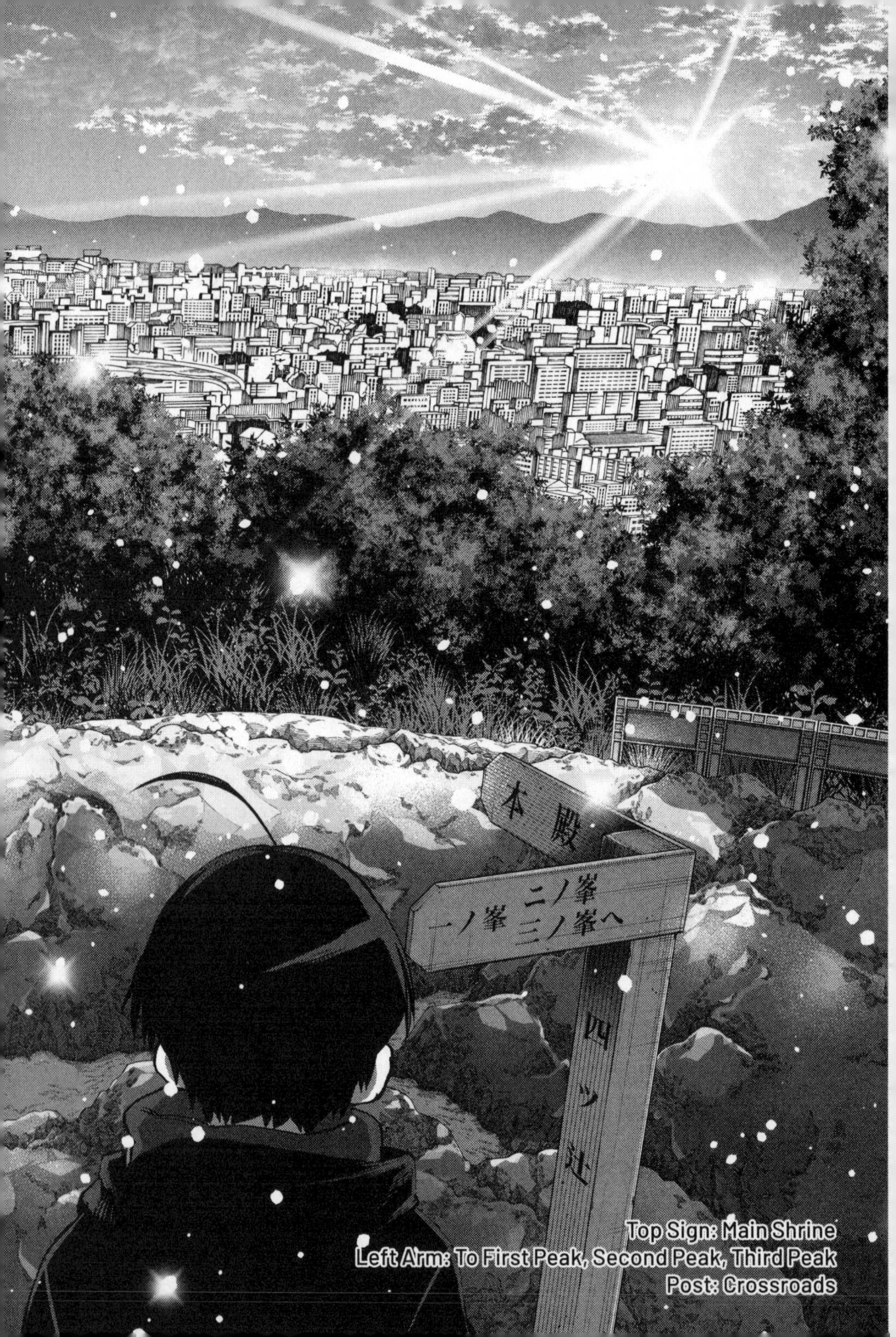
本殿
一ノ峯 二ノ峯 三ノ峯へ
四ツ辻
Top Sign: Main Shrine
Left Arm: To First Peak, Second Peak, Third Peak
Post: Crossroads

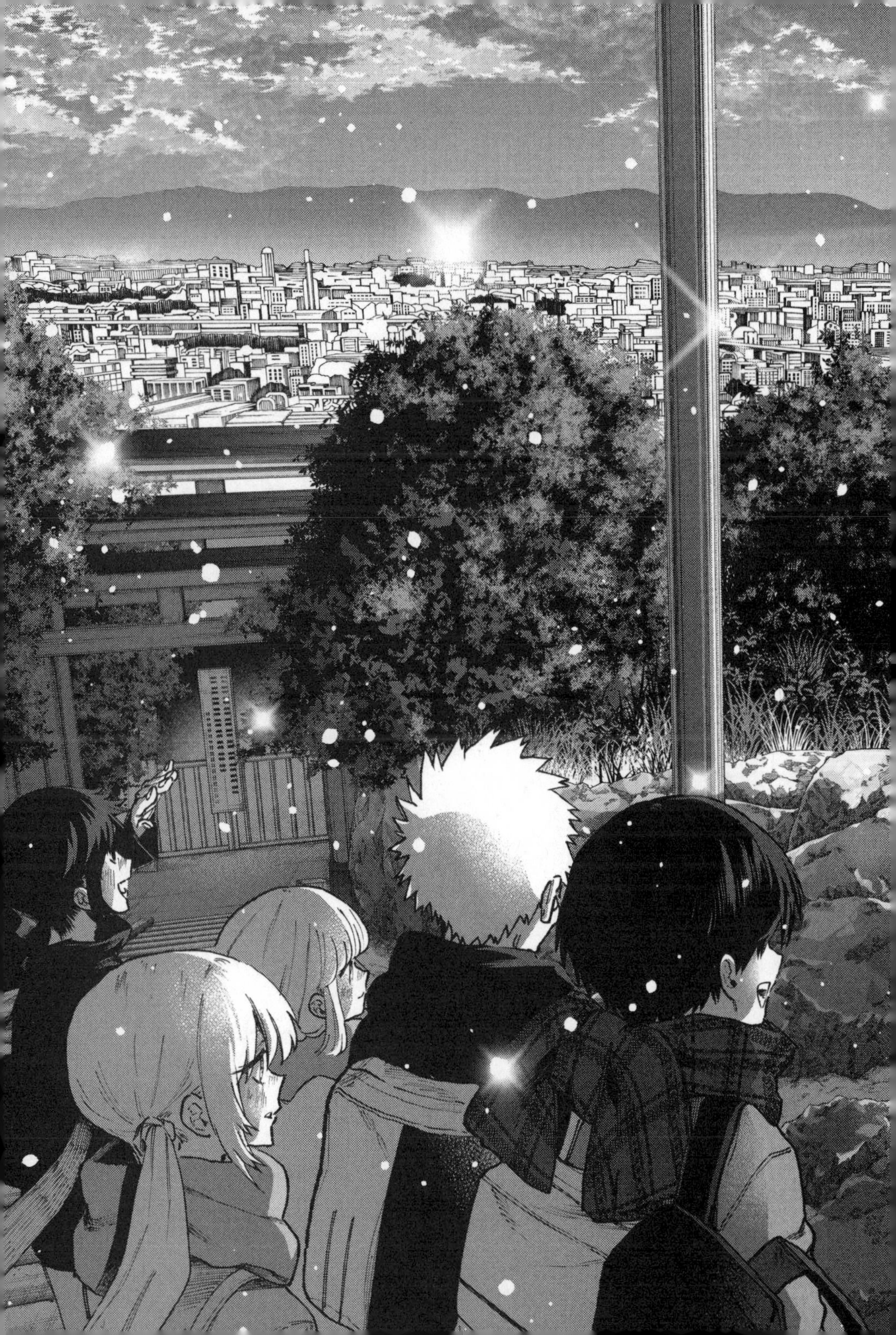

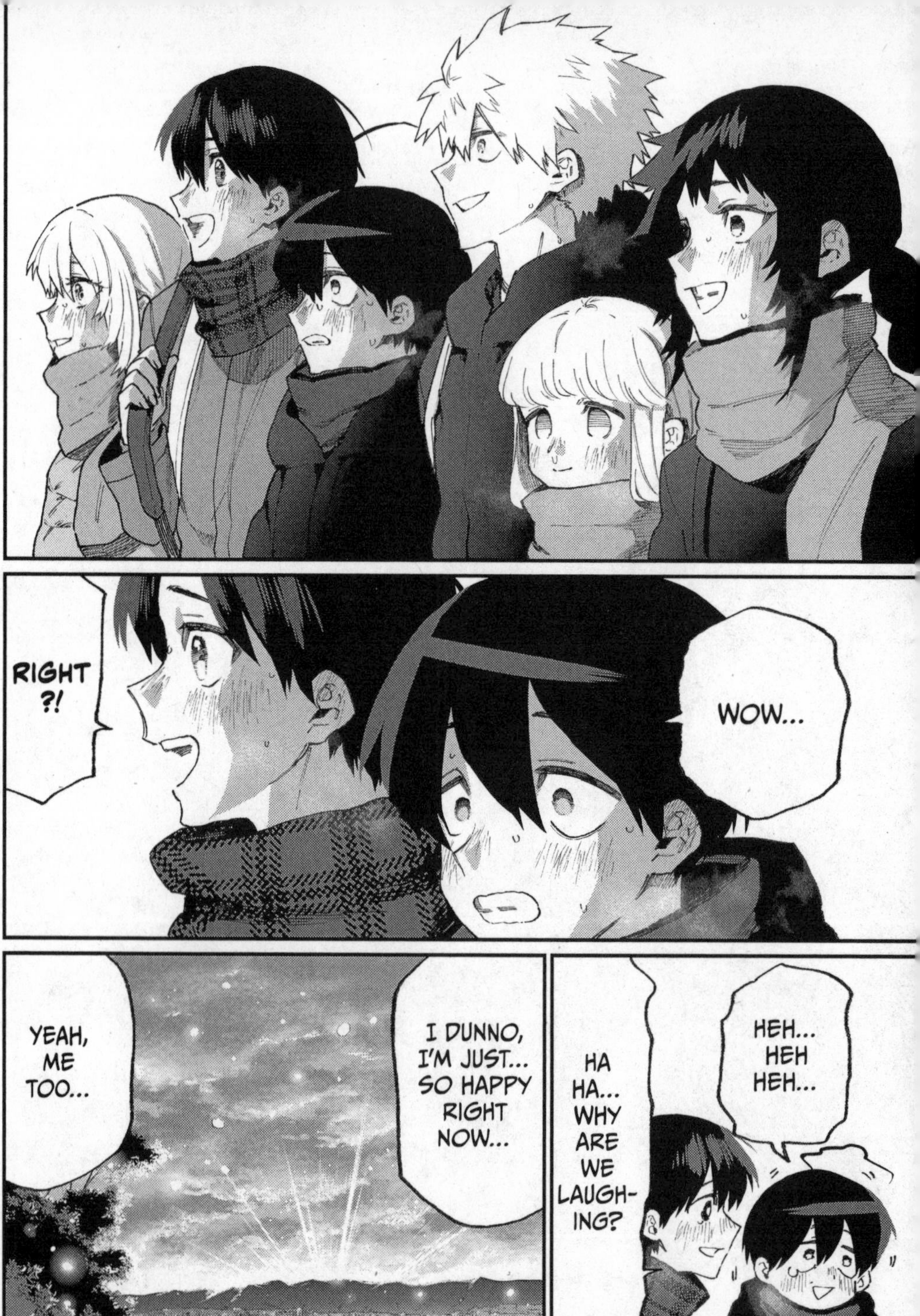
WOW...
RIGHT ?!
HEH... HEH HEH...
HA HA... WHY ARE WE LAUGH-ING?
I DUNNO, I'M JUST... SO HAPPY RIGHT NOW...
YEAH, ME TOO...

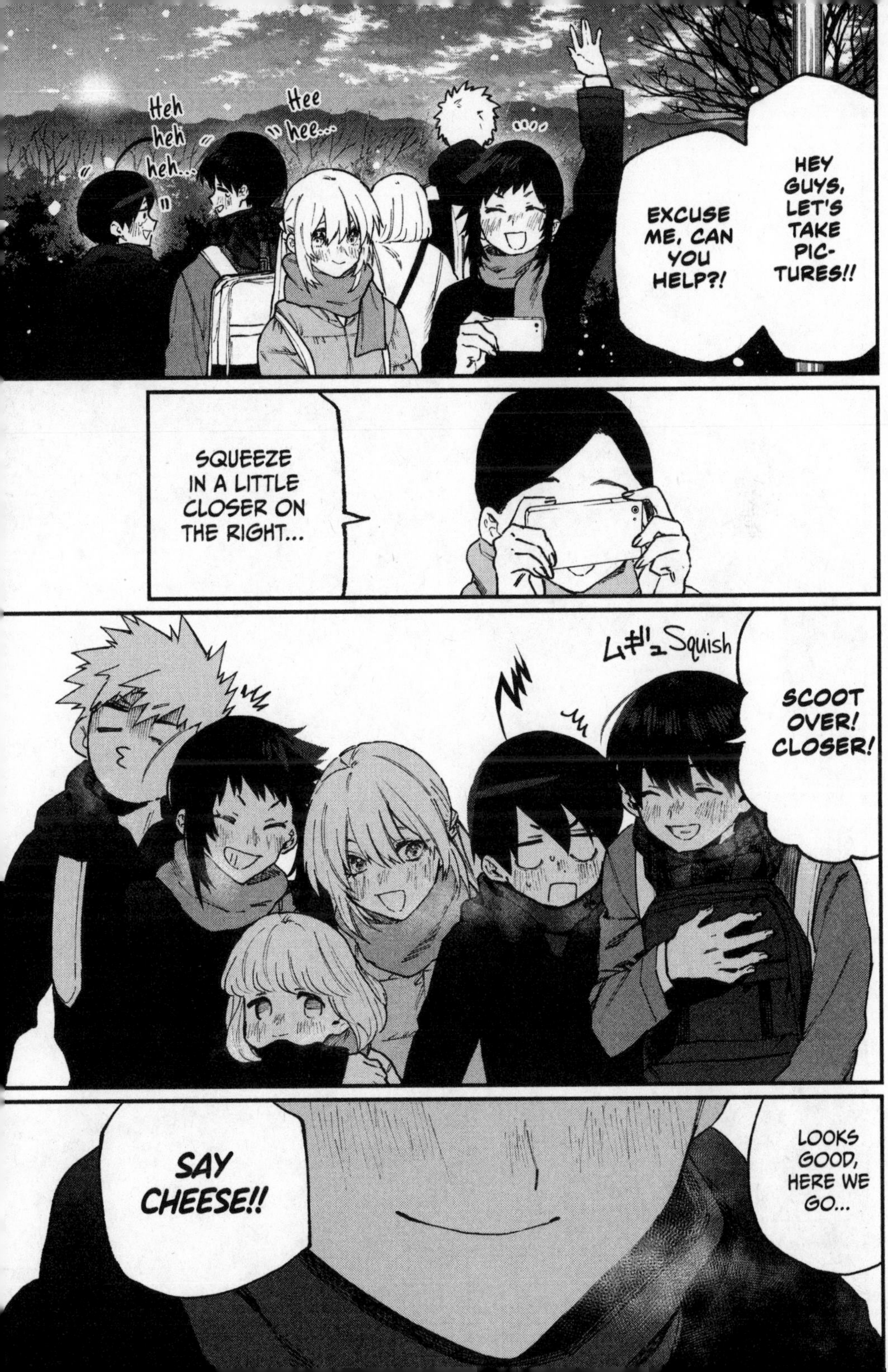
HEY GUYS, LET'S TAKE PIC- TURES!!
EXCUSE ME, CAN YOU HELP?!
...
Hee hee...
Heh heh heh...
SQUEEZE IN A LITTLE CLOSER ON THE RIGHT...
SCOOT OVER! CLOSER!
ムギュ Squish
LOOKS GOOD, HERE WE GO...
SAY CHEESE!!

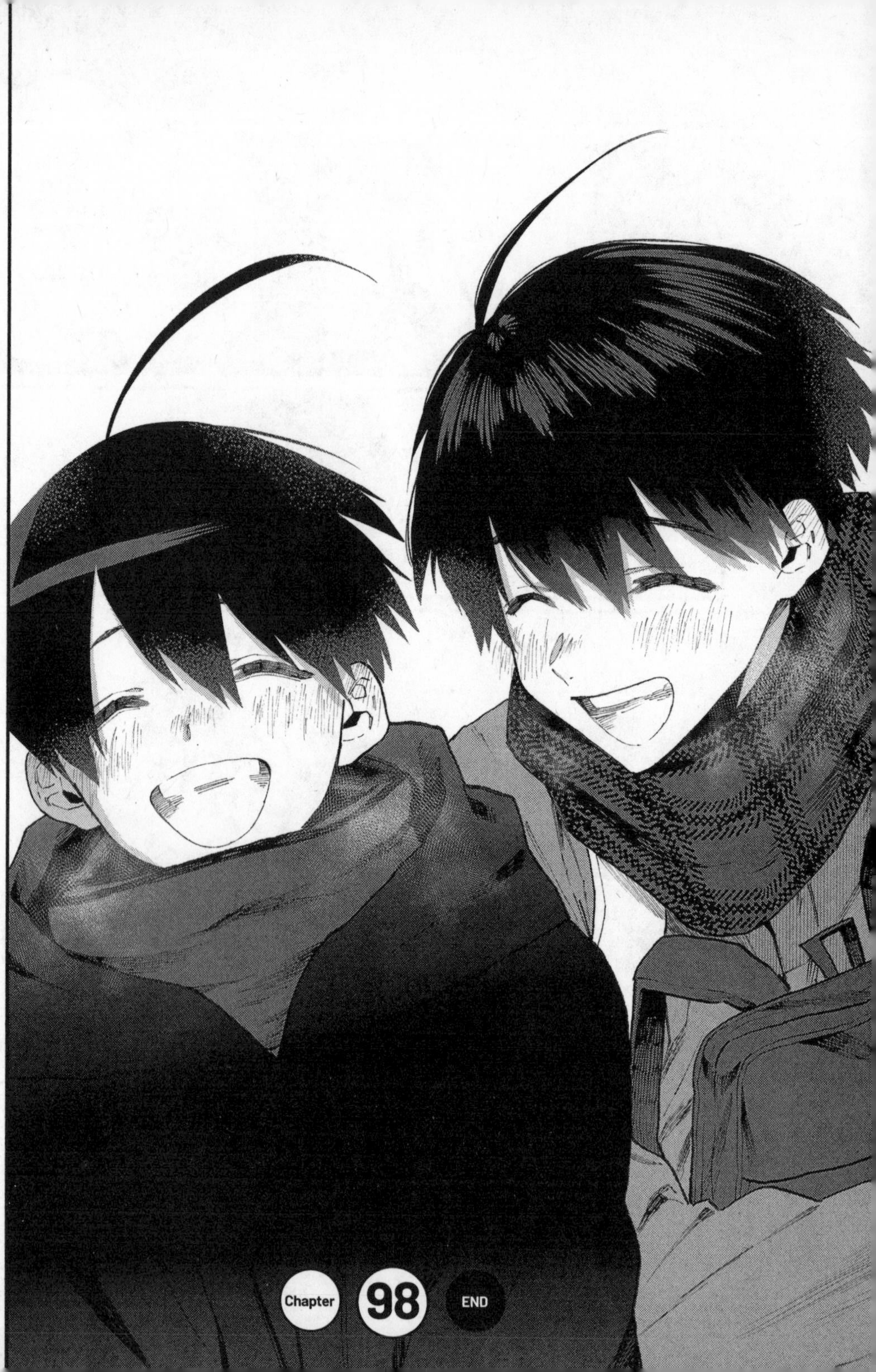
Chapter
98
END

SHIKIMORI'S not just a cutie

MISS

SHIKIMORI

IS NOT JUST CUTE

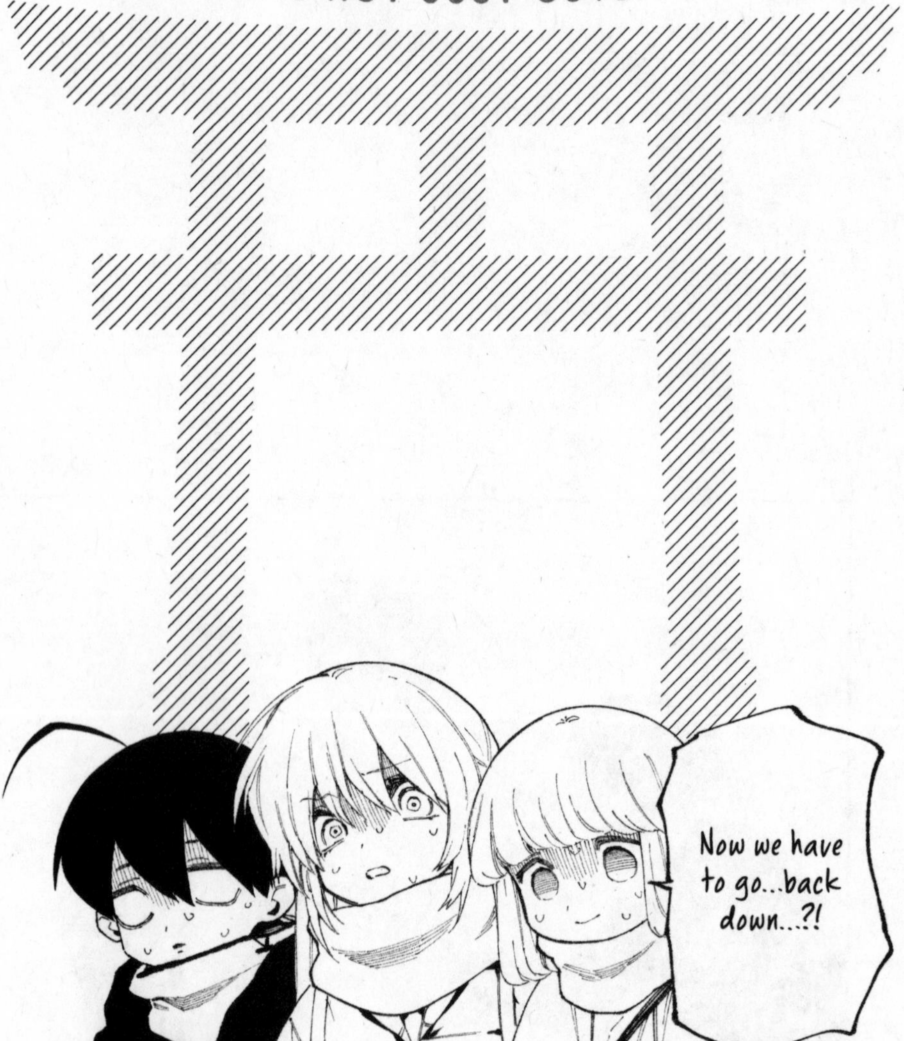
Now we have to go...back down...?!

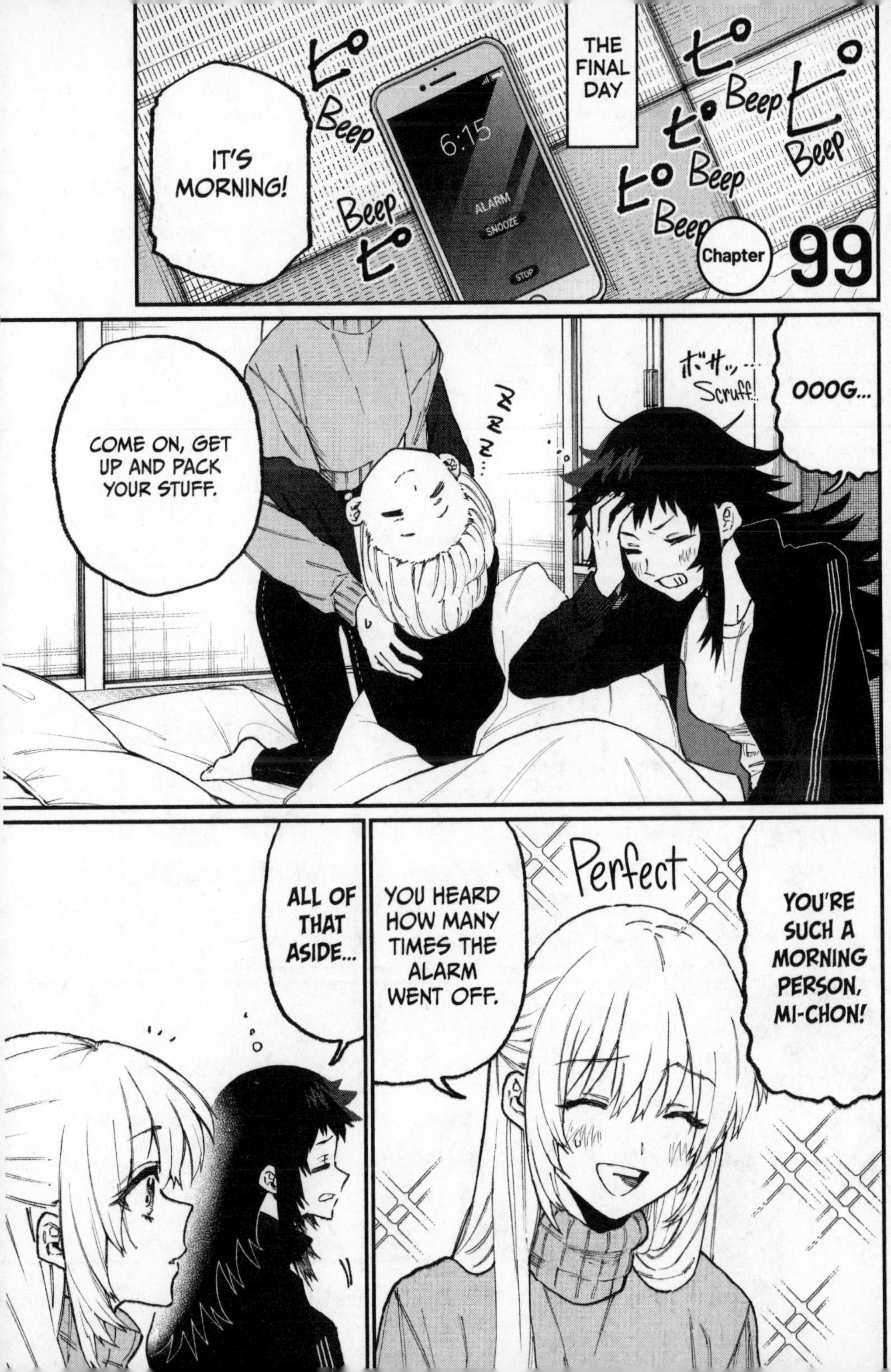
THE FINAL DAY
ピ Beep
ピ Beep
ピ Beep
ピ Beep
Beep
Chapter 99
6:15
ALARM
SNOOZE
STOP
ピ Beep
ピ Beep
IT'S MORNING!
OOOG...
ボサッ… Scruff!
COME ON, GET UP AND PACK YOUR STUFF.
YOU'RE SUCH A MORNING PERSON, MI-CHON!
Perfect
YOU HEARD HOW MANY TIMES THE ALARM WENT OFF.
ALL OF THAT ASIDE...

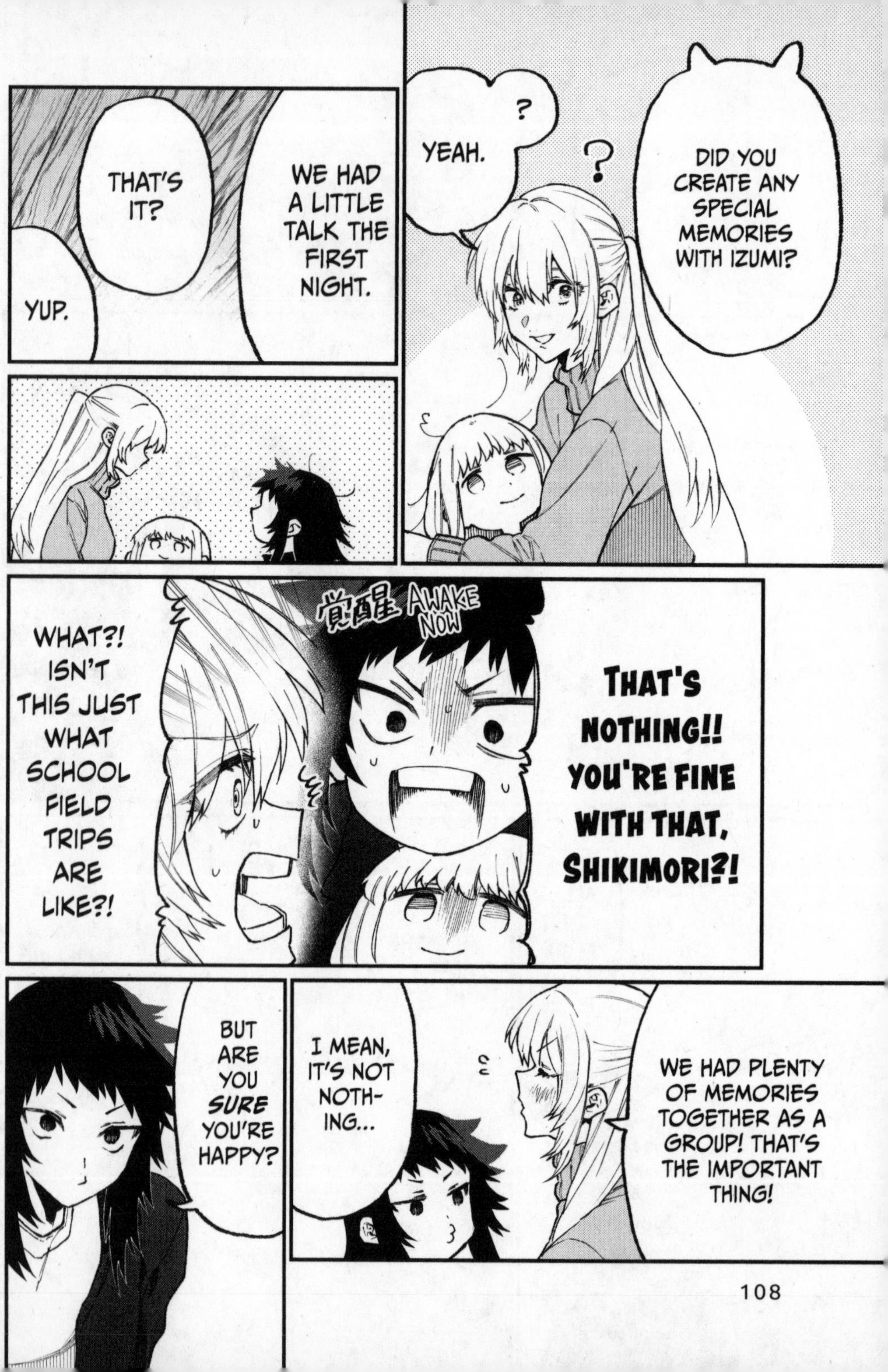
DID YOU CREATE ANY SPECIAL MEMORIES WITH IZUMI?
?
YEAH.
?
WE HAD A LITTLE TALK THE FIRST NIGHT.
THAT'S IT?
YUP.
覚醒 AWAKE NOW
THAT'S NOTHING!! YOU'RE FINE WITH THAT, SHIKIMORI?!
WHAT?! ISN'T THIS JUST WHAT SCHOOL FIELD TRIPS ARE LIKE?!
WE HAD PLENTY OF MEMORIES TOGETHER AS A GROUP! THAT'S THE IMPORTANT THING!
I MEAN, IT'S NOT NOTH-ING...
BUT ARE YOU *SURE* YOU'RE HAPPY?

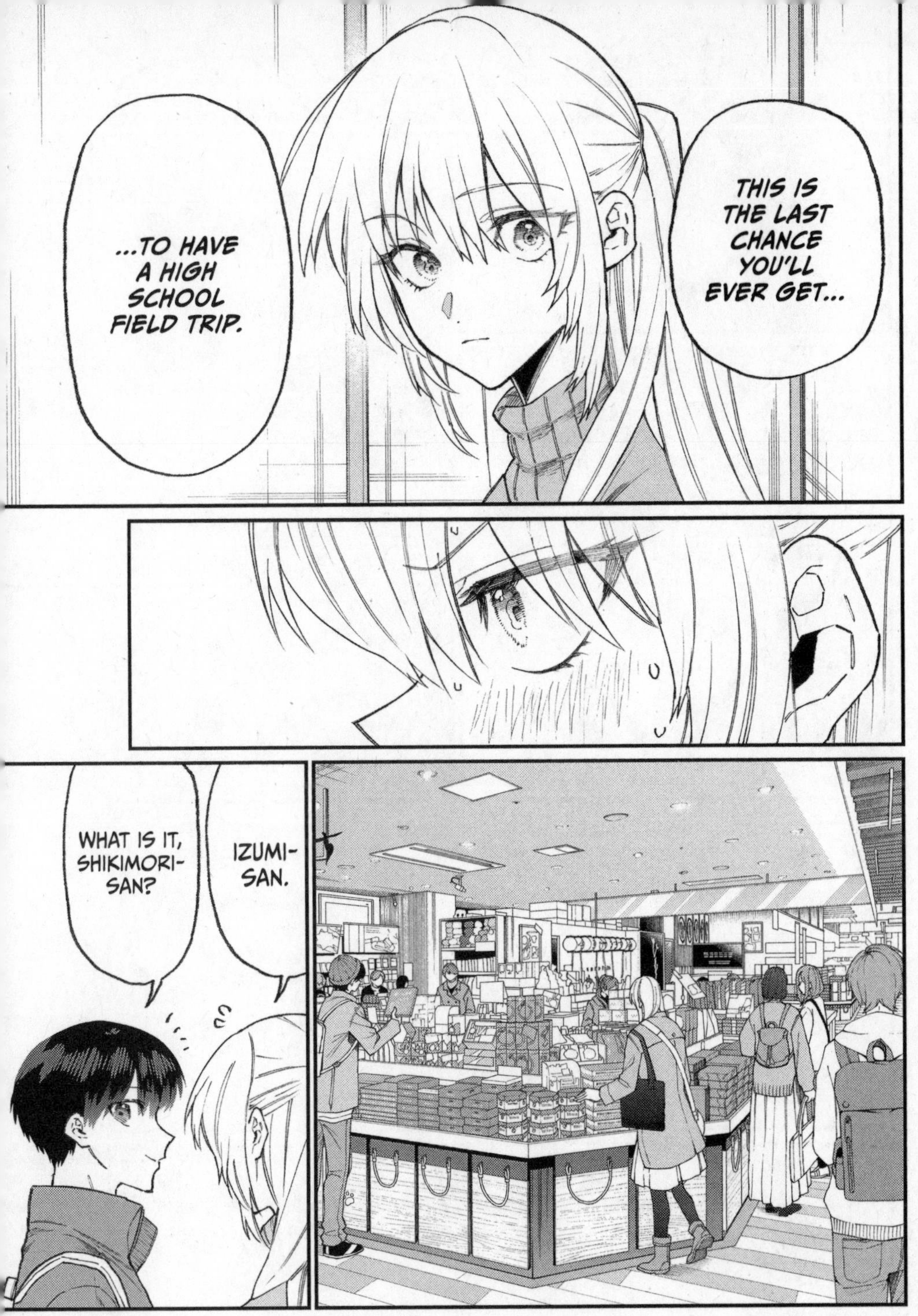
THIS IS THE LAST CHANCE YOU'LL EVER GET...
...TO HAVE A HIGH SCHOOL FIELD TRIP.
IZUMI-SAN.
WHAT IS IT, SHIKIMORI-SAN?

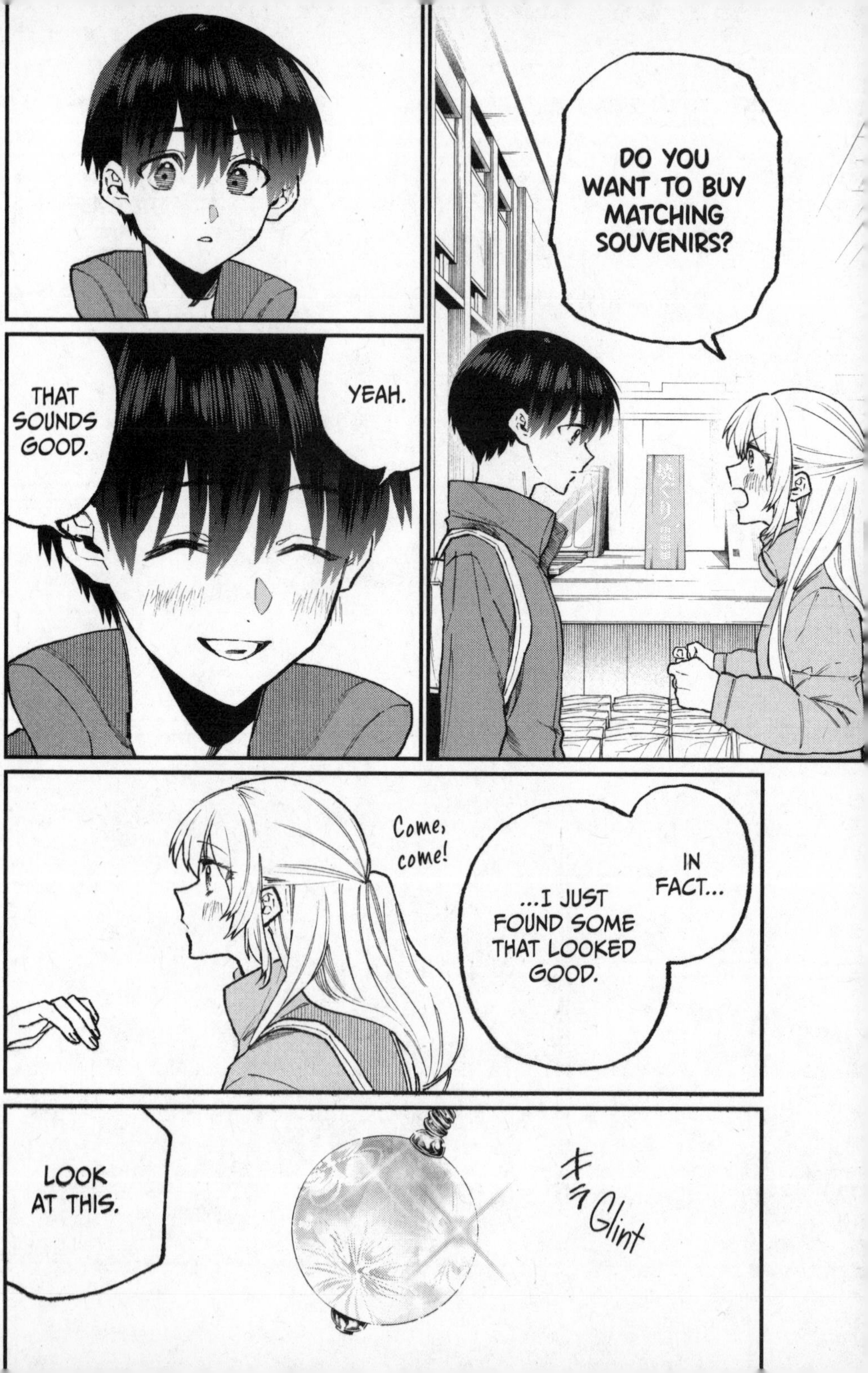
DO YOU WANT TO BUY MATCHING SOUVENIRS?
YEAH.
THAT SOUNDS GOOD.
IN FACT...
...I JUST FOUND SOME THAT LOOKED GOOD.
Come, come!
キラ Glint
LOOK AT THIS.

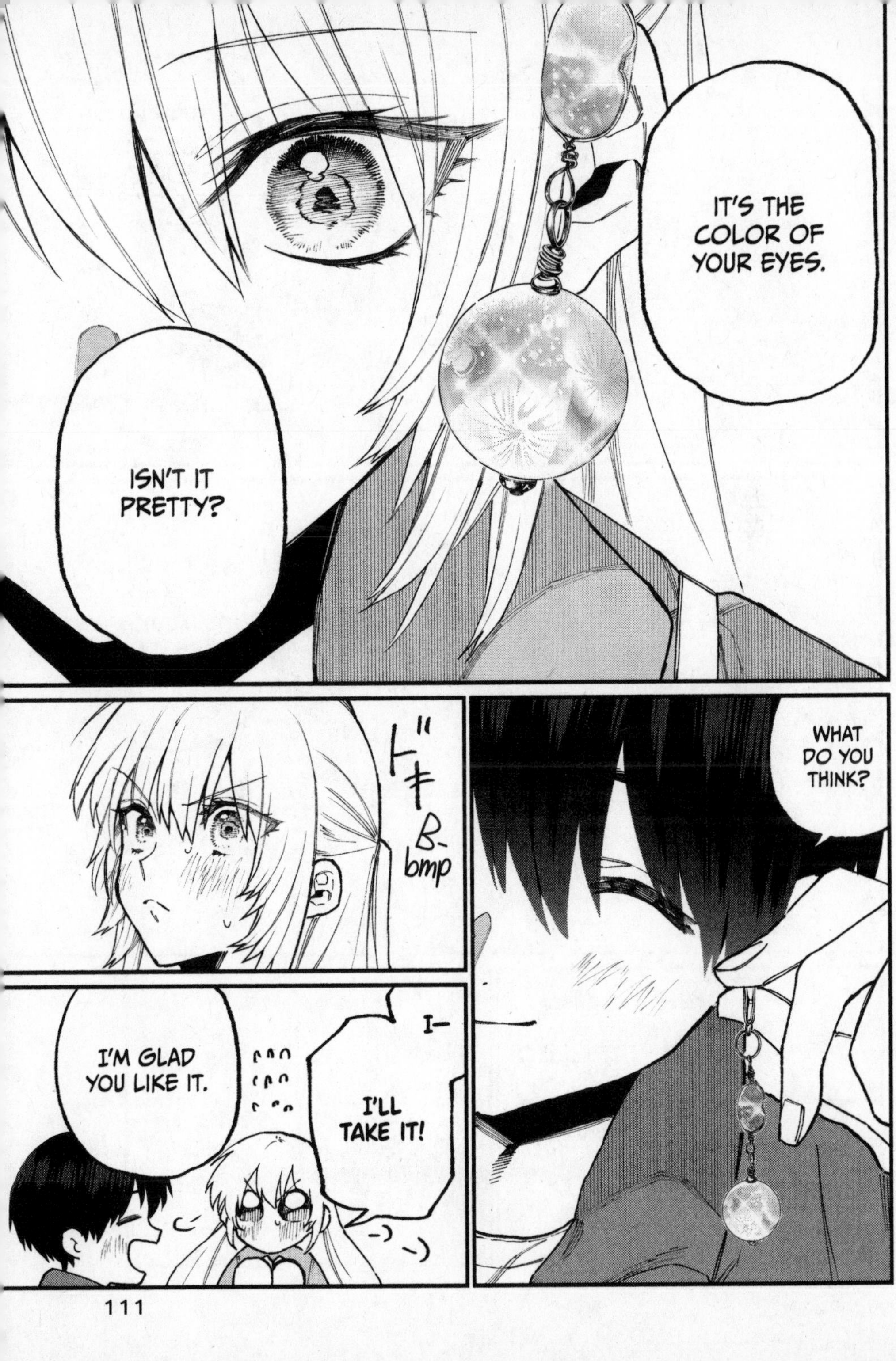
IT'S THE COLOR OF YOUR EYES.
ISN'T IT PRETTY?
WHAT DO YOU THINK?
ドキ
B-bmp
I—
I'LL TAKE IT!
I'M GLAD YOU LIKE IT.

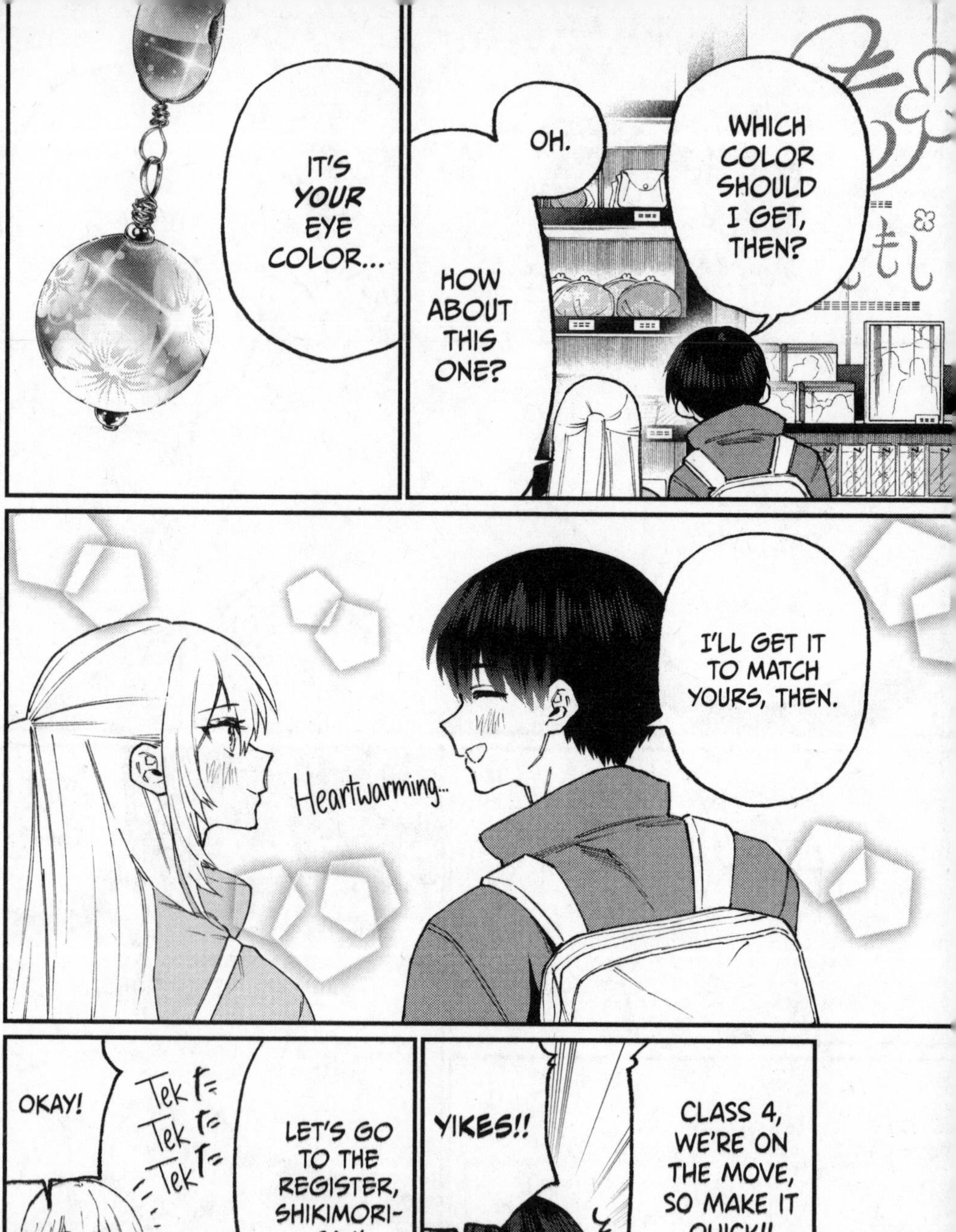
WHICH COLOR SHOULD I GET, THEN?
OH.
HOW ABOUT THIS ONE?
IT'S *YOUR* EYE COLOR...
I'LL GET IT TO MATCH YOURS, THEN.
Heartwarming...
CLASS 4, WE'RE ON THE MOVE, SO MAKE IT QUICK!!
YIKES!!
LET'S GO TO THE REGISTER, SHIKIMORI-SAN!
Tek Tek Tek
OKAY!

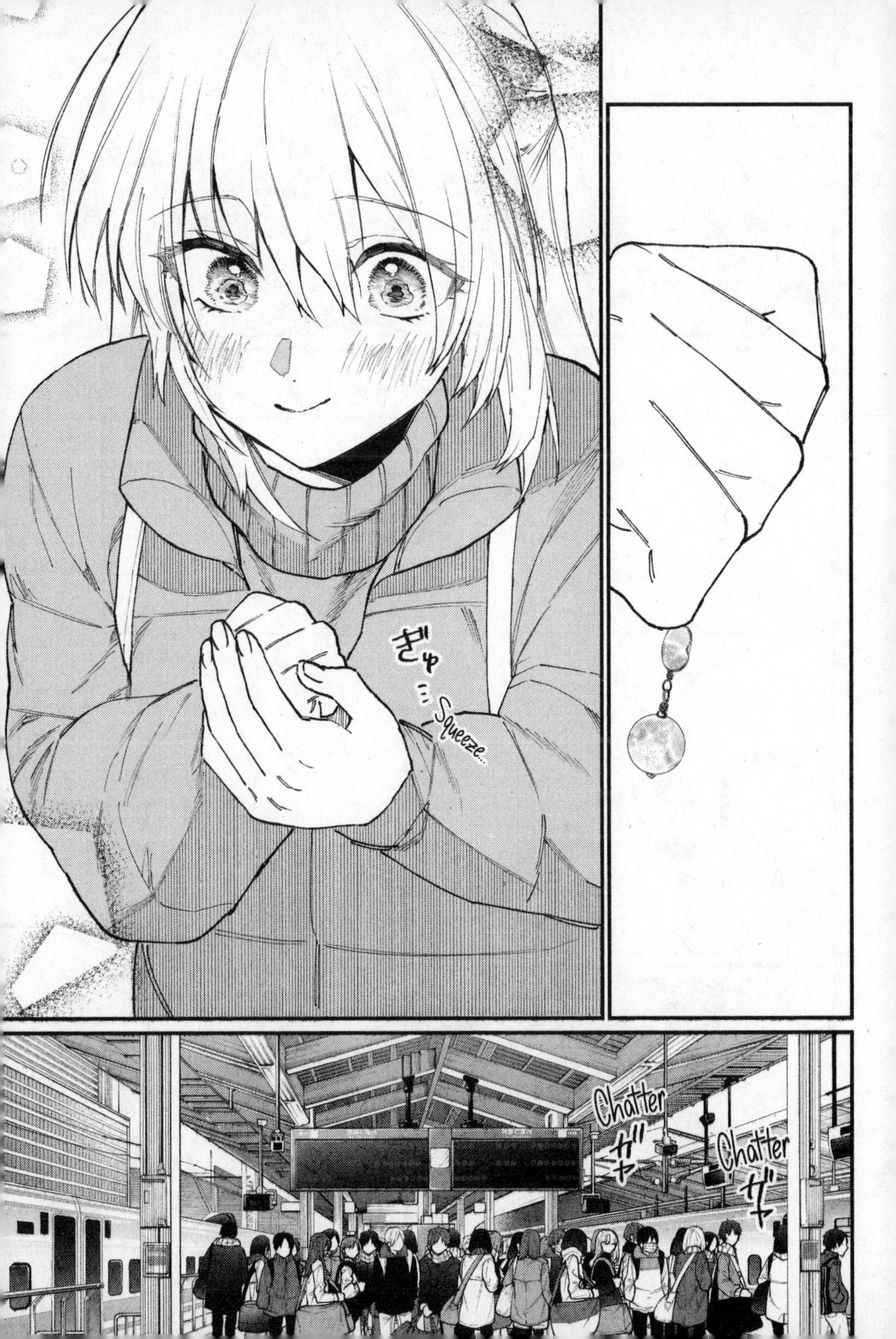
ぎゅ
Squeeze...
Chatter
ガヤ
Chatter
ガヤ

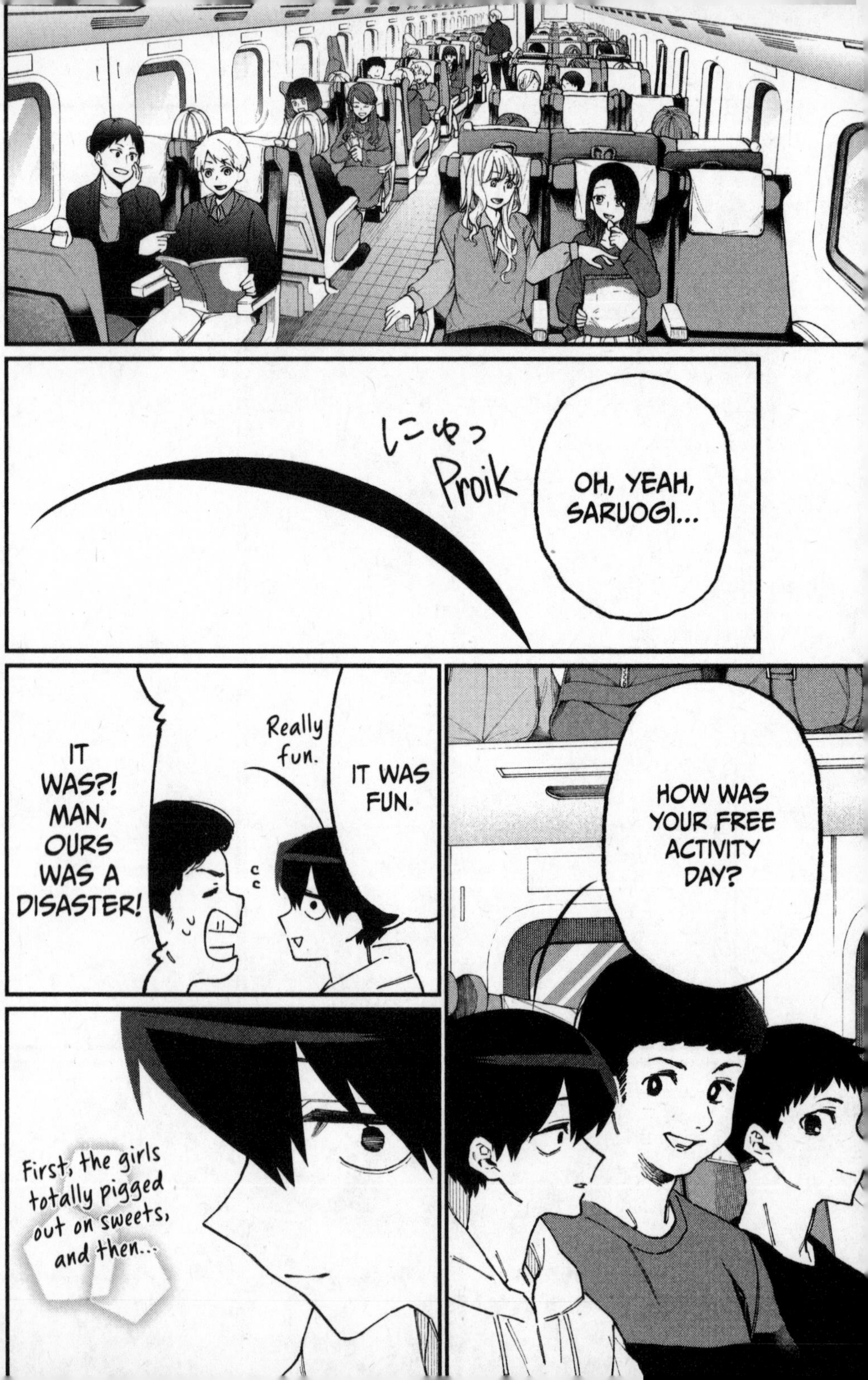
OH, YEAH, SARUOGI...
にゅっ
Proik
HOW WAS YOUR FREE ACTIVITY DAY?
IT WAS FUN.
Really fun.
IT WAS?! MAN, OURS WAS A DISASTER!
First, the girls totally pigged out on sweets, and then...

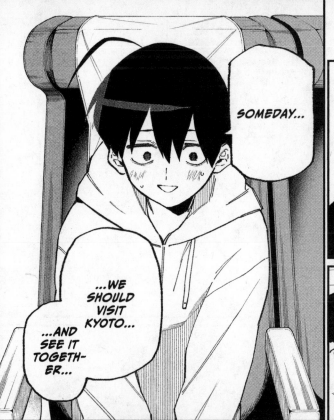

...
...
I THINK...
SOMEDAY...
...WE SHOULD VISIT KYOTO...
...AND SEE IT TOGETHER...
WE COULD DO IT AS A GRADUATION TRIP OR SOMETHING.
HUH?
HOW MANY TIMES DO WE HAVE TO VISIT KYOTO, THOUGH?
N-NO...
LET'S GO!
...

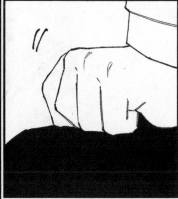

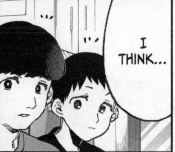

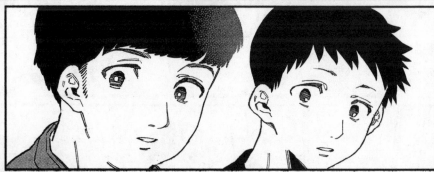

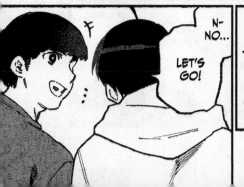

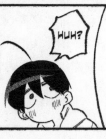

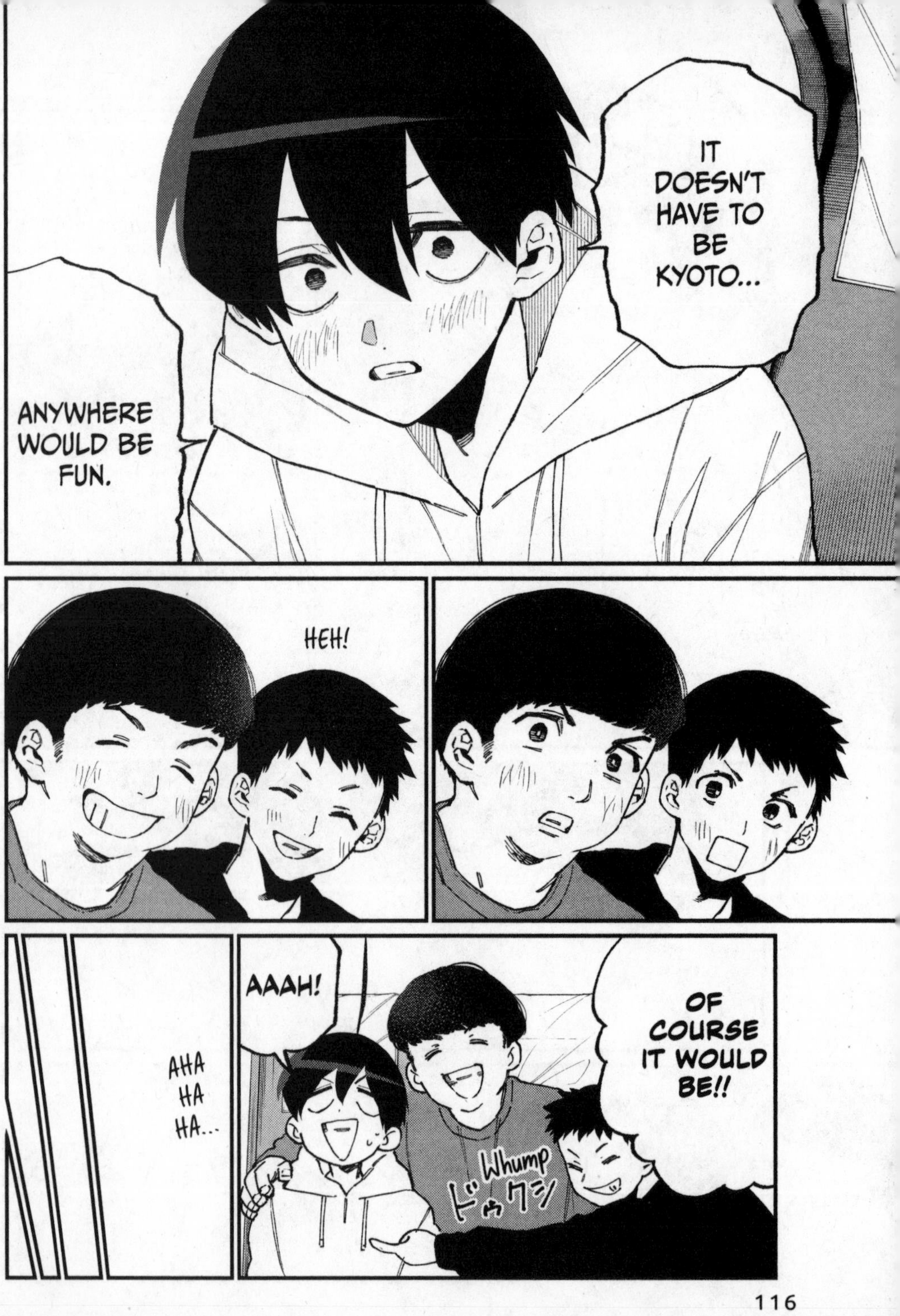
IT DOESN'T HAVE TO BE KYOTO...
ANYWHERE WOULD BE FUN.
HEH!
OF COURSE IT WOULD BE!!
AAAH!
Whump
ドゥクシ
AHA HA HA...

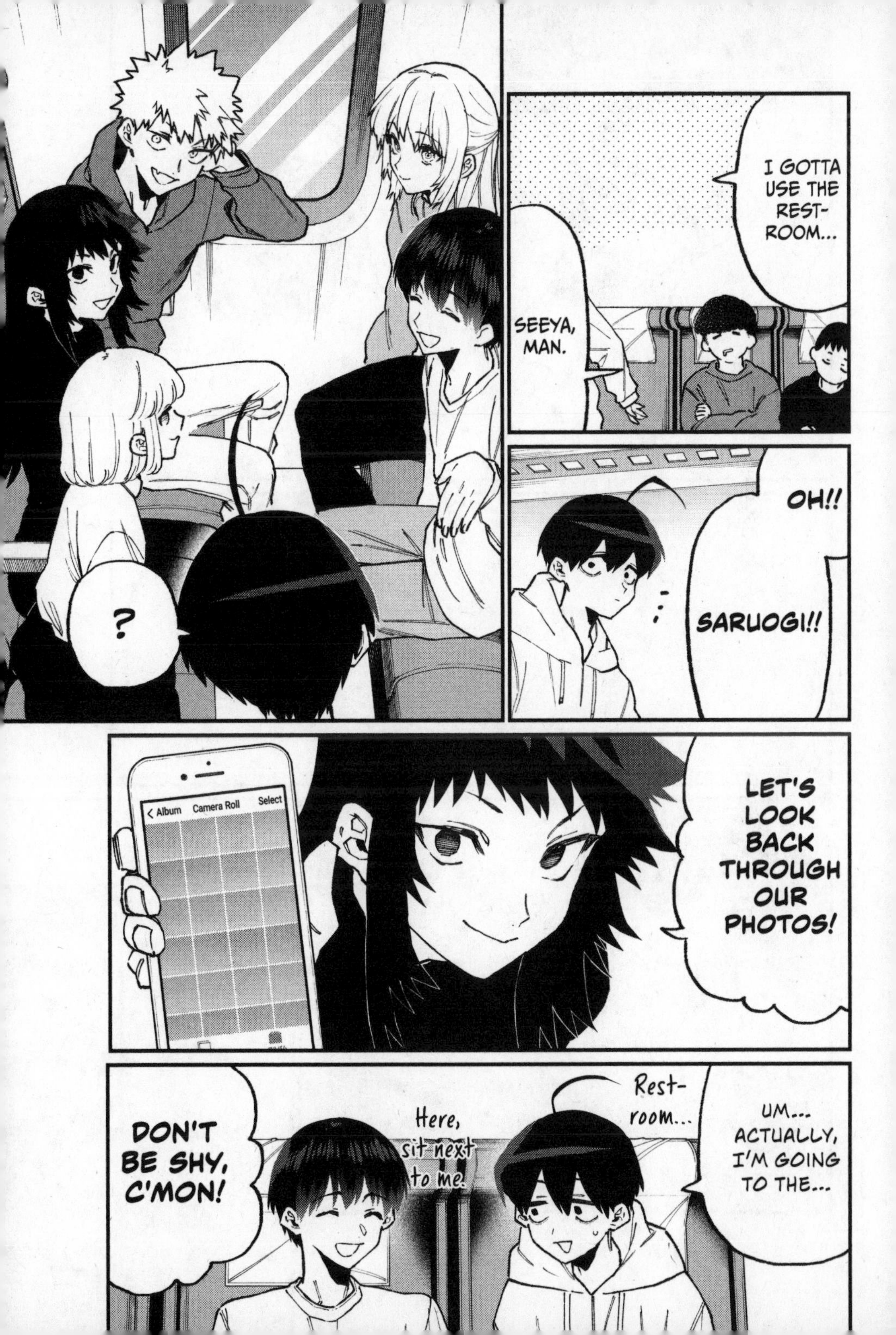
I GOTTA USE THE REST-ROOM...
SEEYA, MAN.
OH!!
SARUOGI!!
?
LET'S LOOK BACK THROUGH OUR PHOTOS!
Album
Camera Roll
Select
UM... ACTUALLY, I'M GOING TO THE...
Rest-room...
Here, sit next to me.
DON'T BE SHY, C'MON!

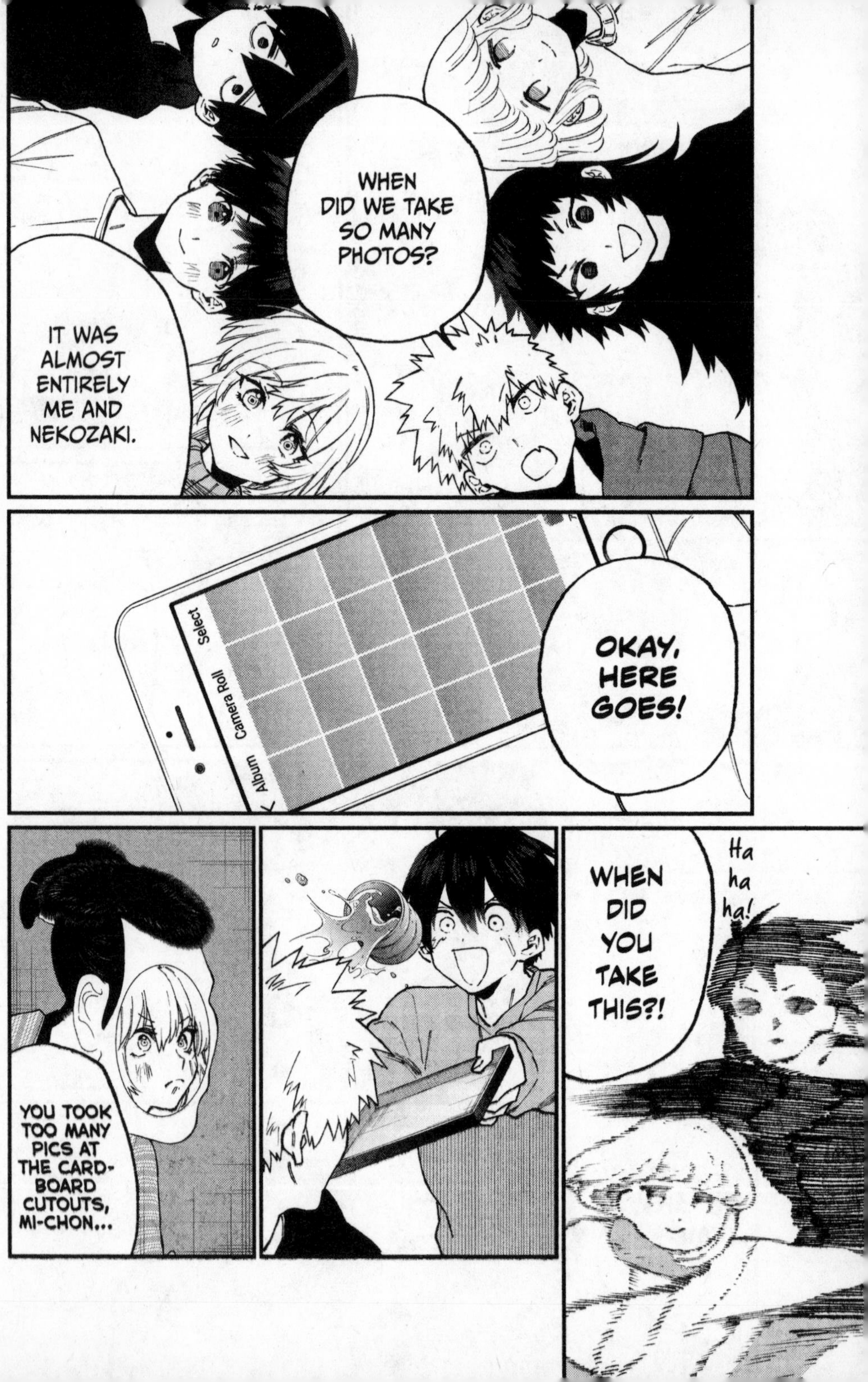
WHEN DID WE TAKE SO MANY PHOTOS?
IT WAS ALMOST ENTIRELY ME AND NEKOZAKI.
OKAY, HERE GOES!
Select
Camera Roll
Album
Ha ha ha!
WHEN DID YOU TAKE THIS?!
YOU TOOK TOO MANY PICS AT THE CARD-BOARD CUTOUTS, MI-CHON...

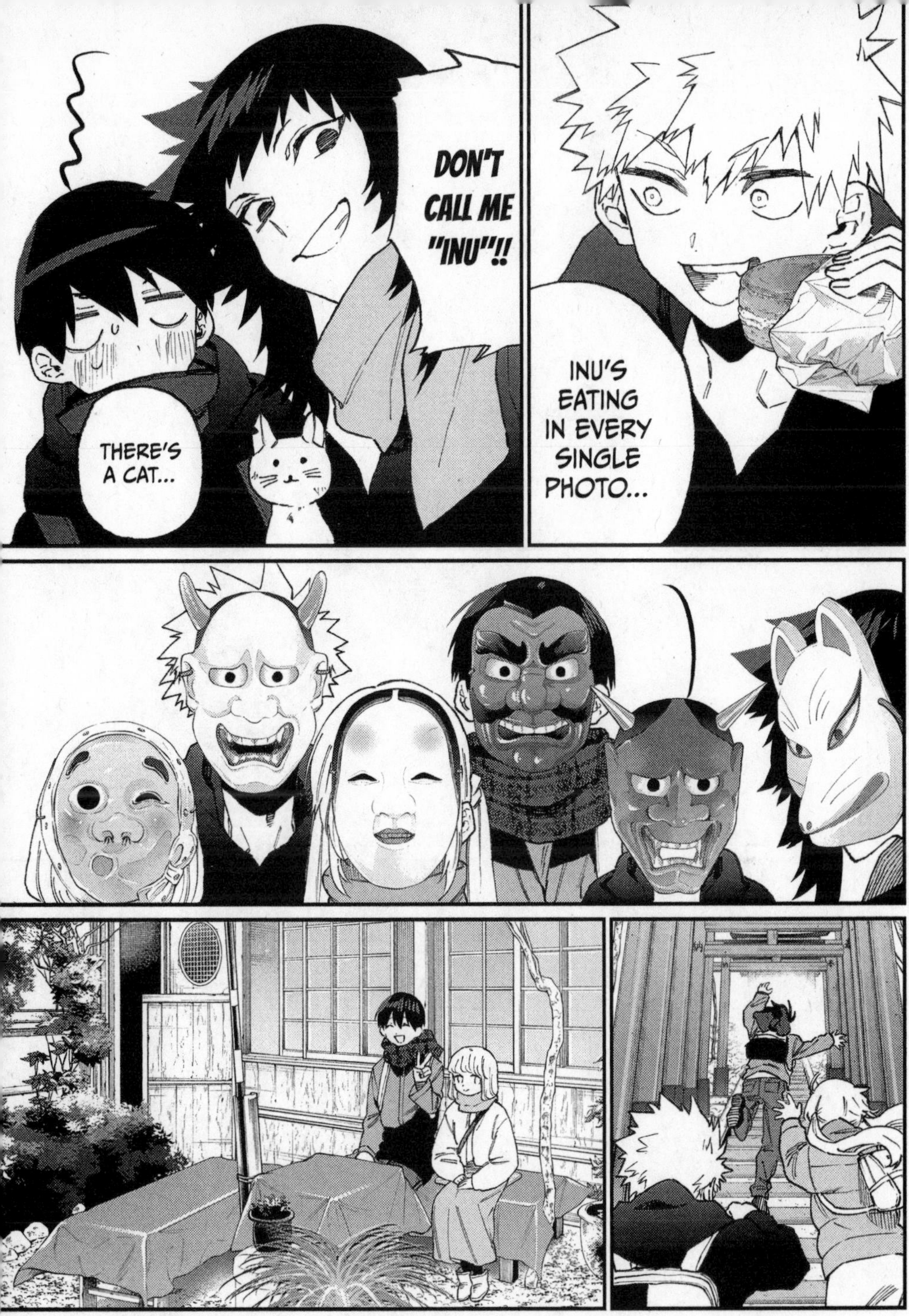
INU'S EATING IN EVERY SINGLE PHOTO...
DON'T CALL ME "INU"!!
THERE'S A CAT...

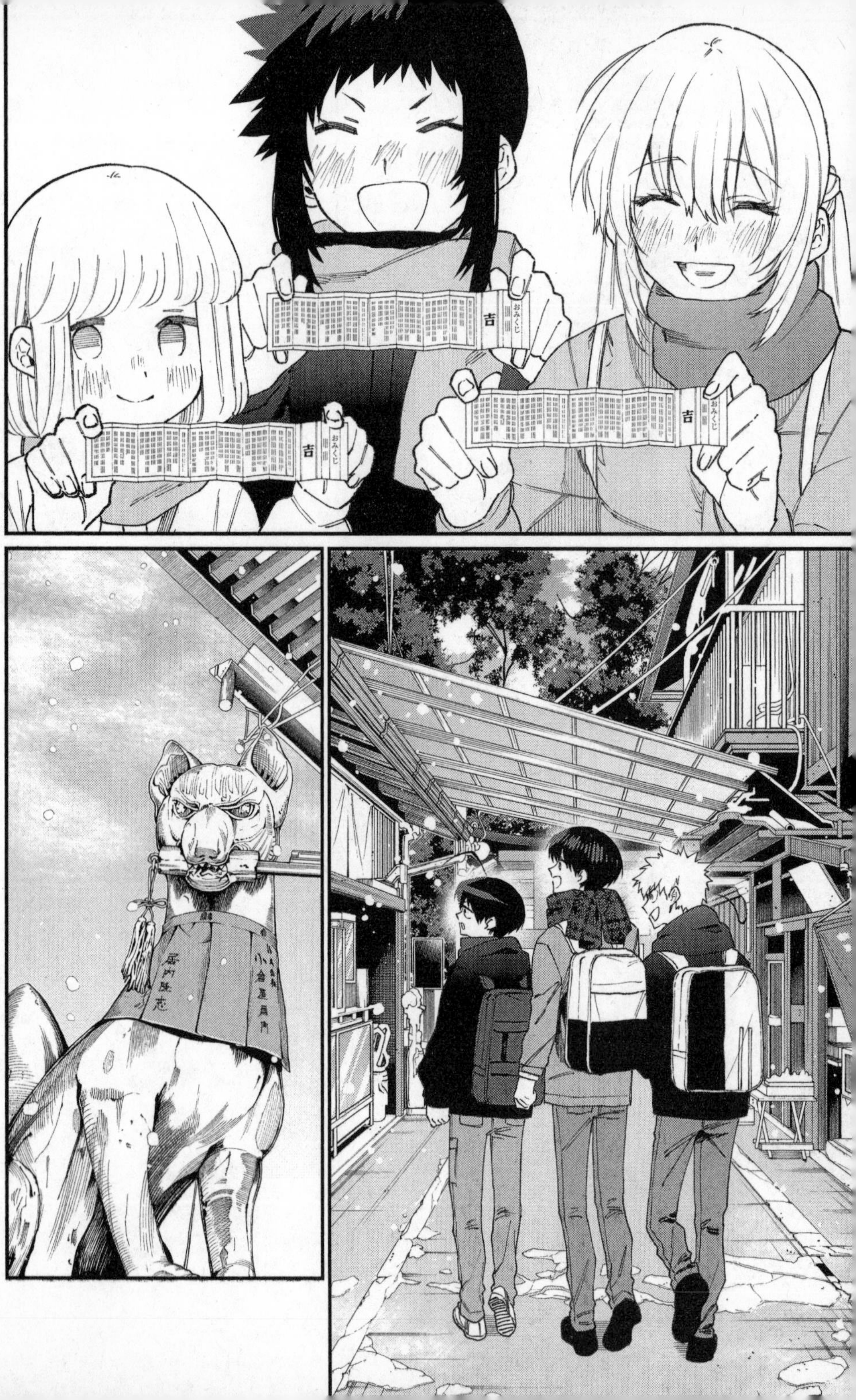
おみくじ
吉
おみくじ
吉
おみくじ
吉

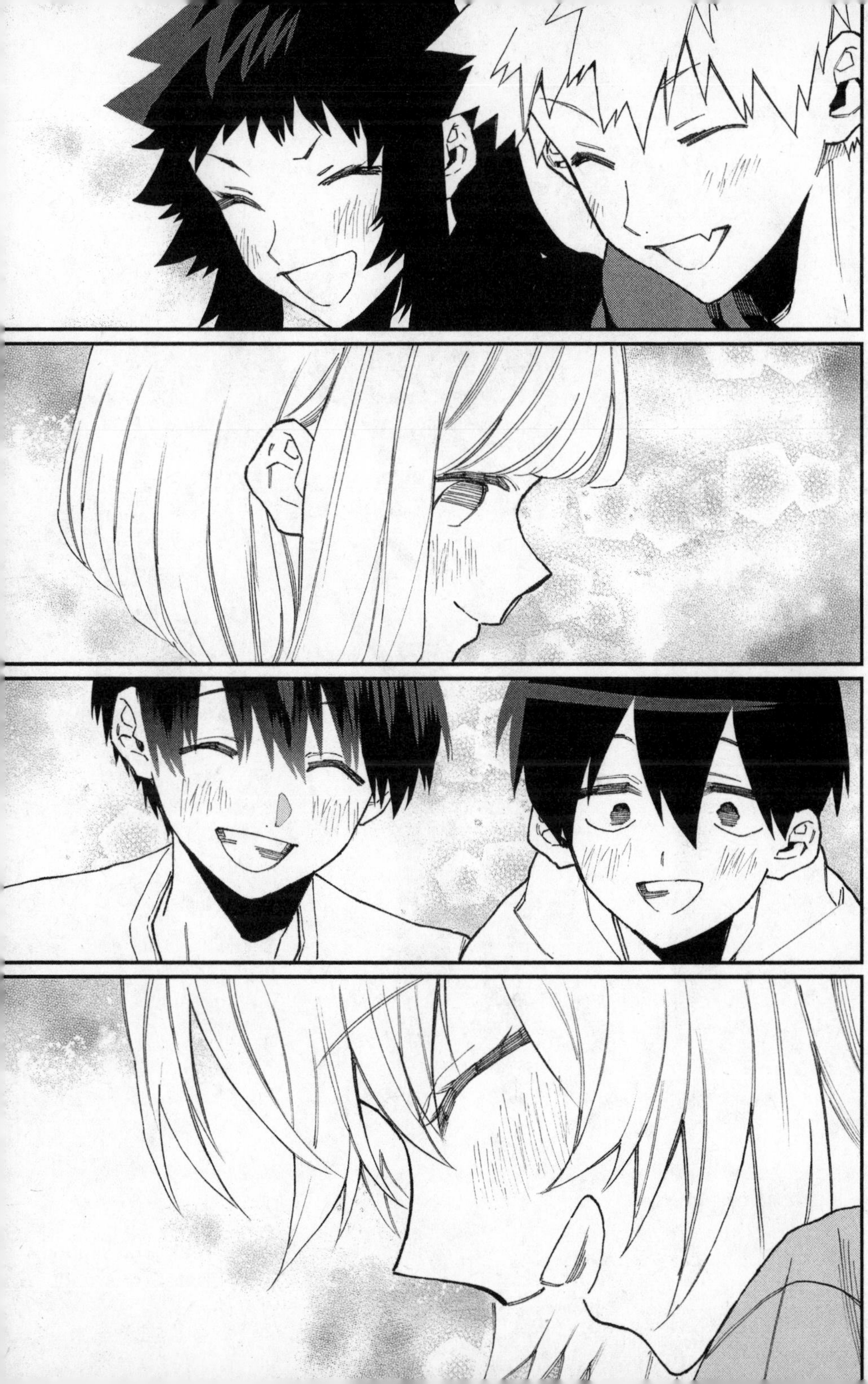

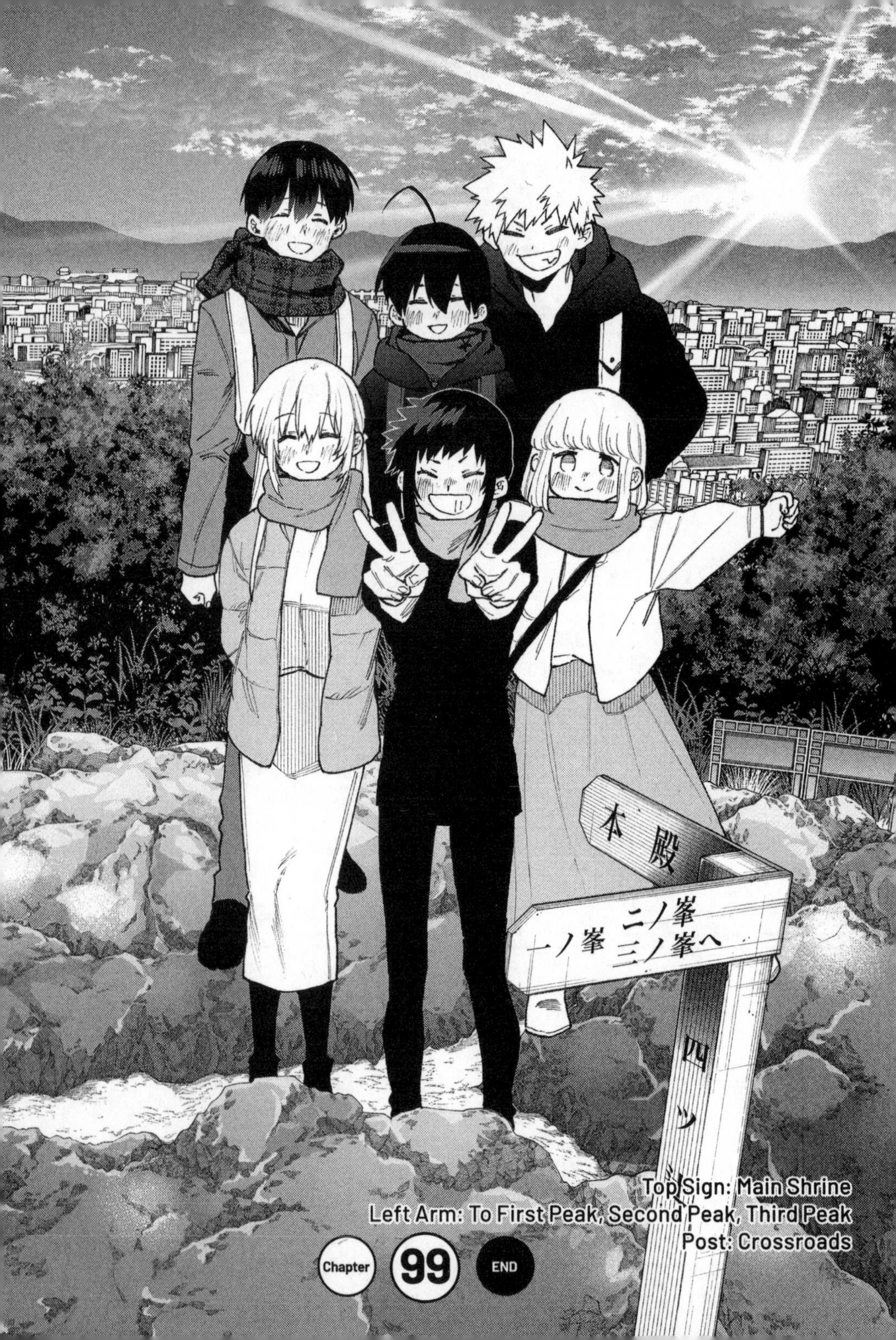
本殿
一ノ峯 二ノ峯 三ノ峯へ
Top Sign: Main Shrine
Left Arm: To First Peak, Second Peak, Third Peak
Post: Crossroads
Chapter 99 END

MISS SHIKI MORI IS NOT JUST CUTE

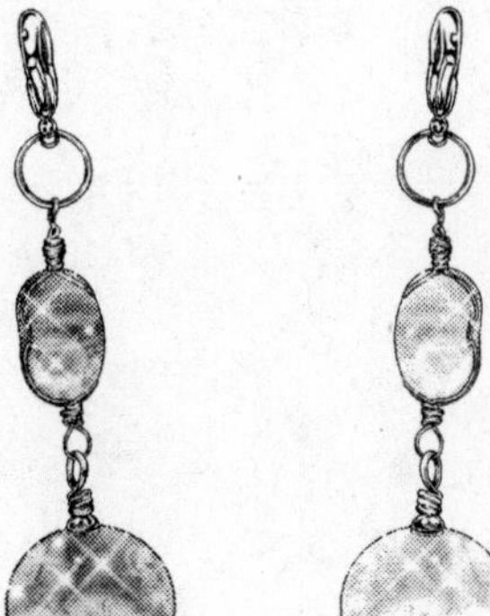

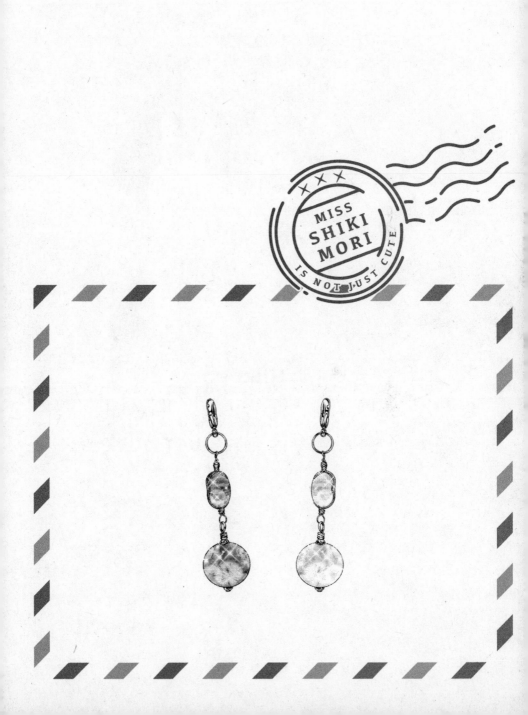

MISS
SHIKIMORI
IS NOT JUST CUTE

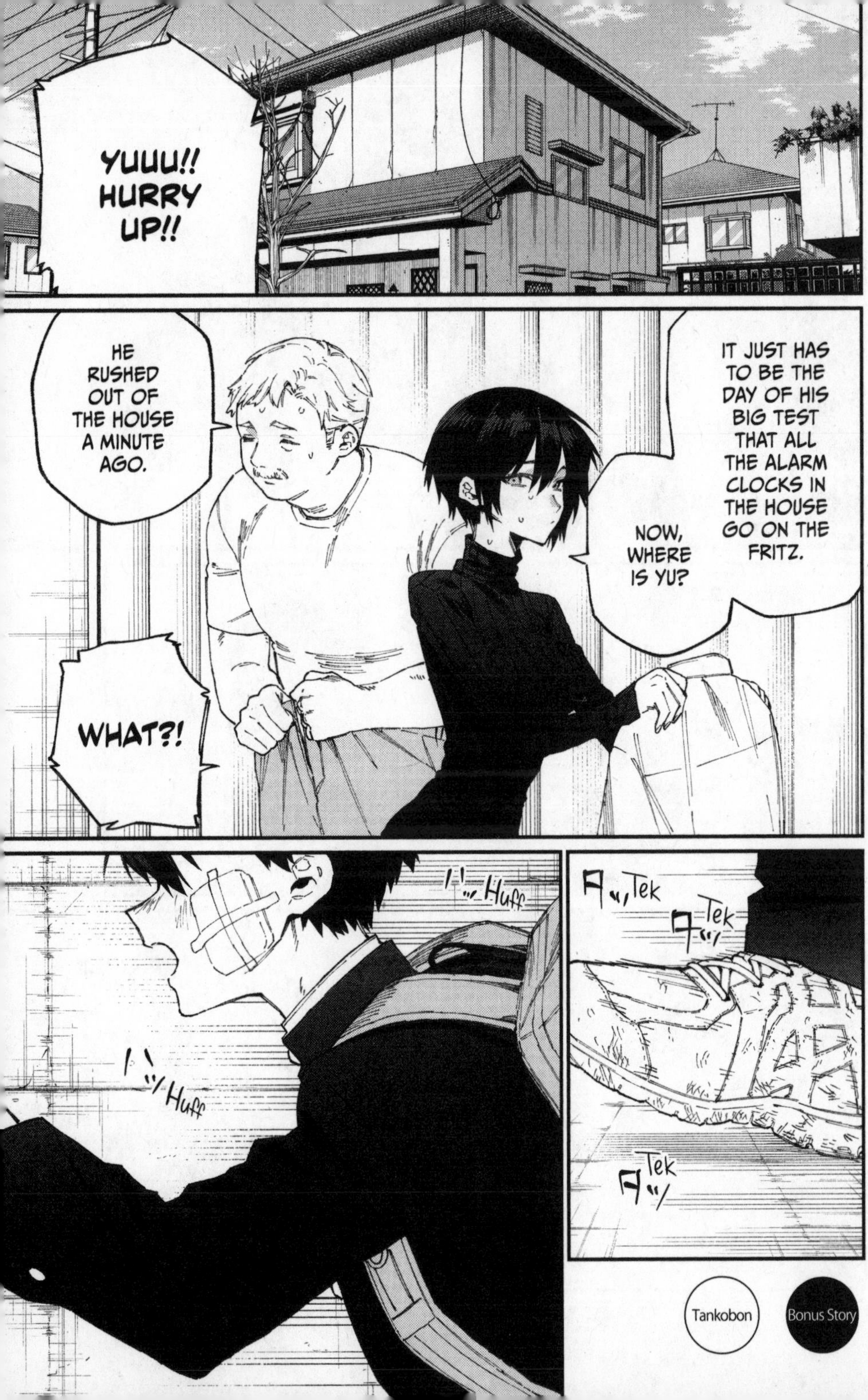
YUUU!! HURRY UP!!
IT JUST HAS TO BE THE DAY OF HIS BIG TEST THAT ALL THE ALARM CLOCKS IN THE HOUSE GO ON THE FRITZ.
NOW, WHERE IS YU?
HE RUSHED OUT OF THE HOUSE A MINUTE AGO.
WHAT?!
Tek
Tek
Tek
Huff
Huff
Tankobon
Bonus Story

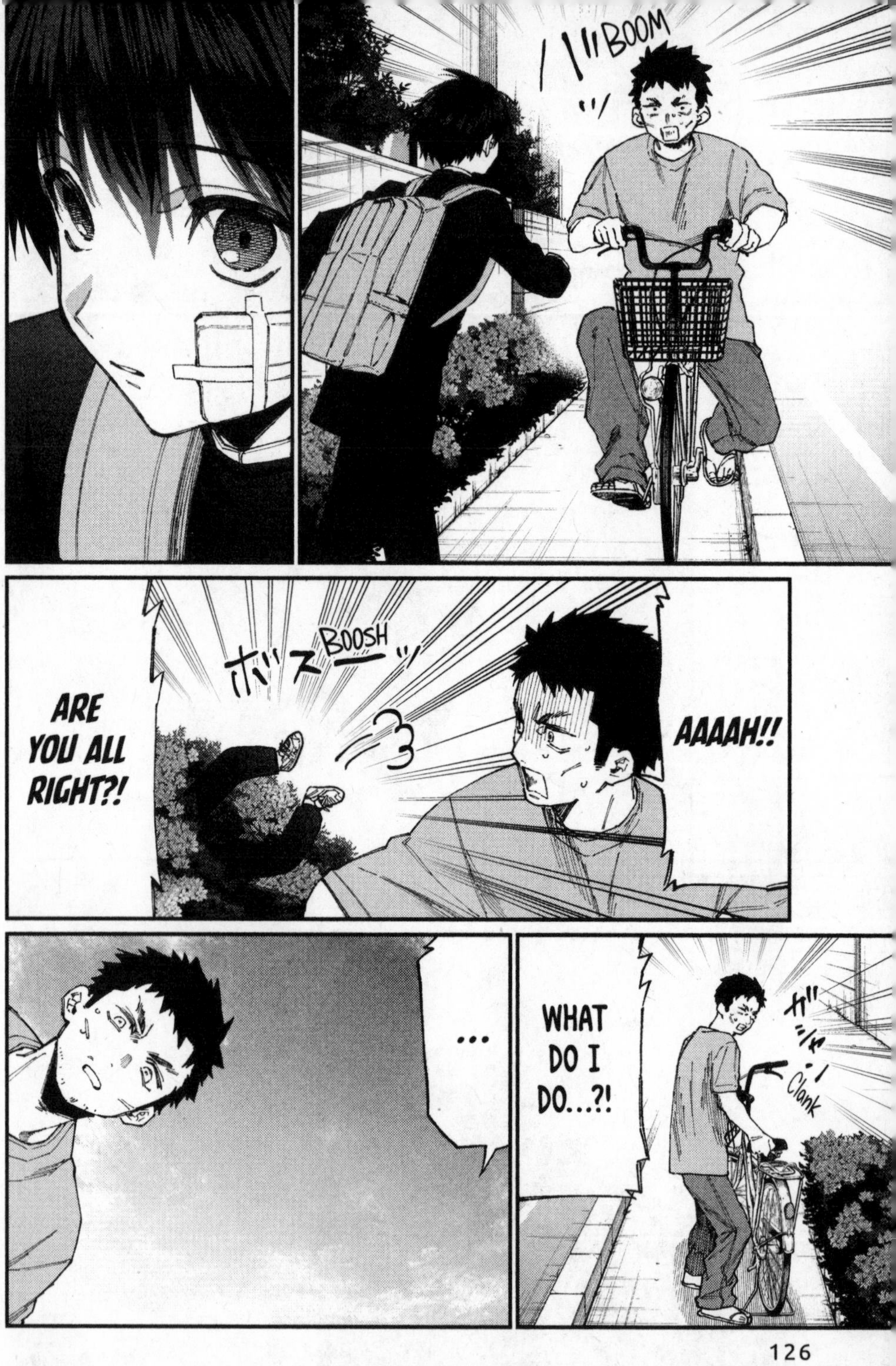
BOOM
ボスーッ
BOOSH
AAAAH!!
ARE YOU ALL RIGHT?!
WHAT DO I DO...?!
ガシャ
Clank
...

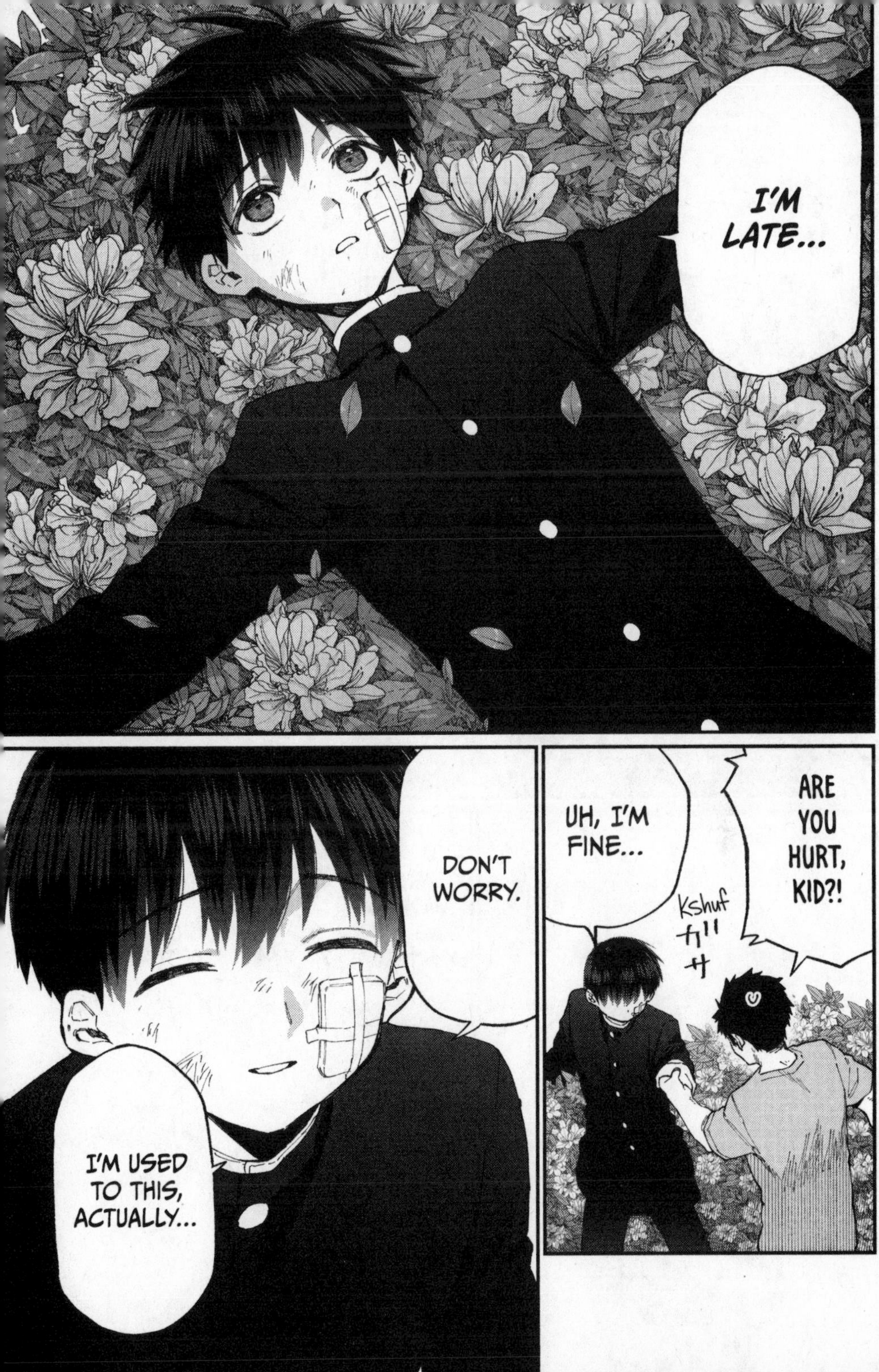
I'M LATE...
ARE YOU HURT, KID?!
UH, I'M FINE...
Kshuf
DON'T WORRY.
I'M USED TO THIS, ACTUALLY...

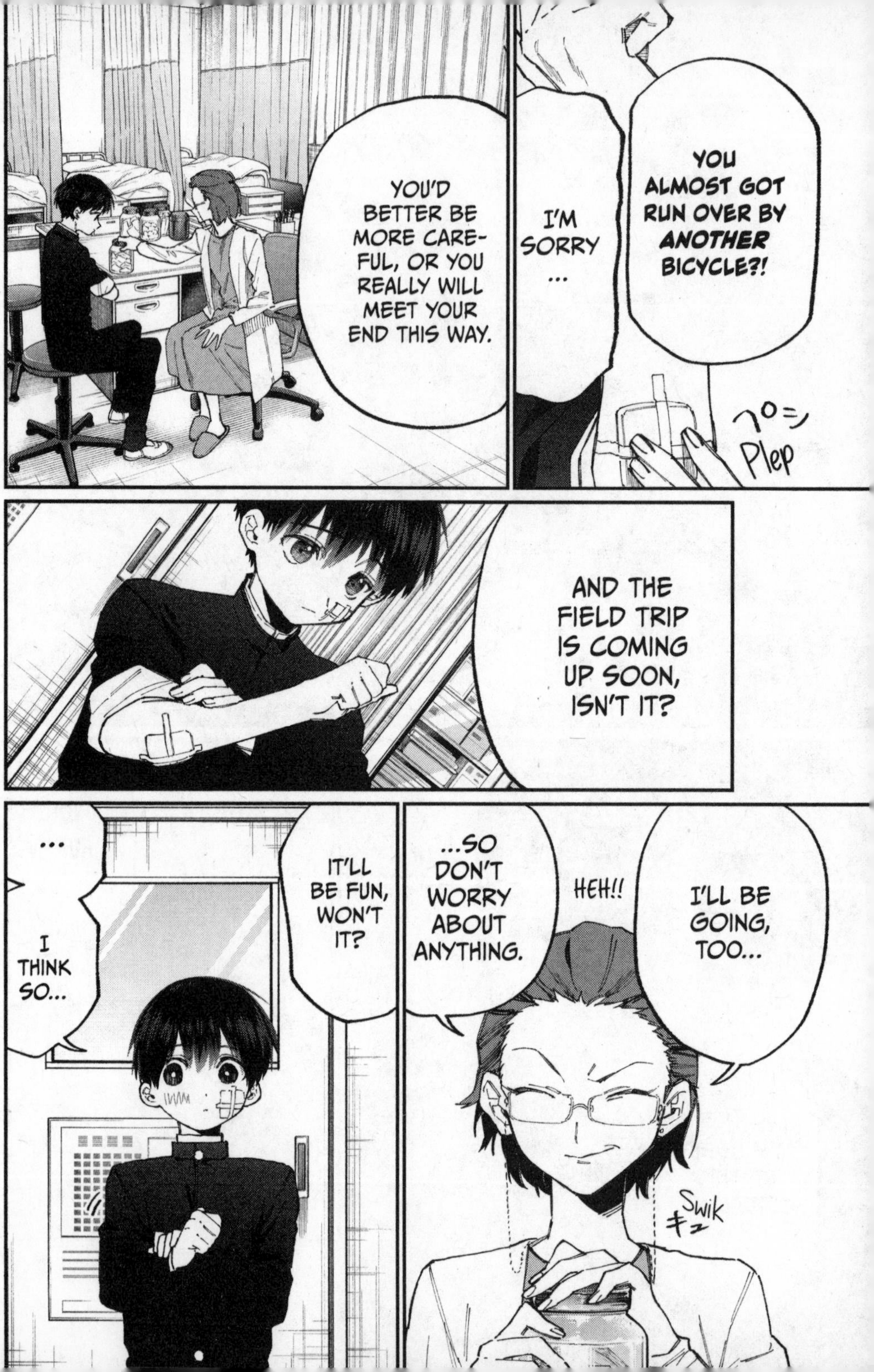
YOU ALMOST GOT RUN OVER BY ANOTHER BICYCLE?!
I'M SORRY ...
Plep
YOU'D BETTER BE MORE CARE-FUL, OR YOU REALLY WILL MEET YOUR END THIS WAY.
AND THE FIELD TRIP IS COMING UP SOON, ISN'T IT?
I'LL BE GOING, TOO...
HEH!!
...SO DON'T WORRY ABOUT ANYTHING.
Swik
IT'LL BE FUN, WON'T IT?
...
I THINK SO...

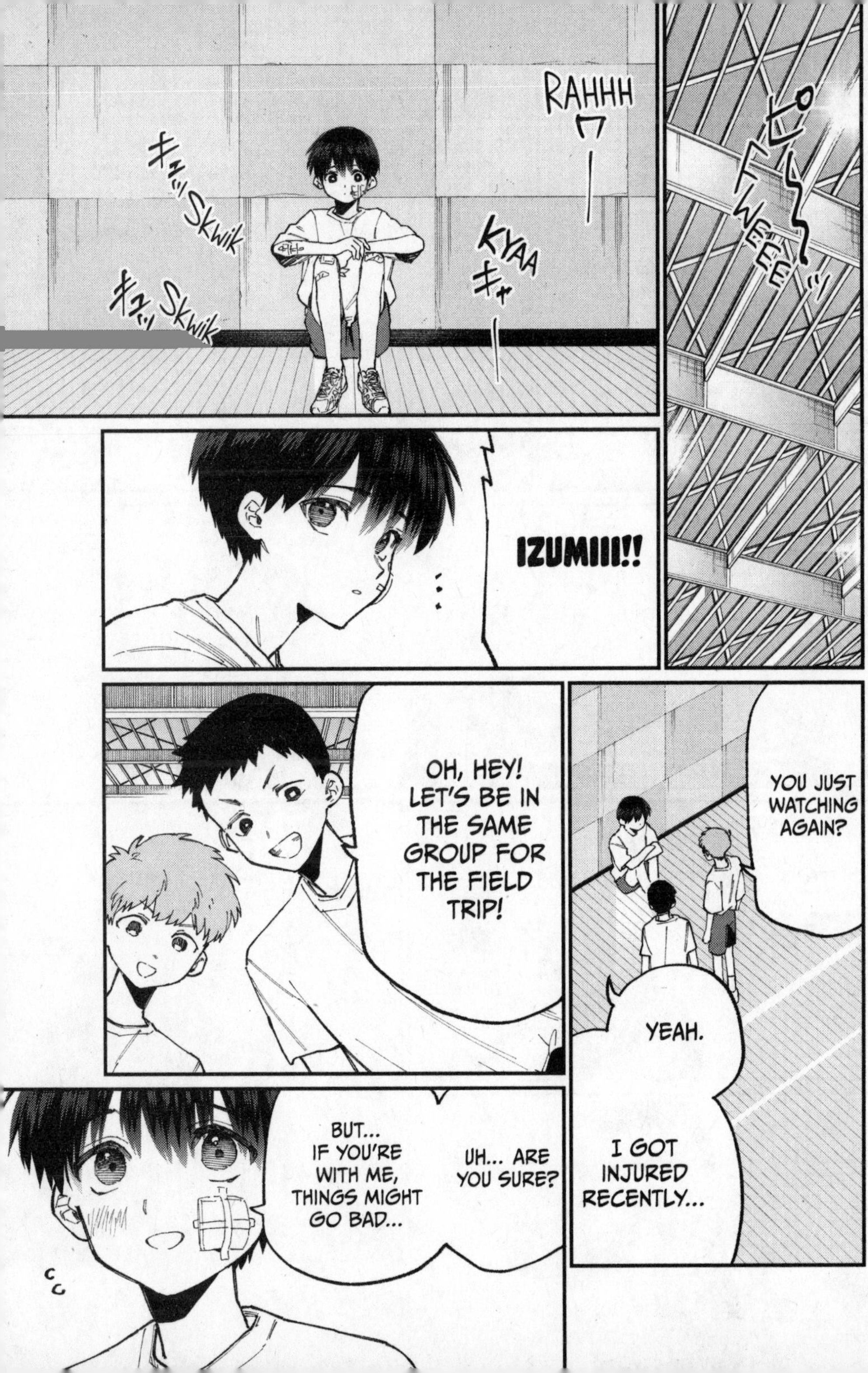

WEEE
RAHHH ワー
KYAA キャー
キュッ Skwik
キュッ Skwik
IZUMIII!!
...
YOU JUST WATCHING AGAIN?
YEAH.
I GOT INJURED RECENTLY...
OH, HEY! LET'S BE IN THE SAME GROUP FOR THE FIELD TRIP!
UH... ARE YOU SURE?
BUT... IF YOU'RE WITH ME, THINGS MIGHT GO BAD...

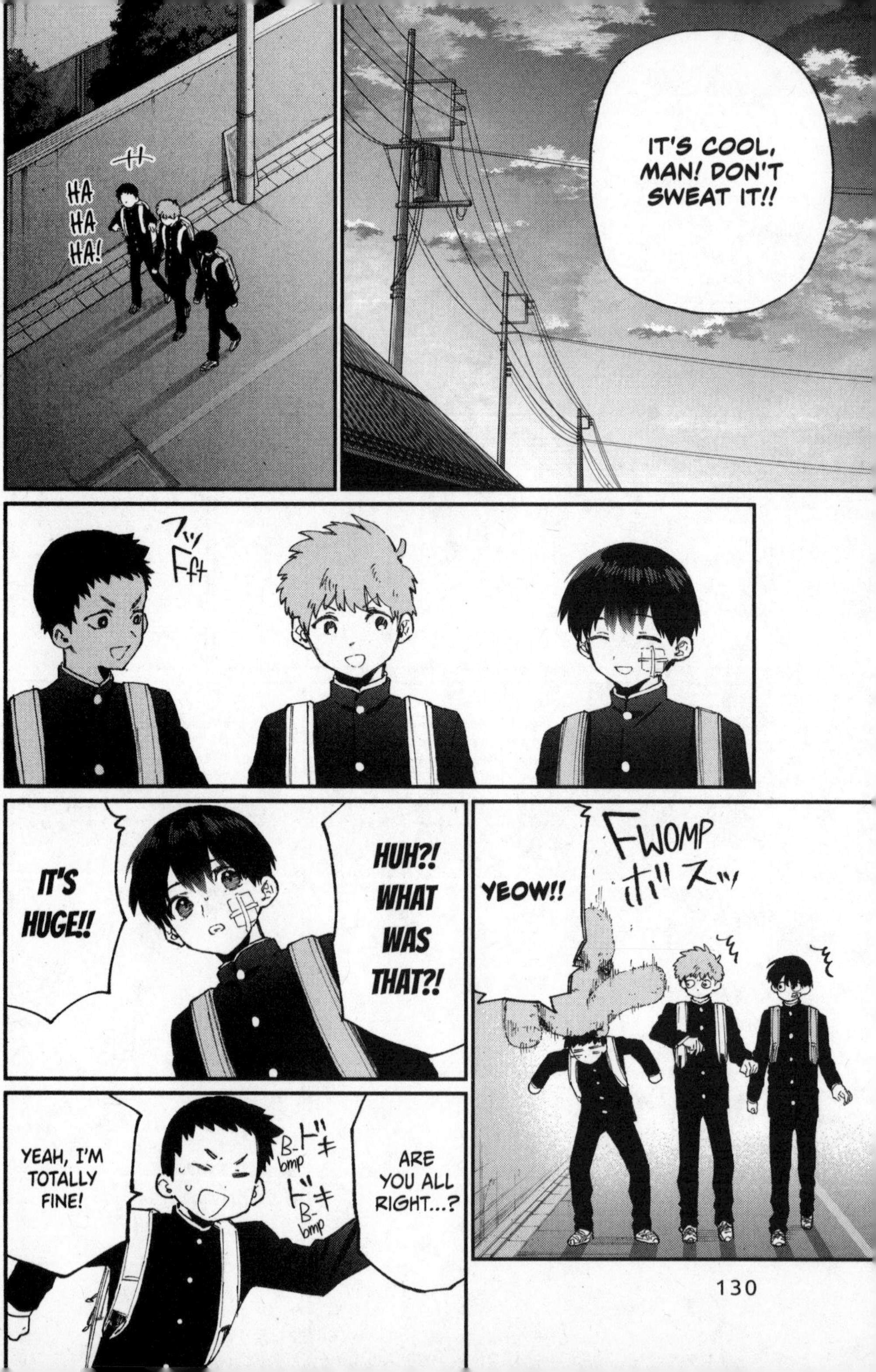
IT'S COOL, MAN! DON'T SWEAT IT!!
HA HA HA!
フッ Fft
FWOMP ボスッ
YEOW!!
HUH?! WHAT WAS THAT?!
IT'S HUGE!!
ARE YOU ALL RIGHT...?
ドキ B-bmp
ドキ B-bmp
YEAH, I'M TOTALLY FINE!

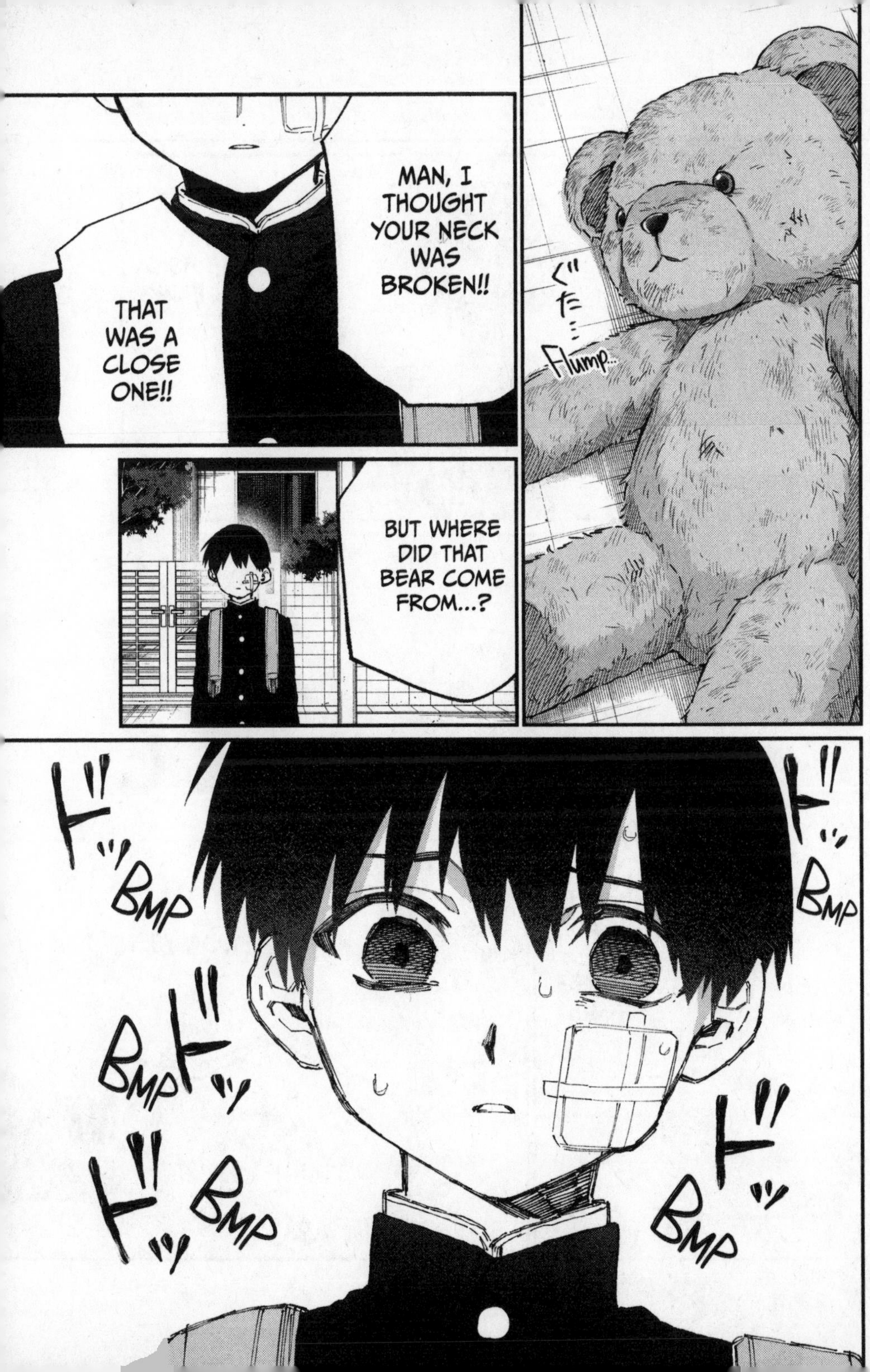
Flump...
MAN, I THOUGHT YOUR NECK WAS BROKEN!!
THAT WAS A CLOSE ONE!!
BUT WHERE DID THAT BEAR COME FROM...?
Bmp
Bmp
Bmp
Bmp
Bmp
Bmp

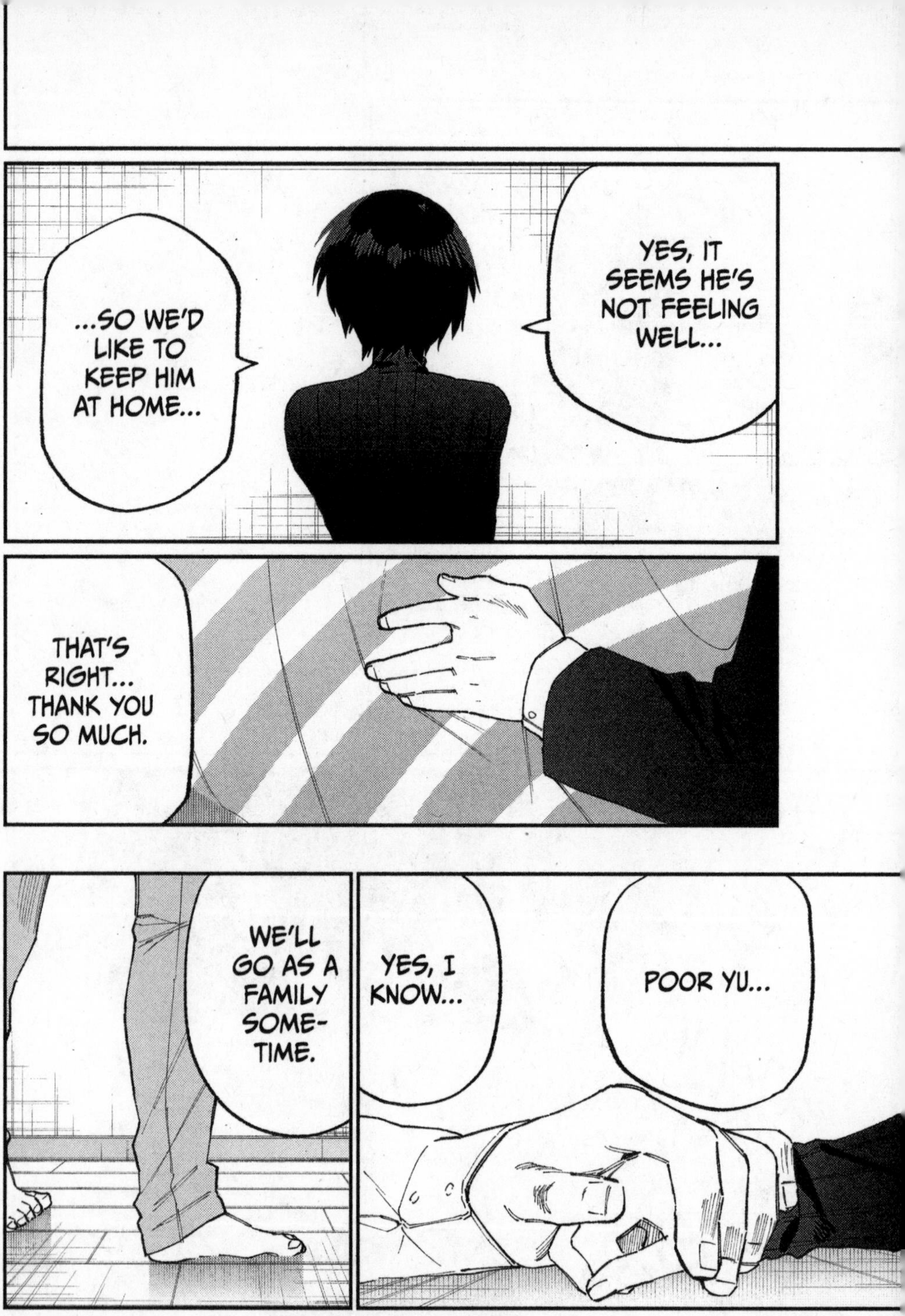
YES, IT SEEMS HE'S NOT FEELING WELL...
...SO WE'D LIKE TO KEEP HIM AT HOME...
THAT'S RIGHT... THANK YOU SO MUCH.
POOR YU...
YES, I KNOW...
WE'LL GO AS A FAMILY SOME-TIME.

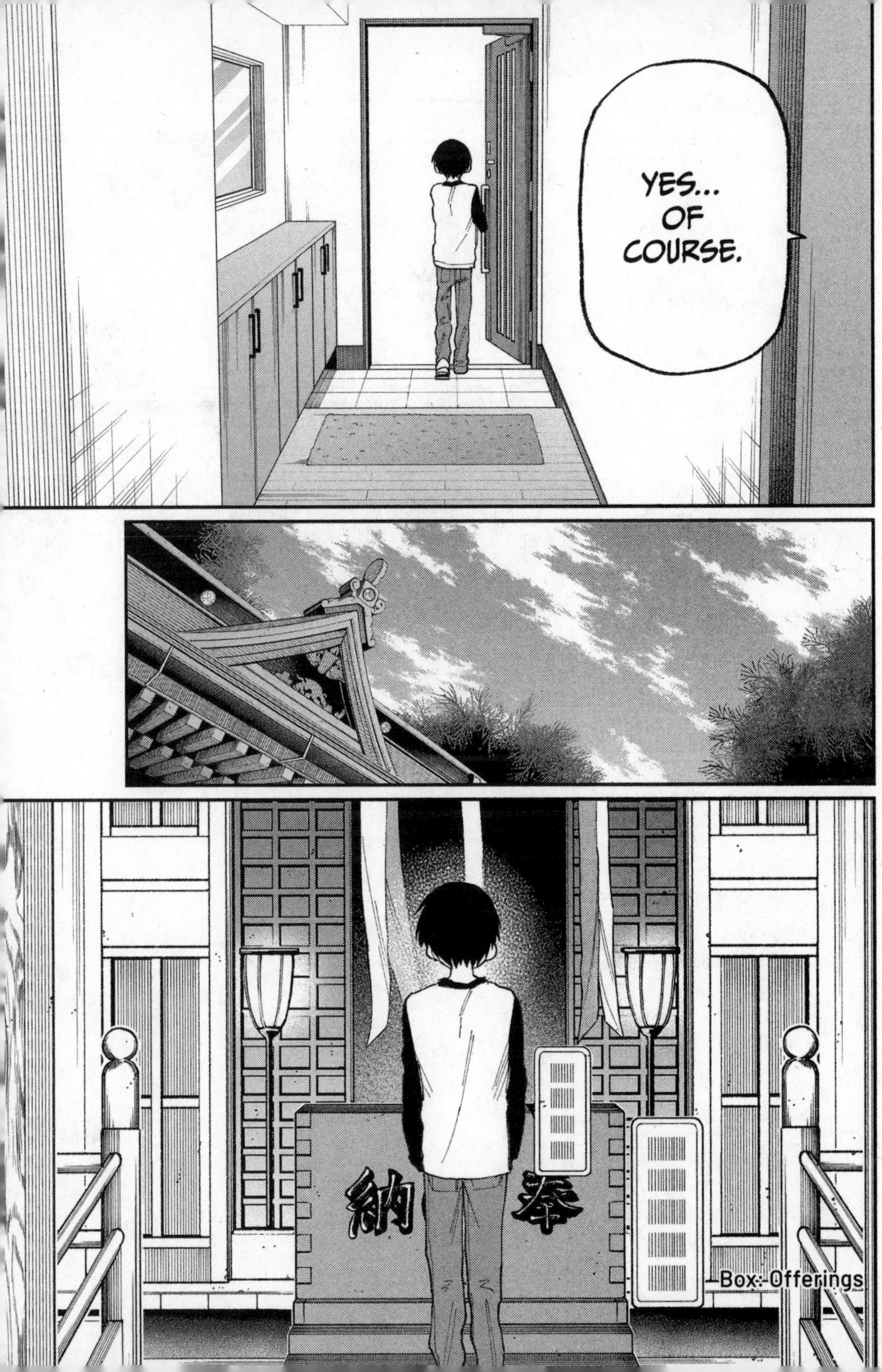
YES... OF COURSE.
納 奉
Box: Offerings

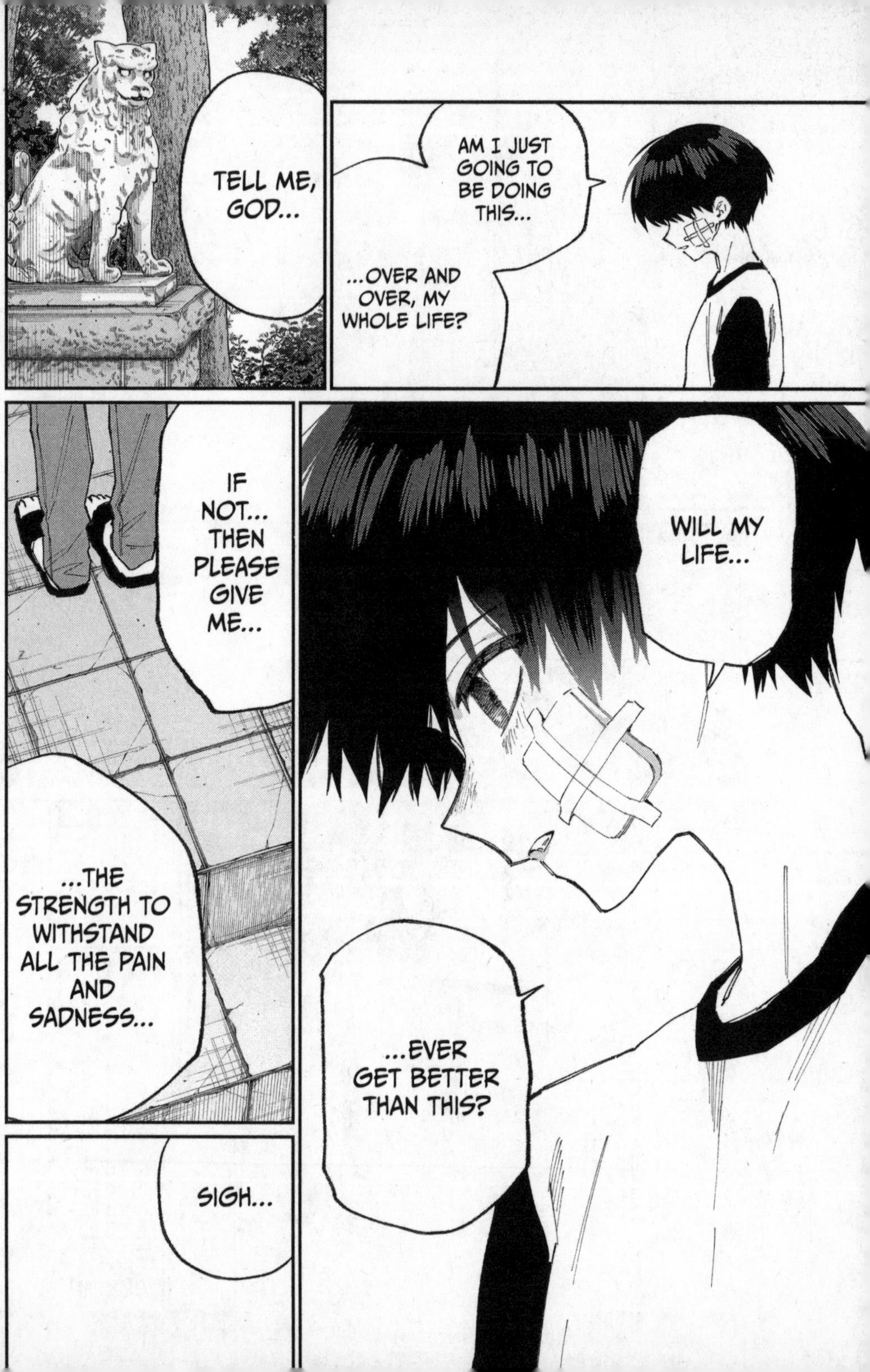
AM I JUST GOING TO BE DOING THIS...
...OVER AND OVER, MY WHOLE LIFE?
TELL ME, GOD...
WILL MY LIFE...
...EVER GET BETTER THAN THIS?
IF NOT... THEN PLEASE GIVE ME...
...THE STRENGTH TO WITHSTAND ALL THE PAIN AND SADNESS...
SIGH...

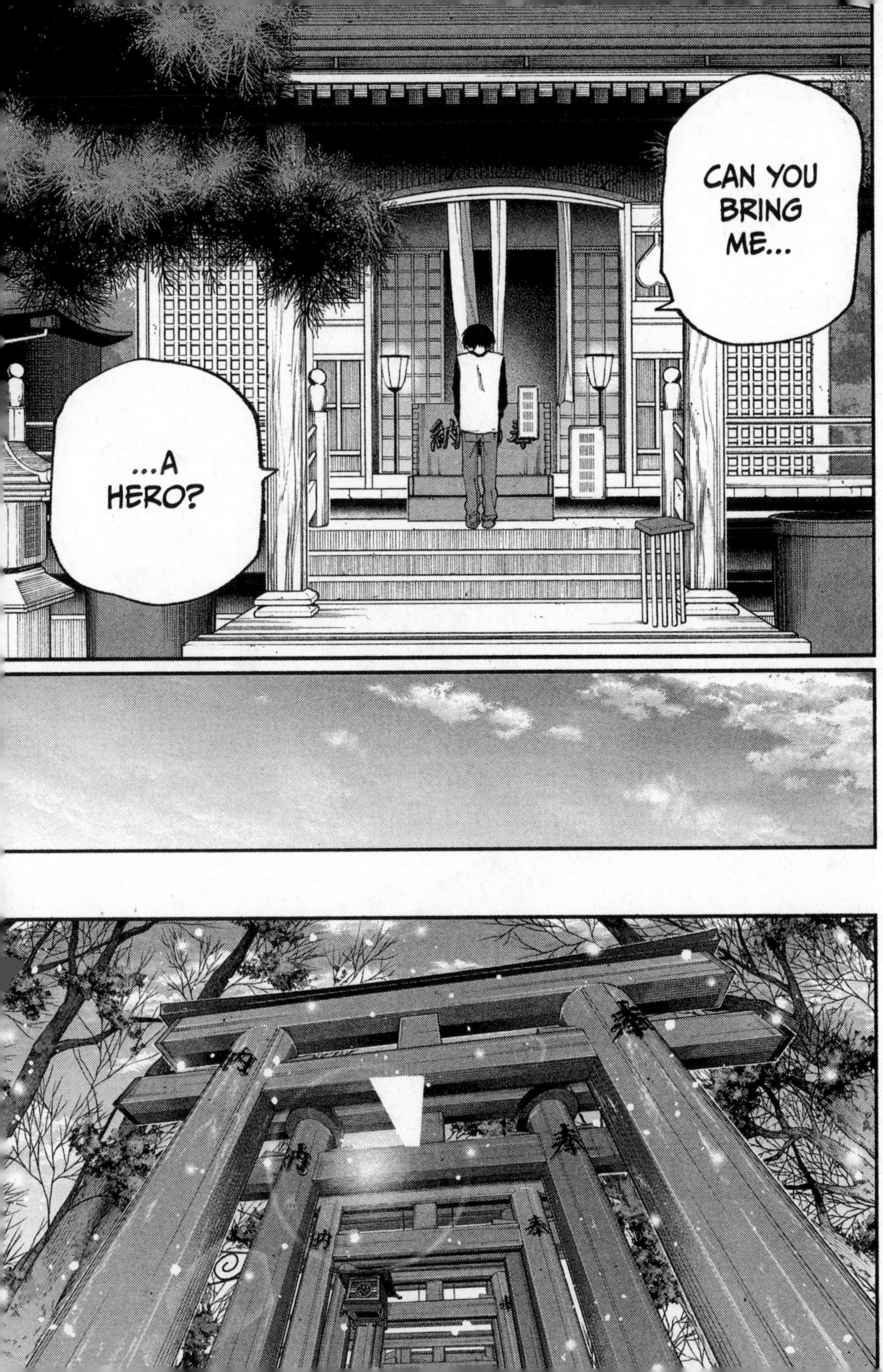
CAN YOU BRING ME...
...A HERO?

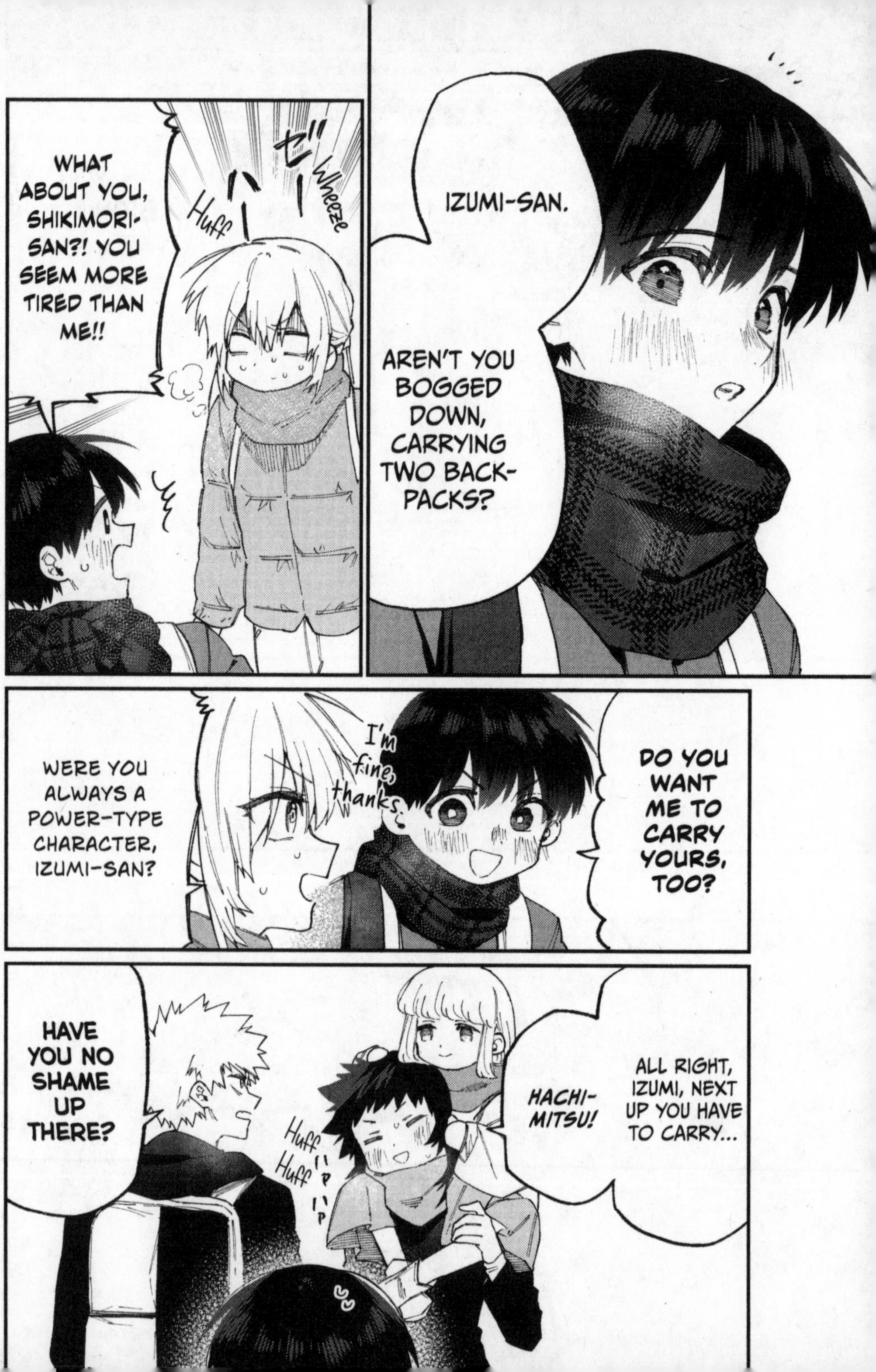
IZUMI-SAN.
AREN'T YOU BOGGED DOWN, CARRYING TWO BACK-PACKS?
Wheeze
Huff
WHAT ABOUT YOU, SHIKIMORI-SAN?! YOU SEEM MORE TIRED THAN ME!!
DO YOU WANT ME TO CARRY YOURS, TOO?
I'm fine, thanks.
WERE YOU ALWAYS A POWER-TYPE CHARACTER, IZUMI-SAN?
ALL RIGHT, IZUMI, NEXT UP YOU HAVE TO CARRY...
HACHI-MITSU!
Huff
Huff
HAVE YOU NO SHAME UP THERE?

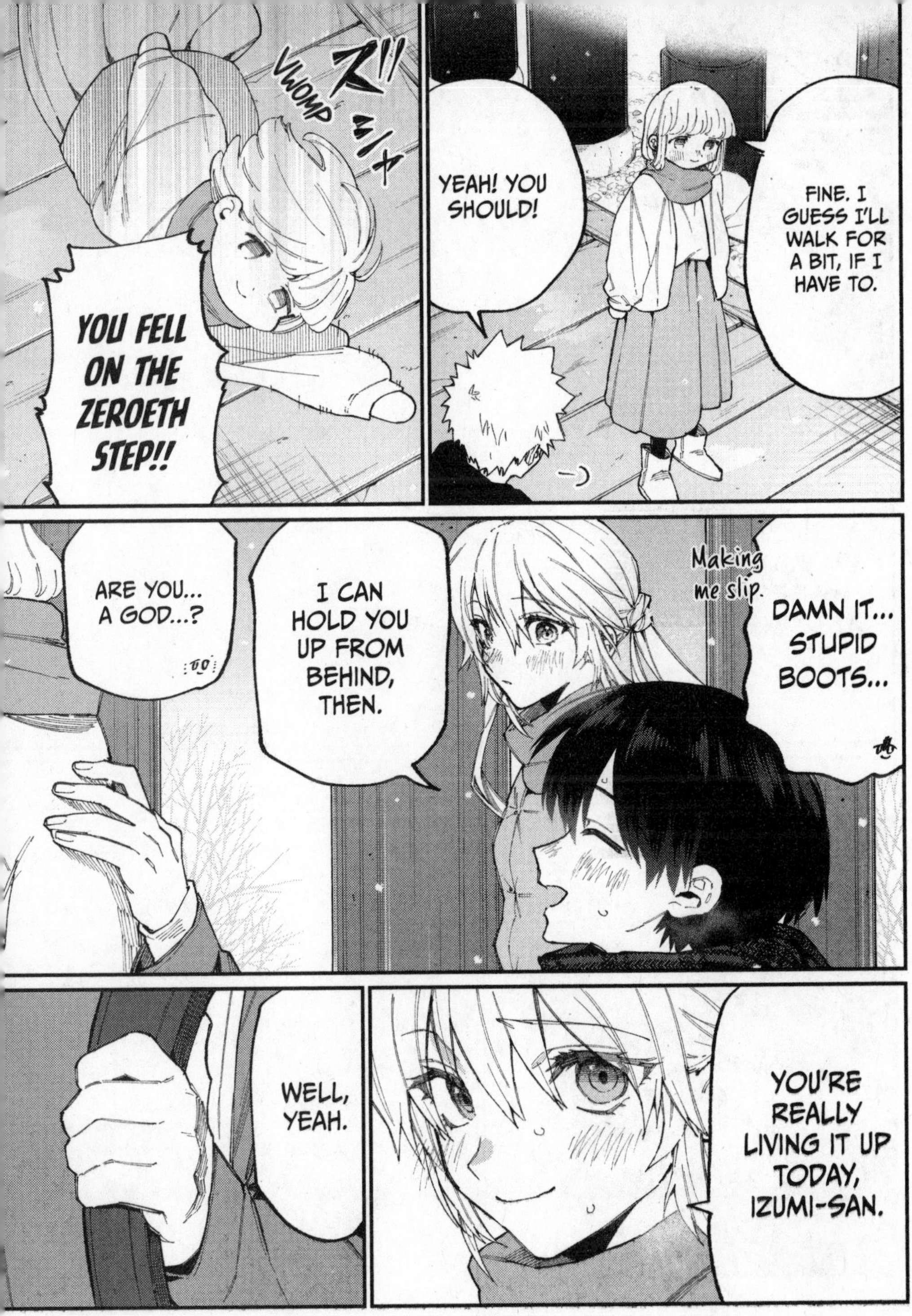
FINE. I GUESS I'LL WALK FOR A BIT, IF I HAVE TO.
YEAH! YOU SHOULD!
ズ
VWOMP
ムシャ
YOU FELL ON THE ZEROETH STEP!!
Making me slip.
DAMN IT... STUPID BOOTS...
I CAN HOLD YOU UP FROM BEHIND, THEN.
ARE YOU... A GOD...?
YOU'RE REALLY LIVING IT UP TODAY, IZUMI-SAN.
WELL, YEAH.

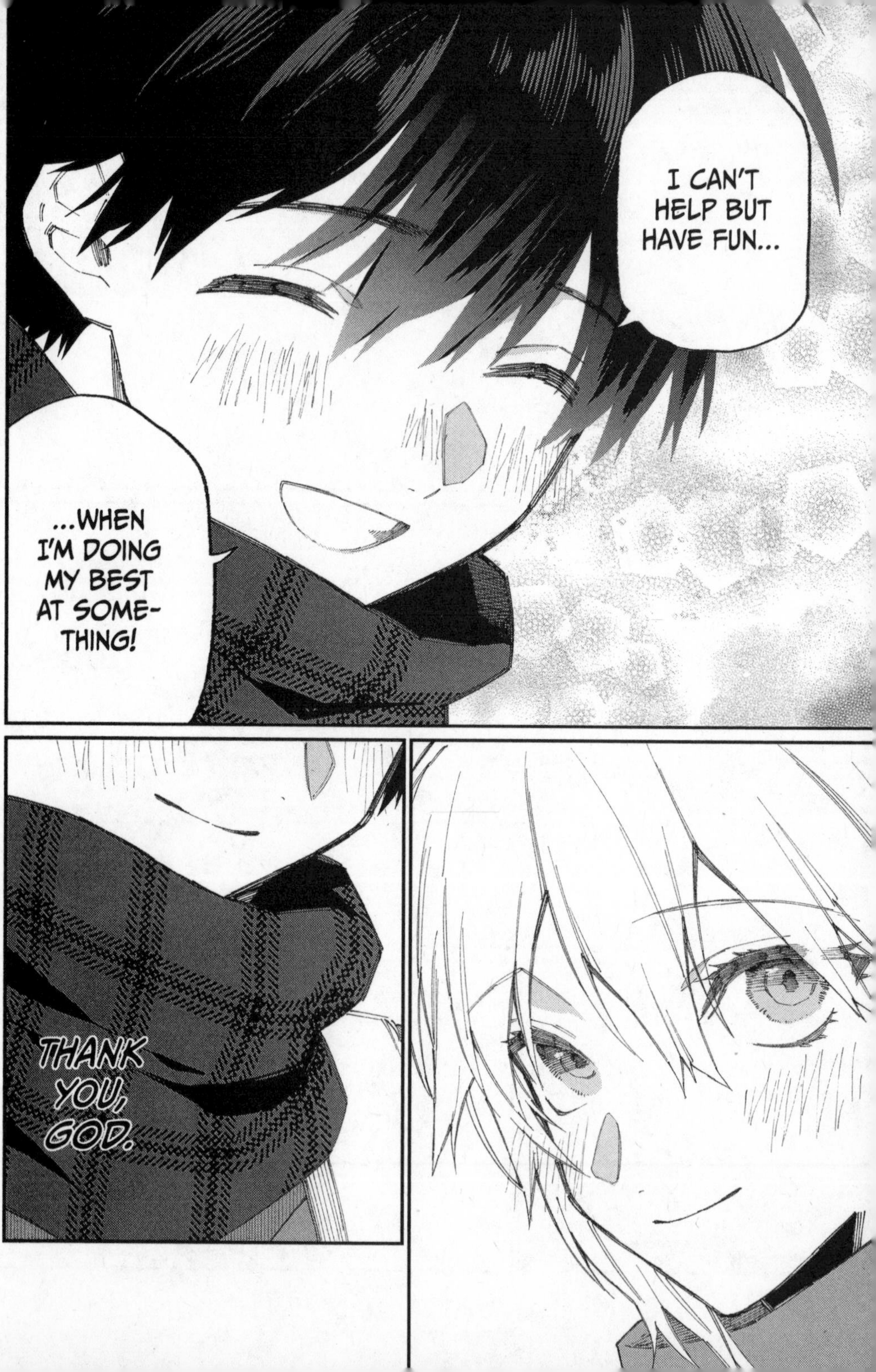
I CAN'T HELP BUT HAVE FUN...
...WHEN I'M DOING MY BEST AT SOME-THING!
THANK YOU, GOD.

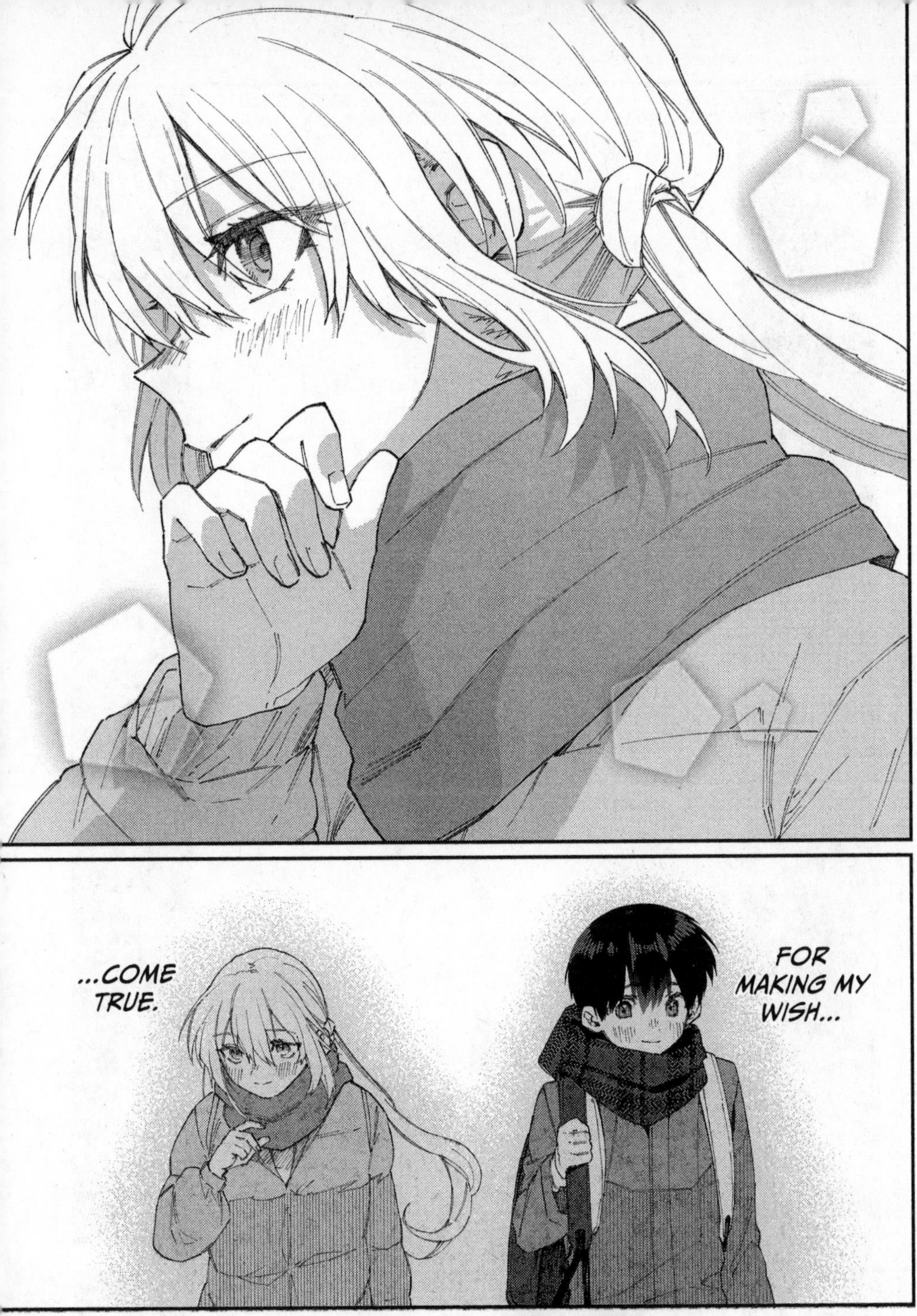
FOR MAKING MY WISH...
...COME TRUE.

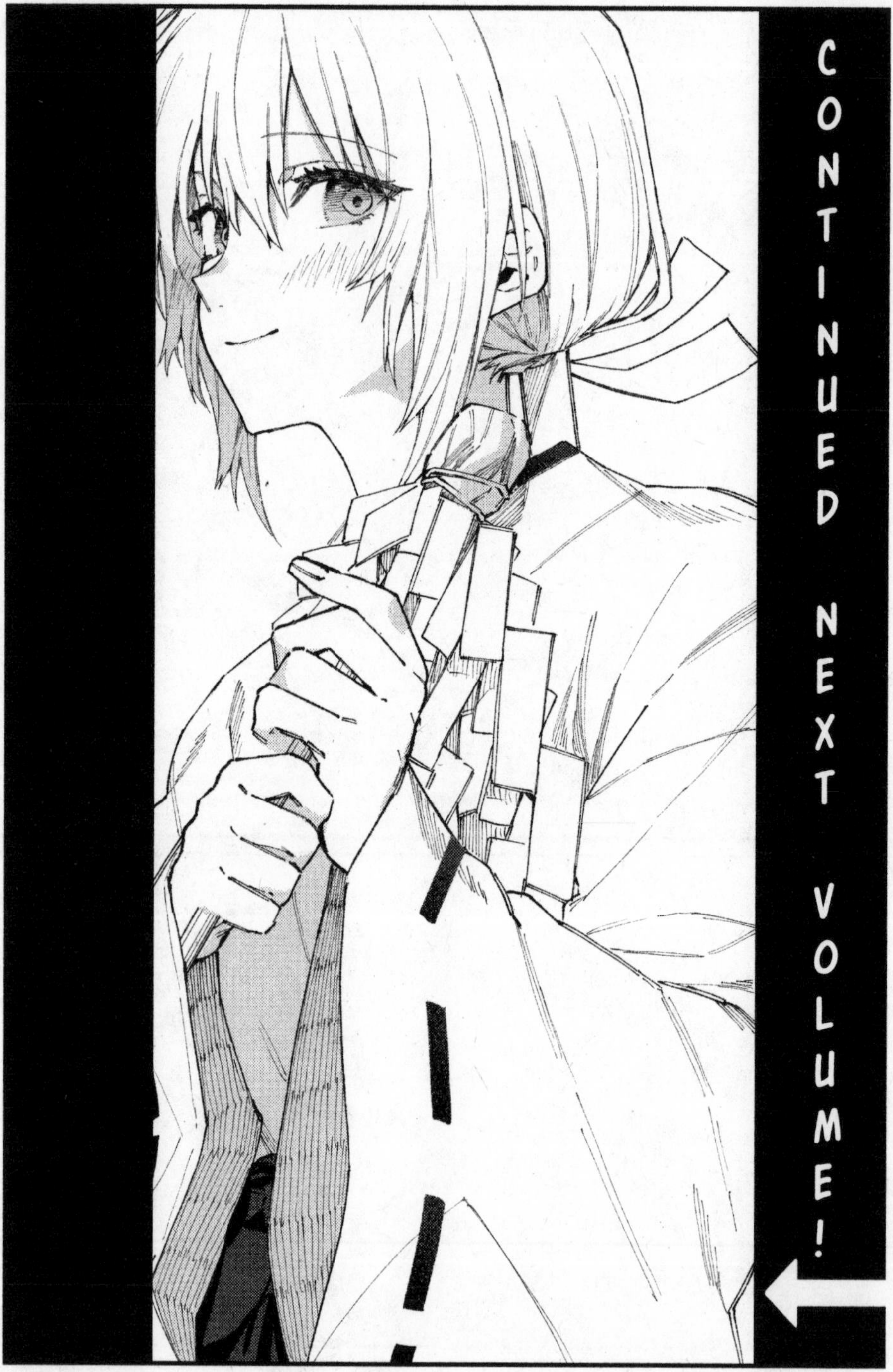
CONTINUED NEXT VOLUME!

Afterword

Thank you so much for buying Volume 10! We've
reached double digits! It's incredible that a story I
started by uploading art on Twitter turned into this.
Whew! I've been blessed by so much support. Thanks
for sticking around, and hope to see you in the future!

Staff: Editors   Design:
Na-san   Hiraoka-san   Kuraji-san
Santo-san   Toki-san
Tsuchida-san Design: Thank you,
              Kuraji-san   as always!

In the milestone 100th chapter

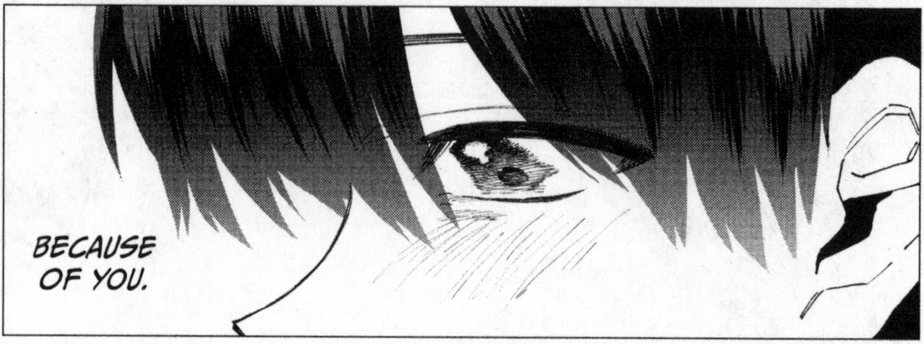
BECAUSE OF YOU.

A huge incident

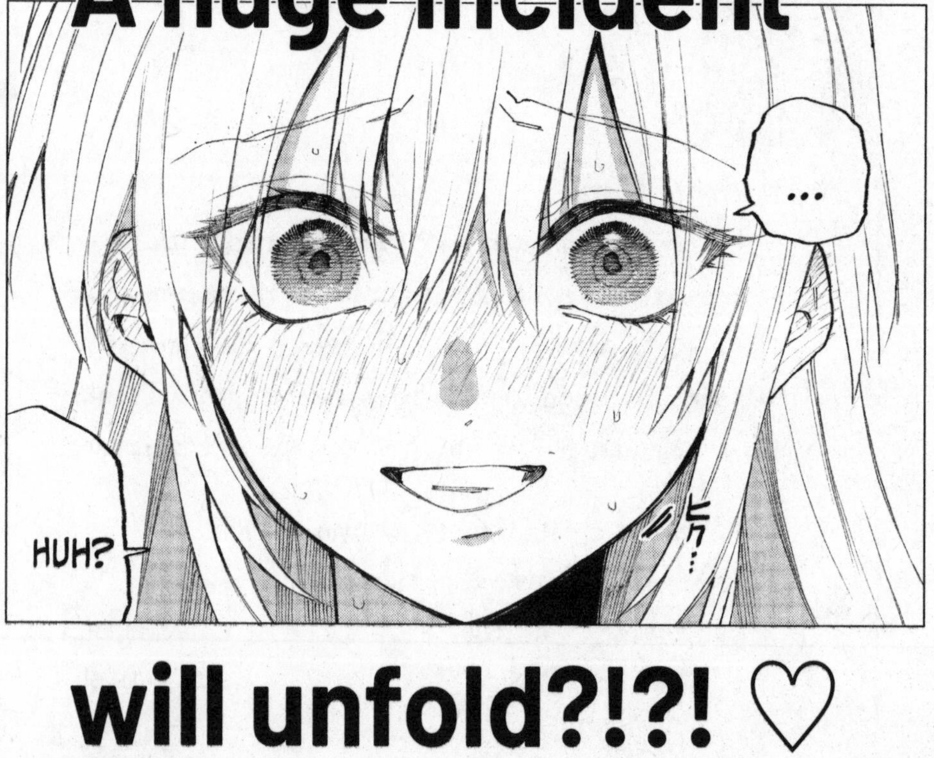
...
ヒク...
HUH?

will unfold?!?! ♡

A brilliant season of youth

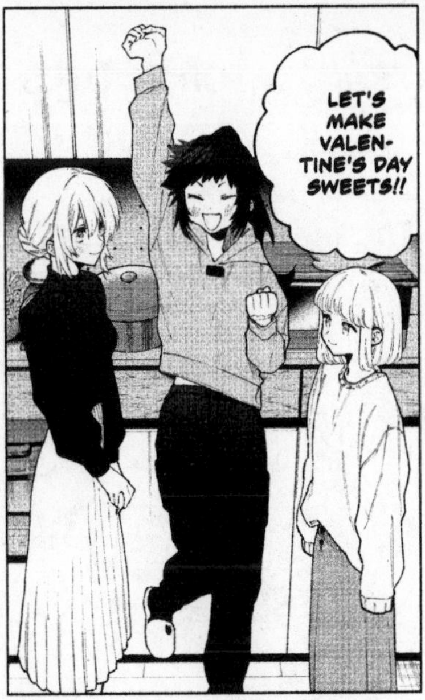
LET'S MAKE VALEN-TINE'S DAY SWEETS!!

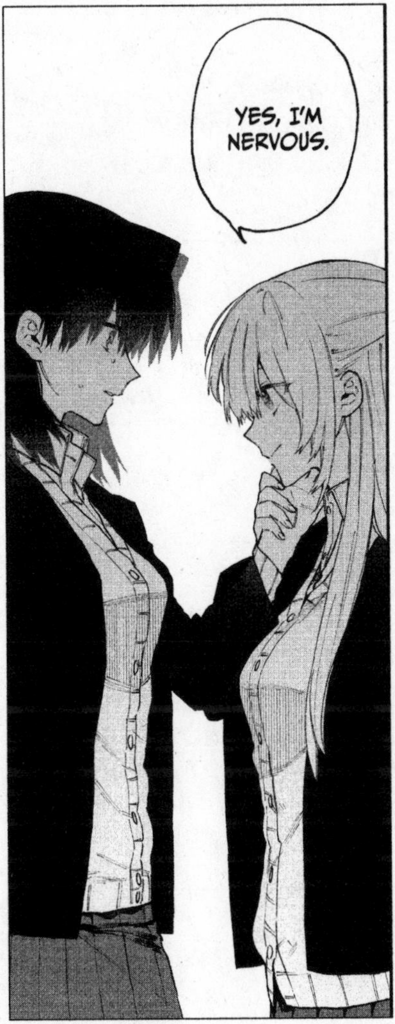
YES, I'M NERVOUS.

plays host

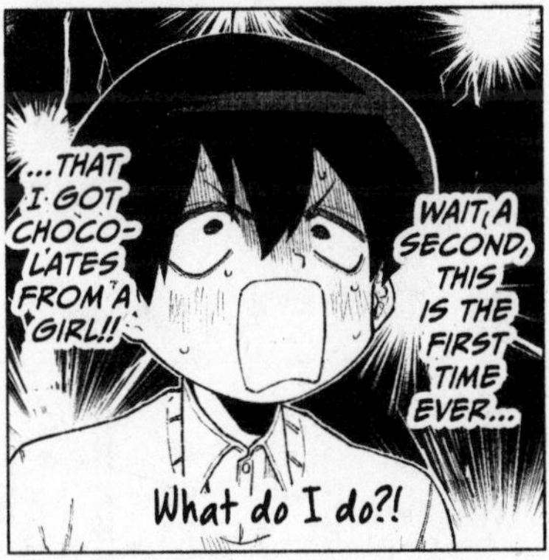
WAIT, A SECOND, THIS IS THE FIRST TIME EVER...
...THAT I GOT CHOCO-LATES FROM A GIRL!!
What do I do?!

to interlocking emotions...

This and more in Volume 11, coming soon!

TRANSLATOR'S NOTES

Maiko, page 6

The traditional title for an apprentice *geisha,* who are most associated with Kyoto. Within Kyoto, *geisha* and *maiko* perform in areas called *hanamachi* (flower towns), with Gion being the most famous and prestigious *hanamachi* in Kyoto.

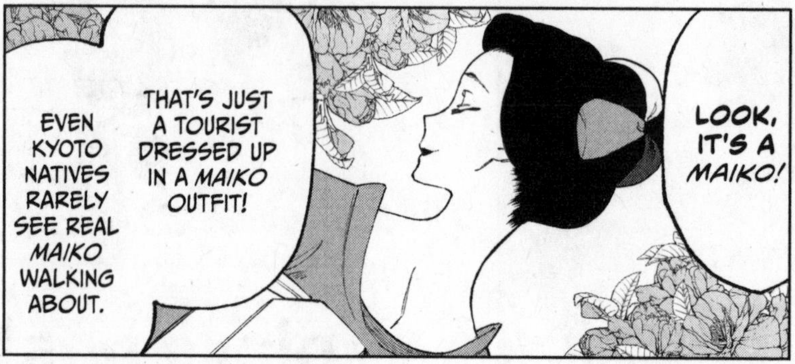
LOOK, IT'S A *MAIKO!*
THAT'S JUST A TOURIST DRESSED UP IN A *MAIKO* OUTFIT!
EVEN KYOTO NATIVES RARELY SEE REAL *MAIKO* WALKING ABOUT.

Yasaka, Kodaji, Chion-in, page 6

Three prominent religious structures out of many to be found in Kyoto, which contains nearly a dozen and a half World Heritage Sites alone, among its 2,000 temples and shrines. Yasaka is a major Shinto shrine, Kodaiji is a Zen Buddhist temple created by the widow of Toyotomi Hideyoshi, and Chion-in Monastery is the headquarters of the Jôdô-shû school of Buddhism, the largest in Japan.

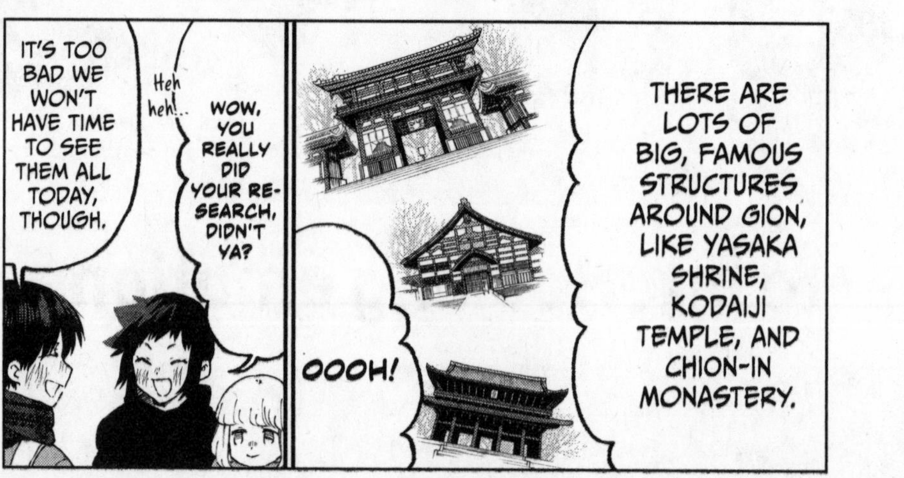
THERE ARE LOTS OF BIG, FAMOUS STRUCTURES AROUND GION, LIKE YASAKA SHRINE, KODAIJI TEMPLE, AND CHION-IN MONASTERY.
OOOH!
WOW, YOU REALLY DID YOUR RE-SEARCH, DIDN'T YA?
Heh heh!...
IT'S TOO BAD WE WON'T HAVE TIME TO SEE THEM ALL TODAY, THOUGH.

Hanamikoji Street, page 12

One of the famous, old-fashioned streets of Gion District in Kyoto, translating to "Flower Viewing Lane."

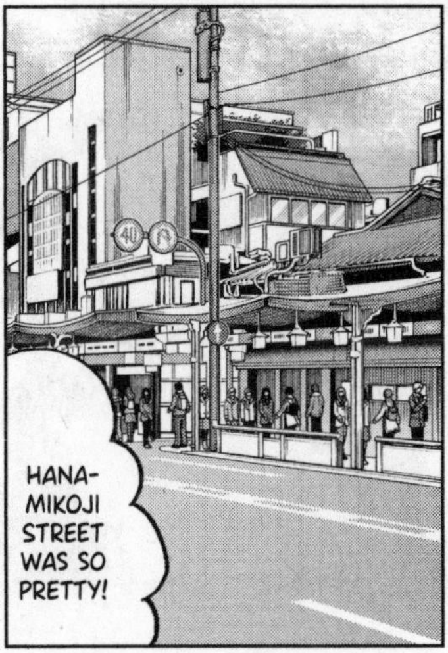
HANA-MIKOJI STREET WAS SO PRETTY!

Yatsuhashi, page 13

A traditional confection of Japan, made of rice flour, sugar, and cinnamon. When baked, they resemble long brown strips that are curved in a u-shape. When eaten raw, they are soft and chewy, and typically folded into a triangular shape, sometimes with sweet bean paste inside.

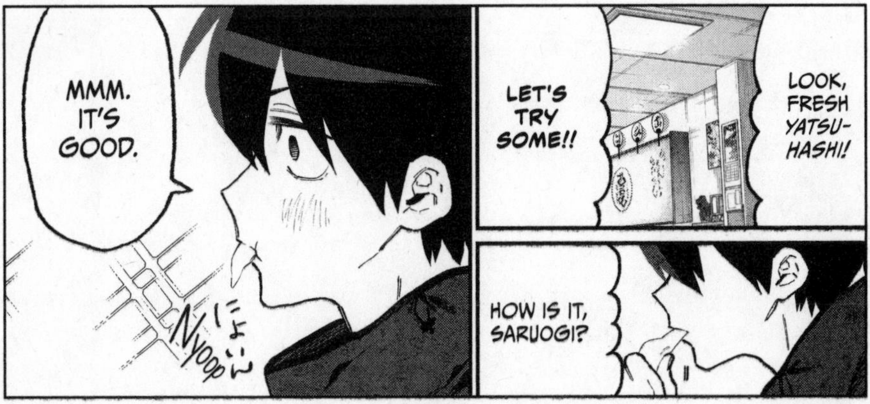
LOOK, FRESH YATSU-HASHI!
LET'S TRY SOME!!
HOW IS IT, SARUOGI?
MMM. IT'S GOOD.
Nyoop

Thousand-armed Kannon, page 25
One of the incarnations of the boddhisatva of compassion and mercy, which is most popular in East Asia. Her thousand-armed depiction is said to indicate her great ability to extend kindness to those in need.

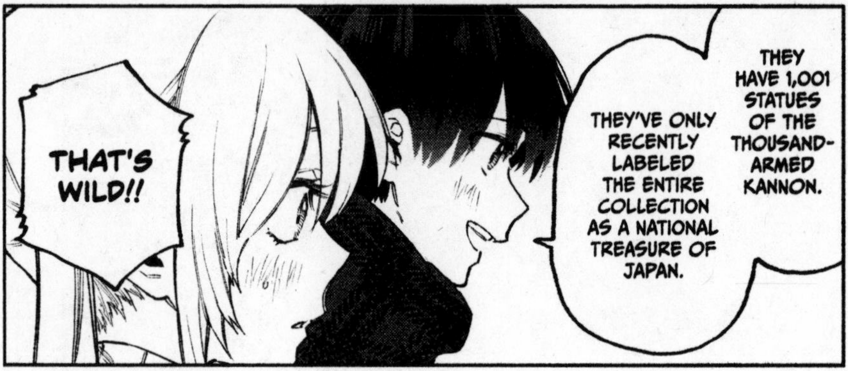
THEY HAVE 1,001 STATUES OF THE THOUSAND-ARMED KANNON.
THEY'VE ONLY RECENTLY LABELED THE ENTIRE COLLECTION AS A NATIONAL TREASURE OF JAPAN.
THAT'S WILD!!

PERFECT WORLD

Rie Aruga

A TOUCHING
NEW SERIES
ABOUT LOVE AND
COPING WITH
DISABILITY

An office party reunites Tsugumi with her high school crush Itsuki. He's realized his dream of becoming an architect, but along the way, he experienced a spinal injury that put him in a wheelchair. Now Tsugumi's rekindled feelings will butt up against prejudices she never considered — and Itsuki will have to decide if he's ready to let someone into his heart...

"Depicts with great delicacy and courage the difficulties some with disabilities experience getting involved in romantic relationships... Rie Aruga refuses to romanticize, pushing her heroine to face the reality of disability. She invites her readers to the same tasks of empathy, knowledge and recognition."
—Slate.fr

"An important entry [in manga romance].., The emotional core of both plot and characters indicates thoughtfulness... [Aruga's] research is readily apparent in the text and artwork, making this feel like a real story,"
—Anime News Network

KC
KODANSHA
COMICS

A SMART, NEW ROMANTIC COMEDY FOR FANS OF *SHORTCAKE CAKE* AND *TERRACE HOUSE*!

Living-Room Matsunaga-san © Keiko Iwashita / Kodansha ltd.

KC KODANSHA COMICS

A romance manga starring high school girl Meeko, who learns to live on her own in a boarding house whose living room is home to the odd (but handsome) Matsunaga-san. She begins to adjust to her new life away from her parents, but Meeko soon learns that no matter how far away from home she is, she's still a young girl at heart — especially when she finds herself falling for Matsunaga-san.

The adorable new odd-couple cat comedy manga from the creator of the beloved *Chi's Sweet Home*, in full color!

Praise for Chi's Sweet Home

"Nearly impossible to turn away... a true all-ages title that anyone, young or old, cat lover or not, will enjoy. The stories will bring a smile to your face and warm your heart."

—School Library Journal

Sue & Tai-chan

Konami Kanata

Sue is an aging housecat who's looking forward to living out her life in peace... but her plans change when the mischievous black tomcat Tai-chan enters the picture! Hey! Sue never signed up to be a catsitter! *Sue & Tai-chan* is the latest from the reigning meow-narch of cute kitty comics, Konami Kanata.

KC KODANSHA COMICS

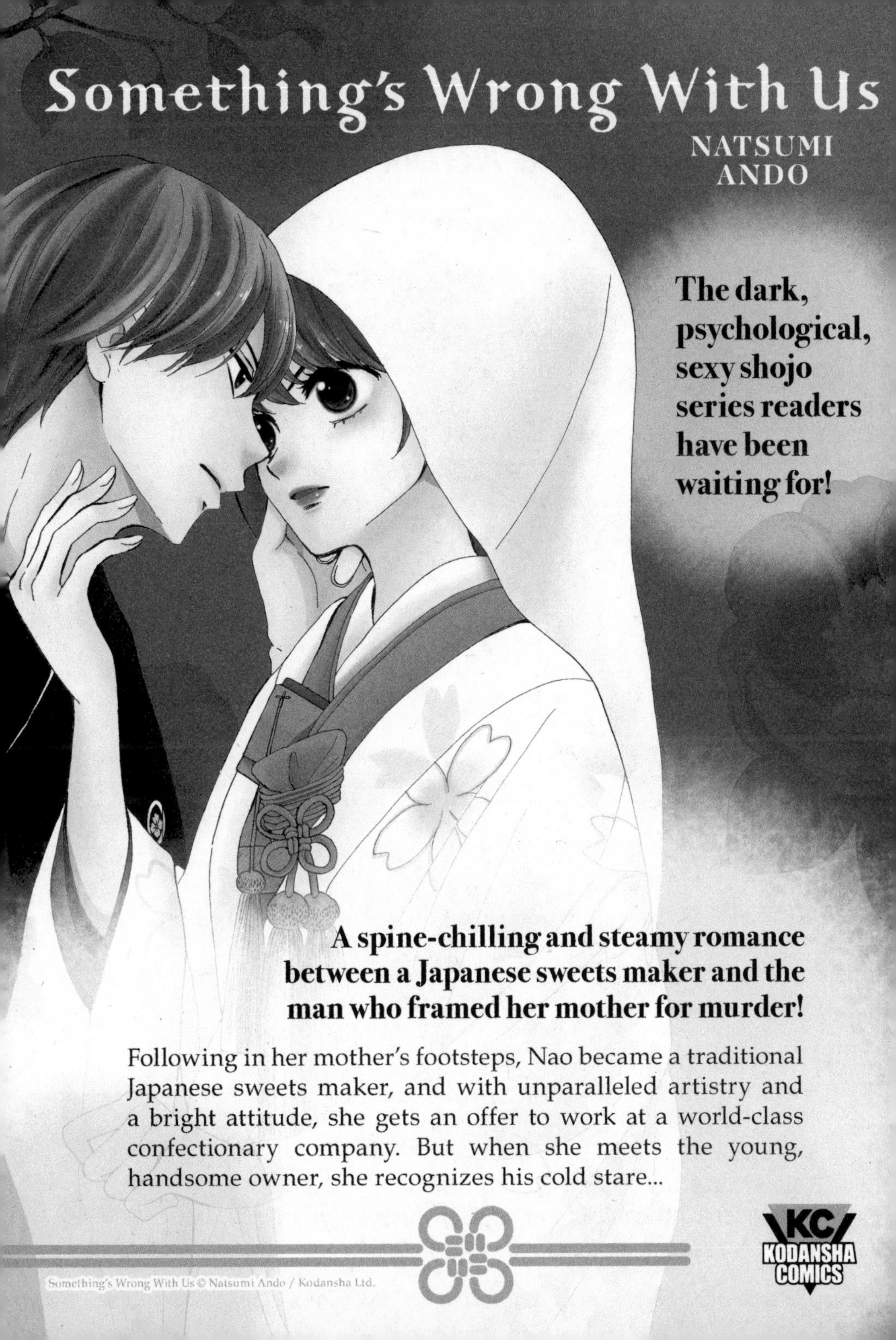
Something's Wrong With Us
NATSUMI ANDO
The dark, psychological, sexy shojo series readers have been waiting for!
A spine-chilling and steamy romance between a Japanese sweets maker and the man who framed her mother for murder!
Following in her mother's footsteps, Nao became a traditional Japanese sweets maker, and with unparalleled artistry and a bright attitude, she gets an offer to work at a world-class confectionary company. But when she meets the young, handsome owner, she recognizes his cold stare...
KC KODANSHA COMICS
Something's Wrong With Us © Natsumi Ando / Kodansha Ltd.

THE SWEET SCENT OF LOVE IS IN THE AIR! FOR FANS OF OFFBEAT ROMANCES LIKE *WOTAKOI*

Sweat and Soap © Kintetsu Yamada / Kodansha Ltd.

In an office romance, there's a fine line between sexy and awkward... and that line is where Asako — a woman who sweats copiously — meets Koutarou — a perfume developer who can't get enough of Asako's, er, scent. Don't miss a romcom manga like no other!

KC KODANSHA COMICS

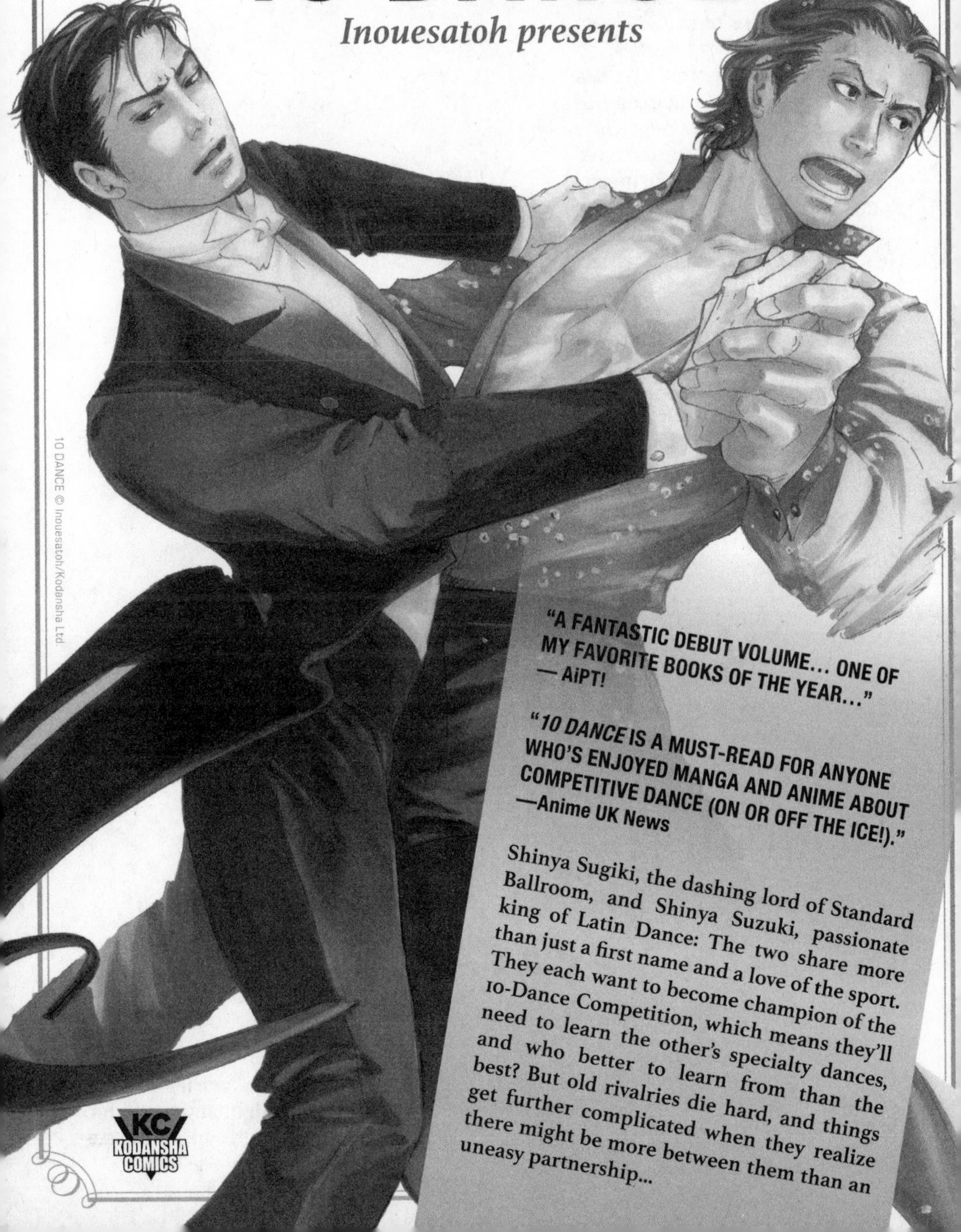
10 DANCE © Inouesatoh/Kodansha Ltd.
"A FANTASTIC DEBUT VOLUME… ONE OF MY FAVORITE BOOKS OF THE YEAR…" — AiPT!
"*10 DANCE* IS A MUST-READ FOR ANYONE WHO'S ENJOYED MANGA AND ANIME ABOUT COMPETITIVE DANCE (ON OR OFF THE ICE!)." —Anime UK News
Shinya Sugiki, the dashing lord of Standard Ballroom, and Shinya Suzuki, passionate king of Latin Dance: The two share more than just a first name and a love of the sport. They each want to become champion of the 10-Dance Competition, which means they'll need to learn the other's specialty dances, and who better to learn from than the best? But old rivalries die hard, and things get further complicated when they realize there might be more between them than an uneasy partnership...
KC KODANSHA COMICS

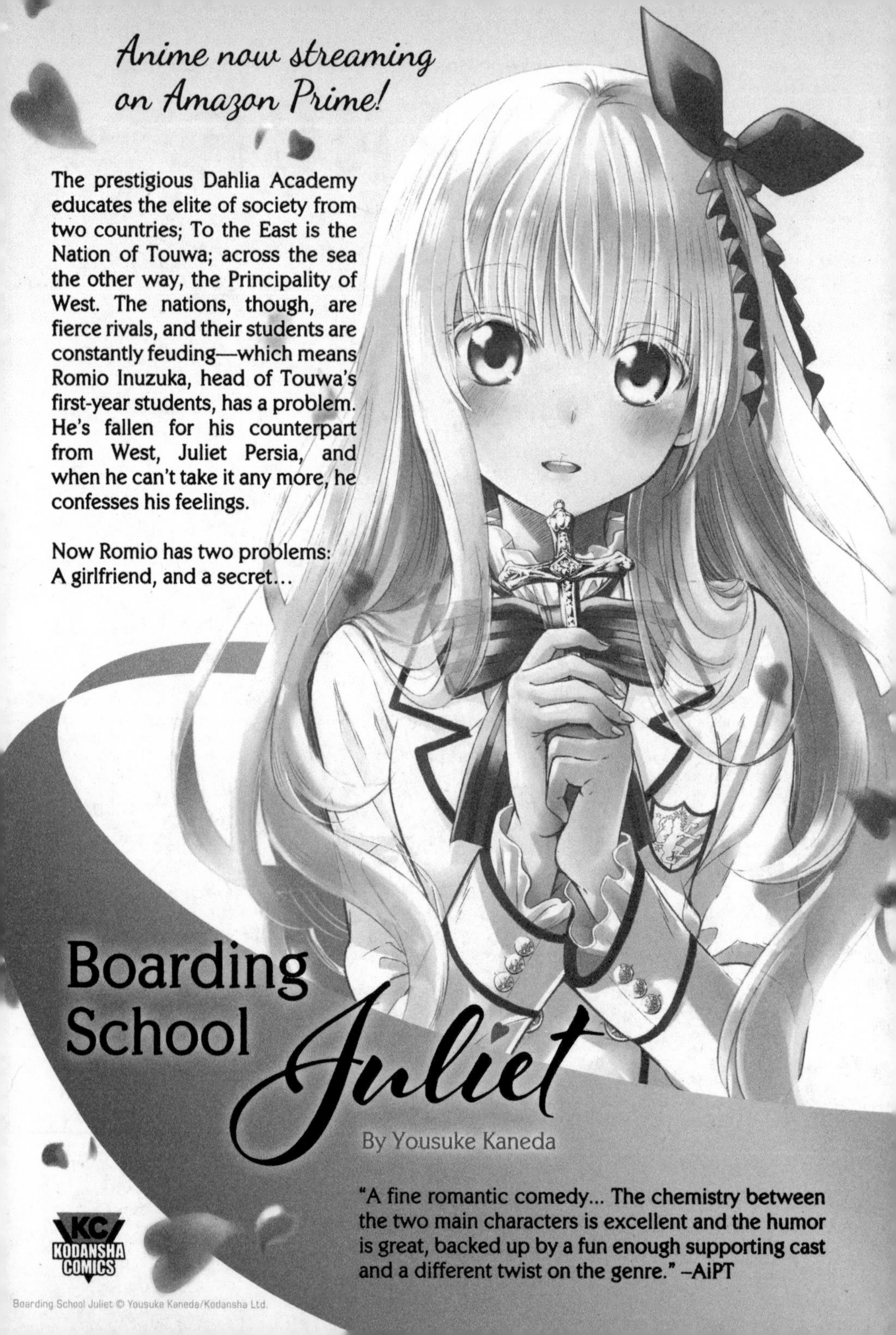
Anime now streaming on Amazon Prime!
The prestigious Dahlia Academy educates the elite of society from two countries; To the East is the Nation of Touwa; across the sea the other way, the Principality of West. The nations, though, are fierce rivals, and their students are constantly feuding—which means Romio Inuzuka, head of Touwa's first-year students, has a problem. He's fallen for his counterpart from West, Juliet Persia, and when he can't take it any more, he confesses his feelings.
Now Romio has two problems: A girlfriend, and a secret...
Boarding School Juliet
By Yousuke Kaneda
"A fine romantic comedy... The chemistry between the two main characters is excellent and the humor is great, backed up by a fun enough supporting cast and a different twist on the genre." –AiPT
KC KODANSHA COMICS
Boarding School Juliet © Yousuke Kaneda/Kodansha Ltd.

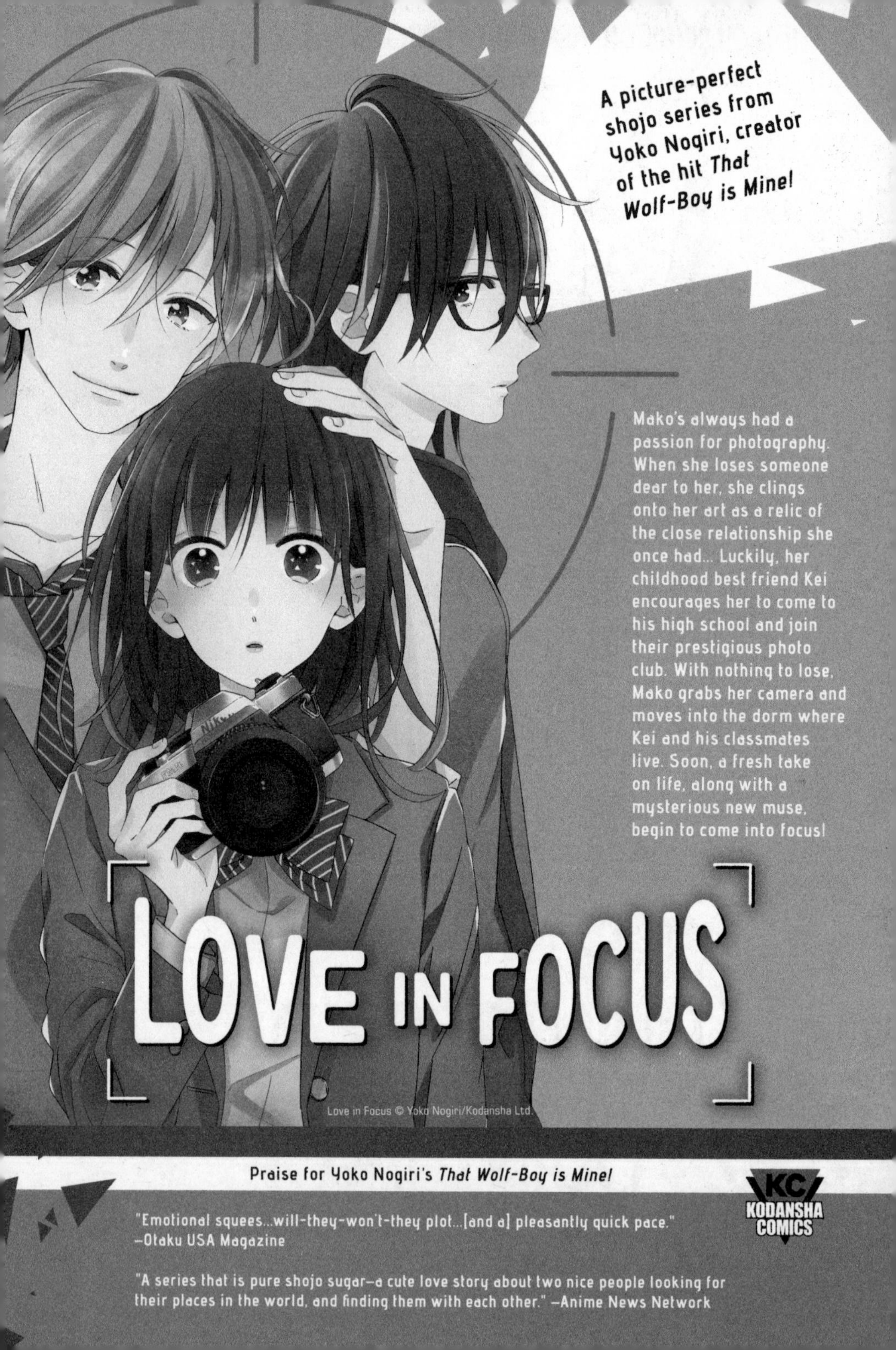

◄ KAMOME ►
SHIRAHAMA

Witch Hat Atelier

A magical manga
adventure for
fans of Disney
and Studio
Ghibli!

Witch Hat Atelier © Kamome Shirahama/Kodansha Ltd.

The magical adventure that took Japan by storm is finally here, from acclaimed DC and Marvel cover artist Kamome Shirahama!

In a world where everyone takes wonders like magic spells and dragons for granted, Coco is a girl with a simple dream: She wants to be a witch. But everybody knows magicians are born, not made, and Coco was not born with a gift for magic. Resigned to her un-magical life, Coco is about to give up on her dream to become a witch...until the day she meets Qifrey, a mysterious, traveling magician. After secretly seeing Qifrey perform magic in a way she's never seen before, Coco soon learns what everybody "knows" might not be the truth, and discovers that her magical dream may not be as far away as it may seem...

KC
KODANSHA
COMICS

**THE MAGICAL GIRL CLASSIC THAT BROUGHT A
GENERATION OF READERS TO MANGA, NOW BACK IN A
DEFINITIVE, HARDCOVER COLLECTOR'S EDITION!**

CARDCAPTOR SAKURA
COLLECTOR'S EDITION
C L A M P

Ten-year-old Sakura Kinomoto lives a pretty normal life with her older brother, Tōya, and widowed father, Fujitaka—until the day she discovers a strange book in her father's library, and her life takes a magical turn...

- A deluxe large-format hardcover edition of CLAMP's shojo manga classic
- All-new foil-stamped cover art on each volume
- Comes with exclusive collectible art card

KC
KODANSHA COMICS

A Kodansha Comics Trade Paperback Original
Shikimori's Not Just a Cutie 10 copyright © 2021 Keigo Maki
English translation copyright © 2022 Keigo Maki

Published in the United States by Kodansha Comics, an imprint of
Kodansha USA Publishing, LLC, New York.

Publication rights for this English edition arranged through
Kodansha Ltd., Tokyo.

First published in Japan in 2021 by Kodansha Ltd., Tokyo.

ISBN 978-1-64651-590-5

Printed in the United States of America.

www.kodansha.us

9 8 7 6 5 4 3 2 1
Translation: Stephen Paul
Lettering: Mercedes McGarry
Editing: David Yoo
Kodansha Comics edition cover design by My Truong

Publisher: Kiichiro Sugawara

Director of publishing services: Ben Applegate
Director of publishing operations: Dave Barrett
Associate director, publishing operations: Stephen Pakula
Publishing services managing editors: Madison Salters, Alanna Ruse
Production managers: Emi Lotto, Angela Zurlo
Logo and character art ©Kodansha USA Publishing, LLC